drunken *angel*

ALAN KAUFMAN

V!Va
EDITIONS

Published in the United States by Viva Editions, an imprint of Cleis Press Inc., 2246 Sixth Street, Berkeley CA 94710.

Printed in the United States.
Cover design: Scott Idleman/Blink
Cover photograph: Tetra Images
Text design: Frank Wiedemann

First Edition.
10 9 8 7 6 5 4 3 2 1

Trade paper ISBN: 978-1-936740-02-4
E-book ISBN: 978-1-936740-06-2

Library of Congress Cataloging-in-Publication Data

Kaufman, Alan.
  Drunken angel : a memoir / Alan Kaufman.
     p. cm.
  ISBN 978-1-936740-02-4 (hardback)
  1. Kaufman, Alan. 2. Alcoholics--Biography. 3. Kaufman, Alan--Sexual behavior.
  4. Fathers and daughters. I. Title.
  HV5032.K38A3 2011
  362.292092--dc23
  [B]
                                   2011025641

It's very thrilling to see darkness again.

—Diane Arbus

PART ONE

1

ON A LAMP STAND BY HIS BED MY FATHER KEPT A small stack of *True Men's Adventures* and *Stag*, magazines with illustrated feature stories bearing titles like "Virgin Brides for Himmler's Nazi Torture Dungeons" and "Hitler's Secret Blood Cult" or "Death Orgy in the Rat Pits of the Gestapo."

I couldn't tear my eyes away.

The covers showed buxom, naked young women—Jewish, I presumed—in shredded slips, their panting and perspiring busts crisscrossed with luscious-looking whip welts, hung by wrists from ceilings, about to be boiled, others spread-eagled on torture tables, dripping red cherry cough drop–colored blood as shirtless bald grinning sadists manned obscene instruments.

Is this what my birth looked like? Had my mother, a French-born Jew, been a virgin torture bride for the pleasures of the medical Gestapo? And is that why she still constantly revisits doctors and goes to the hospital to have surgeries? To my libido, it was logical.

To her, my hungers were disgraceful. "You're hungry? You don't know what hunger is," she told me, mopping her flushed face with her apron, when I requested more bread.

I was too fat, she said. "Look at you! You should be ashamed! You have breasts like a woman. In the war I hid in basements and attics, starving, and all around me German soldiers with dogs. I was just a little older than you. Hungry! What do you know? Your waist is bigger than mine!"

But what about the Gestapo rat pits, I wondered, shutting my eyes, trying to imagine her hung over cauldrons, like the ones bubbling on the stove, or chained to a wall, naked and starving, a thin figure with voluptuous breasts, a moan parting her lips. Shifting uncomfortably in my seat, I grew hard under the dinette table.

The magazines' cheap black-and-white newsprint guts contained boner-inspiring photo art, grainy flicks of scantily clad women of ill repute, black bars printed over their eyes. You saw pretty clearly their cleavages, could form a mental movie. I knew that sex was bad things one did and I knew the mags were sinful, but reading was the only thing I seemed to excel in at school; I failed most subjects. I read the mags compulsively, desperately, yet with a curious mentholated sense of remove, the coolness of sin, the way others pray, for fantasy, escape from the circumstances of my life, for I did not yet understand about libraries, that you can be only eight years old but based on honor take home books, since there was no honor in my world where I was a groveling larva trying just not to get crushed.

My father played cards and bet on horses. He brought home stolen hi-fi consoles and portable TVs, purchased hot, or hung out with his brother, Arnold, and the kids, who were mainly jailbirds and hoods. And if I could, I stole too—you couldn't trust a kid like me, for now and then I took change from his pockets, filched cupcakes and comics from the candy stores.

When an actual book fell into my hands, street-found, some yellowish crumbling paperback, Ted Mack's *The Man From O.R.G.Y.*, or George Orwell's *1984*, I handled these with proprietary reverence, inscribed the title page with "Property of Alan Kaufman" and a little poem plagiarized from Pop, who had it scrawled in the only two books he kept, a Webster's and this antho of best prose from Nat Fleisher's *Ring* Magazine:

"I pity the river, I pity the brook, I pity the one who steals this book."

It seemed like great poetry to me. I wondered if he made it up, was some kind of poet. This, the first poem I ever learned, stolen from my dad, made me want to write others.

I tried. When I showed my efforts to my teacher, she put across the top: "Excellent! You're a real writer!" Even my mother encouraged this idea, and kept my poems stashed in her secret drawer of precious things, folded away among silken panties and bras—my very first archive.

My poems, writing and reading, became erotically tinged, a way to earn love as I couldn't by other means. Writing seemed to befriend me. I felt less lonely, began to dream, and from the page a voice seemed to speak directly to me and to no one else.

Be a writer, it told me.

When I learned that even I could join the library and check out books six at a time, my mother said I would run up fines she couldn't pay, don't I know how poor we are, but I went anyway, returning home with arms full of new sentries to post around my bed. A kind of literary fortress stood guard over my hopes: Ernest Hemingway, James Jones, Leon Uris, Thomas Wolfe, Dylan Thomas, Irwin Shaw, a new bulwark against my mother, who entered my room raging and lashing at me with a belt for my defiance as I cringed in the corner crying and glanced at the books for courage. Could sense Hemingway and Dylan Thomas there in the room, encouraging. Alone, vowed someday to join them. At night, with a flashlight under my blanket tent, I mouthed artful words I barely understood, until, now and then, narratives took form, more real than my reality, and obliterated the grimness of the day and loneliness of my night.

2

DEVOURING STAG ZINES FELT DIFFERENT FROM
struggling through Shaw's "The Girls in Their Summer Dresses" or
Hemingway's "The Battler." Books made me feel healthy and like a
boy. Books fed my Angel. But the magazines bred a secret world of
shame, a growing hint of uncontrolled chaos, a black drunkenness
of the senses, and I plundered them with the rapt terror of forbidden
realms I intuited a boy my age shouldn't be privy to.

This was a worldview of transgressive pornographic global
evil I shared with my parents, a dark adult-only newsstand read
on life, one with the sickening graininess of a Weegee *Daily
News* photo that I felt myself too young to have, for at nine it
crazed me to think that out there in the glass-strewn Bronx
streets were devil worshippers, gangsters, Nazis, Commies,
rapists, torturers, spree killers—scary men in sweat-drenched tees
roaming with razor-buckled garrison belts wrapped around their
fists, waiting to pounce on me. Yet knowing this made me feel
closer to Mom and Dad, even as it gutted deep runnels in my soul,

hidden labyrinthine fear sewers that began to fester and stink.

The mags were spellbindingly addictive. I could not just read one about statuesque blondes bound to altars for ritualized rape and torture and then put down the mag and go sing along with Howdy Doody. I would need to read until the stories ran out and then, jonesing like a junkie, wait until Pop brought some more home. But even the next hit of *Stag* was insufficient. Slowly, I descended into the bottomless pit.

Pop frequently replenished his stock but I was not allowed to read them until he'd been through them first. An illiterate with a fourth-grade education, it could take him days.

When home, Pop lay abed in his boxer shorts and white T-shirt, asleep and farting noxious fumes until nightfall, when he would rise and go to his job at the main post office on 33rd Street and Ninth Avenue in Manhattan, work a shift from midnight to 8:00 a.m., at which time he emerged, squinting, into the early morn and headed over to Times Square for a breakfast of burger patties and Orange Julius, and then a browse in the mag racks for the latest number of *True Men's Adventures*.

When these arrived I planned my commando raid. Waited for my mother to bustle out with shopping cart, complaining about what a good-for-nothing he was, letting his poor wife go out in the rain; how he couldn't care less about her kidney stones or high blood pressure.

"Oh, yeah?" he'd yell back from his throne on the bed, half asleep, face crushed to a pillow. "And what the hell you think I been doing all night? Working to put food in your big goddamned insulting mouth!"

"Oh, to hell with you!" she called back and slammed out.

While Howie lay in bed watching TV, I would gently nudge open my parents bedroom door with fingertips, peer in at my father's calloused feet, listen for his sleep breathing and crawl in on my belly slowly, noiselessly. Slithered undetected, slid the new mags off the rack, and crawled out, booty in hand.

Dad's gonna kill you, Howie would say. He didn't look at the mags, didn't dare. Lay on his bed reading comics, watching TV. A good boy.

We had twin beds, side by side. Lying on mine, I compulsively read them from cover to cover, all the way to the Frederick's of Hollywood ads. The horrifying stories, stimulating, strange, stirred vague longings, desires that I could not identify but felt increasingly frightened of and sickened by, though I couldn't stop, aware as I read of the stirring between my legs.

All this made me feel nightmarishly arrant in the watching invisible eyes of the world and of the writers I admired, as if Hemingway could see me from his throne in the sky library and shook his head in disappointed disgust.

Yet, I did not know what sex was. My birds and bees were satanic torture rites and Goering's Pain Slaves.

I did not even know about coupling. Didn't exist. The stag mags only alluded indirectly to coitus, draping the act in coded euphemisms.

When kids made screwing jokes, I hadn't a clue what they were referring to, just couldn't guess. Babies came from torture chambers, where now and then my mother lay moaning and bloody on some hospital table, surrounded by Nazi surgeons, an incorrigible torture bride getting her insides scrubbed, stabbed, and stitched. In front of the TV, her eyes grew soft watching movie people kiss. "You should get yourself a nice girl someday," she'd say, turning to me. "One with a lot of money."

There were the magazine women in bras and corsets idling

bored on chairs, with black-barred eyes, and the citizens of weird disintegrated streets like the ones around Times Square—denizens of a neon zone I knew well, for my brother and I had been enrolled in singing lessons at a Broadway talent school since my mother's loss at term of a nameless baby girl who would never live to be our sister. We were five at the time of our first class. Year after year we went. This was also about the time my mother began to beat me, at first intermittently and then, as I grew more able to protest, incessantly, with a rolling pin, clothing hanger, or belt. She would then collapse in the bathroom behind a locked door, crying hysterically as she lay on the tiles. I would stand behind the door, ear pressed to the wood, tugging on the doorknob, pleading with her to please open up, Oh, Mommy, let me in, always at about one o clock in the morning, well after my father had gone to work.

She would groan, "Let me die here!"

"Mommy, please!!"

And sometimes the door opened and stumbling out she'd rush to a window, throw it open, threatening to jump. I would beg, weep, until I reasoned so persuasively that little by little I coaxed her back. It may have been such incidents that convinced her of my theatrical ability, because twice a week my mother dressed us in matching blue suits, white shirts, and red bow ties, all things between us being equal, shined our shoes to a high gloss, and marched us, the American flag twins, from the subway to the talent school. The school was located in Times Square next door to a shooting gallery, around which hovered the hookers who looked just like the stag-mag ladies, though sans black bars of identity concealment—hard-edged, angry, feral women, unwashed, with fumey, bloodshot eyes, smoking and talking loudly, calling out to passing men. I sensed that they might have something to do with the sexual menace.

Upstairs, in a classroom with several other children, my brother and I listened to a man named Donald ramble on about the glories of the footlights. Donald played scratchy records on a phonograph and we all stood at our desks warbling up and down the scales. I was riveted by the Camel Cigarette billboard across the street of a man with a hole-mouth from which big gray wobbling puffs of ring-shaped smoke dissolved over Broadway. Then, lesson done, my mother hauled us into a penny arcade, which had a voice-recording booth and where for a dollar she cut a plastic single of Howie and me trilling "Tea for Two." Sometimes she took us into Hubert's Freak Museum to see photos of Sealo the Seal Boy or Alberto Alberta, the half-man, half-woman, or Congo the Jungle Creep. Then, back to the Bronx, where as reward she let us stay up late and sprawl on her bed while she snored in the armchair and my brother lay on his back, reading comics.

With my father's mags out, I had myself a real smut fest.

Snarling black panthers wearing collars adorned with swastikas bared fangs at the near-naked breasts of a spread-eagled and mana-cled "Reich Sex Prisoner" as flesh-gobbling tattooed and feathered cannibals gleefully hog-tied a stripped redhead in prep to become a "Living Sacrifice for the Amazon Snake God"—an immense boa-sized cobra that slithered toward its bug-eyed and screaming victim across a cave floor strewn with skulls.

3

IN THE STAGS THERE WERE CRIME STORIES.
Real-life photos of cold-eyed sex slayers, killers captured after their latest interstate spree. The young men always seemed to have buzz haircuts, deadpan remorseless faces defying the mug-shot photographer to find even a smidgeon of pulpit decency in their soulless lonesome eyes.

They had raped and mutilated scores of young women with beehive dos, flaring nerdy horn-rim glasses, and sleeveless blouses that always buttoned to the neck, the affronts and outrages detailed in graphic terms, except for the rapes, which were described in police blotter officialese: "Lab tests showed that the victims had been repeatedly penetrated."

As yet I had no idea that a penis entered a vagina, or that a breast might be suckled for reasons other than milk. In such accounts, the stabbings became the sex: eroticized knifings, orgasmic woundings.

I only learned about sexual congress at age nine, when my

mother decided to decamp with my brother and me on a cross-country exodus to Los Angeles to enlist a talent scout whose ad had appeared in the back of one of my father's stag mags.

After a four-day transcontinental Greyhound haul we arrived exhausted at the home of a drunken failed actor and director who pretended to audition us, knocked Howie from the box, declared me star material, and offered to help enroll me in Warner Brothers Talent School in exchange for a small fee of ten thousand dollars.

Realizing that she'd been duped, my poor mother marched us out of there and launched on a tearful, zigzagging suicidal meander from state to state, motel to motel—lying whole days in dark rooms, crying, while Howie and I wandered hand in hand, gnawed by hunger, through whatever city or town we happened to land in, and in one of these—Miami—I learned from a dark-skinned Cuban boy named Juan, who spoke near-perfect English, that my father stuck his penis, which Juan called "dick," into my mother's vagina, which Juan called "cunt."

He was slender, good-looking, older than me—maybe ten or eleven—and we had settled into a game of trapping scorpions as they wandered in the grass lawn of the motel. We threw matches onto their backs, or jabbed them with sharp sticks, or crushed them into goo with rocks. The scorpions certainly deserved painful deaths, we reckoned, seeing how poisonous they were.

Juan asked, gaping lewdly: "You seen your father fuck your momma?"

Heart pounding at the sound of the F word, I gaped back. "I dunno."

"I saw my poppa screw my momma other night. You ever see them do it?"

"Do what?"

"You know, man! IT!" Into a circle made with one hand he

jabbed a finger of the other, hard, fast, in and out. "Screwing! Your
daddy put his dick in your mommy's cunt!"

Instantly, I saw what he meant and began to cry.

"It's not true!" I protested. "My dad don't do that to my mom."
But it sounded hollow. Juan jabbed his stick thoughtfully up and
down on a scorpion's back as it writhed in its own leaking fluids.
Then he stood up, smiled wickedly, and implanted in my consciousness a nightmare that would lead to my eventual ruin. "Why I lie to
you, man? Everybody do it! When you grow up, so will you."

4

UNTIL HOLLYWOOD, HOWIE HAD BEEN A WARM, talkative kid. After the thumbs down, he clammed up. I became his emotional conduit, as if appointed to feel for both. I was Mother's little genius, earmarked for escalating special treatment.

Whenever she laid into me in the motel rooms, screeching, he stood by, silently watching, half hidden by the doorway, sucking his thumb, big dark eyes grown wide with terror as I called out: "Howie, help! Make her stop!" But what could he do? Trapped and helpless as we were in the rat pits of her fury?

Out there, on the road, when my father was nowhere about, she beat me mercilessly. This went on, day after day, in motels with names like The Sandman and The Costa Rica and Holiday Bungalow. Muffled by the happy squealing clamor of families in bathing suits frolicking in the pool, my shrieks for help fell on deaf ears.

Back in the Bronx, she woke me at late hours when Pop would be gone—and the harder I screamed, the louder she struck. No mercy shown once she was engaged. My only hope to play dead, stifle my cries, though this always proved impossible, as she managed to find that one spot in the elbow or knees which provoked more pain than I could bear.

She caused me to break, plead, to no avail. With a shrieking sense of injury, at such times I was not a self or a person but a blinding blur kinesthecized by tears. My shadow, on the ground or on a wall, seemed more real than me.

My mother bought the magazines too. I read them when she was out. A shadow world grew in my thoughts. Desires so forbidden their sheer weight crushed me. Often they took the shape of a beautiful adult woman, trussed and blindfolded, helpless to resist my caresses, endearments, or cruelties. She couldn't shrug me off or slap me away. She couldn't hit me with a hanger. She had to let me touch her and kiss her as I liked. She had to let me rub against her, love her as I wanted, for as long as I wished. Such thoughts triggered hard-ons so painful that only repeated ejaculations brought relief.

Turning ten on the road, moving around from motel to flop-house, I began to fear that I was a serial killer, one of those baby-faced blue-eyed butchers gazing back from the dingy newsprint pages of my parents' mags.

I masturbated constantly. Following which I experienced a wave of remorse, sometimes horror. This drew me further into myself.

Barred from decent human society, I was left only with books and with stray dogs, pigeons, hoboes, parks, endless streets, the cold round sun, hunger, and the black-smudge ink traces on my fingers from the smut mags and paperbacks I browsed in the candy stores.

If I was in fact a potential killer, I had best stay hidden from sight, away from women especially, who I feared could at any moment unleash their rage on my exposed elbows and turn me into the tortured son of the Nazi torture bride.

Life had once been a nice place to visit but I didn't want to live here anymore. I felt everything too intensely, became twisted, writhing, a knot of fierce furtive agony. Around women, I grew subdued, pitilessly shy. At school could barely bring myself to speak. We moved from city to city, state to state, the perennial new kids on the block. When money ran out, we wound up in a San Francisco Mission Street flop, out-of-state indigents. Soon after we arrived in the city, my father traveled there to join us. I suppose my parents missed each other, though I suspect she was in flight from the life he had made, which was no life. Naturally, he arrived penniless. Now there was no money and a fourth mouth to feed.

To make ends meet, my mother worked as an au pair temp and every night my father went out into the foggy streets to walk her home. They returned with a can of spaghetti and a bottle of orange soda: dinner for four.

I remember this as a time of lice-crawling despair and sinister strangers. There was not even money for the stags. I recall a couple named Joanne and Bob, young Linkhorn drifter types, descendants of poor Dustbowl refugees who'd thought, same as us, to find Paradise in California, who had befriended my parents and paid frequent visits to our squalid little room to find relief from their own dirty hole on the next floor up.

Once, to prove how tough she was, Joanne threw me face down on the bed, thrust a knee into my back, and jerked my arm behind, twisted until I howled but still didn't relent, even when I begged her to stop.

"You little shit!" she said with a laugh. "Go on! Kick and scream! It won't help you! Do it!"

My parents and her husband stood by guffawing. It was as if I was now a stag story. Stretched for sacrifice. I swore then I'd never let that happen again. From there on, I must serve as my own shield and sword.

5

WE RETURNED TO THE BRONX, TO STAY FOR GOOD. Fed on fat and starch, morbidly obese, with large femalelike breasts that the teen boys would squeeze until we wept, Howie and I had the hell beat out of us.

There was a guy named Billy the Barrel, an adult, who would waylay me en route to the schoolyard, force me into doorways to fondle his testicles. He pressed up against me, panting hard, a hand on my throat, grunted: "Hold them harder. Hold them fuggin' balls."

There were others, strangers, men who chased me down, pinned me against hot metal fin-tailed Buicks and Chevys as indifferent passersby walked on. They whimpered excitedly, squeezed until my breath strangled, grinding their groins against me, their thick cold tongues squirming in my ear.

Struggle was futile. In their arms I went limp, let them do what they wanted until it was done, and once escaped, hurried off to try to return to my body, which I'd left when their hands trapped me, flown off while still in the predatory embrace, to hover over it all in a kind of disembodied aerial astonishment.

Fled, I sat in the cool shadows of some alley, hid among trash cans where no one would think to look, and amid the refuse and stink searched for signs of something lost, a sense of me as good, to retrieve if I could even as I knew that I couldn't, that what had just occurred had happened too often. That with my big breasts and my helplessness I must have been some sort of girl who was supposed to be a boy, or why else would they touch me that way? And then grew amazed, sickened, cursing myself for my passivity. And fantasized about what I should have done, Stab them with a big knife like Jim Bowie, with a sword like Zorro, run them through! Or shoot them dead like the Lone Ranger. Saw myself shouting and punching, wanting to be a hero, but felt only a coward. And slowly, the numbing helplessness and shame filtered through until it was all over me, every part, an invisible infection about which I could not speak to anyone, for what would they think? My father? If he knew? What would he say? Forget about it! And my mother? How would she look at me as I told her about the men touching me in that way?

Forget about it.

BOOK TWO

6

BY AGE FIFTEEN, AFTER YEARS OF SCHOOLYARD training in gutter violence and sports, my body shot up, gained muscle, lost fat. I became a skilled, ruthless fighter who laughed at pain, relished blood, savored mayhem.

Known around the hood as "Moony," I prided myself on bruises and scabs. I grew my hair and sideburns long. My curled lip sneered and my eyes grew sharp.

Billy the Barrel still came around, thinking I'd forgotten his enforced ball-holding. Saw me once and called out: "Hey, there's fugging Moony. Look who got big. You still a punk! Get the fug outta here!"

At stickball, with a bat wagging in his fists, cigarette dangling from his lips, he shot off his mouth at some scared kid whom he'd coerced into a game of pitching in. "C'mon, ya moron!" he screeched at the kid. "Throw me something I can hit! C'MON!"

When he spotted my approach, his face grew grave, he turned

away from the pitch, and the ball bounced off his arm as he tossed the cigarette aside to aim his bat at my forehead.

"C'mere," I said, smiling. He swung. The bat broke against my arm with a loud crack. I laughed. To this day I can feel my hand clamped on his hair, slamming his head into cement studded with glass shards. Had a broken bottle neck going for his eye when hands from behind pulled me off as others hauled him to his feet and hurried him away, bawling, blood gushing through his fingers. Never saw him again.

Other times, I broke teeth. One guy's face exploded against my fist. Another with a knife out, who'd picked on my brother, got beat to a pulp outside a pizza joint, against a car. Once, this huge baboon named Fat Joe put out word on the street that he was gunning for me. I put word back that we should meet in a dead end off the Concourse at such and such a time. He brought an entourage, who stood silent witness as I turned his ape face into a swollen mask of blood.

On a family visit to Uncle Arnold's place in the Castle Hill Projects, we brought big bags of White Castle hamburgers, quarts of Coca-Cola. Cousin Dennis had just returned from serving a stretch. At the time he and his brother Harvey were engaged in heroin dealing, car theft, robberies, and other felony crimes. Ivy, another brother—in all there were nine—had a serious monkey on his back. Entering their home felt like crossing over the threshold of a demonic haunt where crazed devils lived. The edginess of that household was amazing.

While my Aunt Ray sat in the dining room screeching that Arnie should drop dead, Arnie and my father—in full sight of Ray and her circle of sympathetic girlfriends—enjoyed the living room, oblivious to her rants. Arnie wore boxer shorts, wifebeater tee, and house shoes, while my father looked real sharp in an Italian knit, sharkskin slacks, and Florsheim gator loafers.

They blew smoke rings on fat White Owl cigars, remonstrated about lost bets, and argued back and forth about the Yankees. Sometimes their voices dropped and they talked about things I wasn't meant to hear. Bored, I tried wandering down the hall to my cousins' room but Pop's voice cracked like a whip above my head: "Hey, dummy! Where you think you're going?"

"I'm bored. I wanna go see my cousins."

"Get your ass over here NOW!"

"Let 'im go see them pieces of shit," said Uncle Arnold. "It'll be a good warning to him."

"YOU'RE THE PIECE OF SHIT, NOT YOUR SONS!" Ray shrieked. Her bottle brunette big-hair girlfriends, in pantsuits, nodded in accord.

"Awright," my father said. "But if they try to give you any dope, you let me know. I'll go in there and knock them dumbheads off. You morons in there hear me?"

From my cousins' room came laughter.

"Keep your nose clean!" my father warned me.

"Yeah, sure," I said insolently and knocked on the door. Heard Dennis call: "Who's that?"

"It's me."

"Hey, Cousin Alan! C'mon in, man!"

I entered, found them in their Skivvies, stretched on cots, smoking Camels, having themselves a little chitchat, or plotting heists.

"Cousin Alan!" said Dennis. "How's it goin', man? Have a seat, relax."

Down one side of his mouth ran a scar I hadn't seen before.

"It goes," I said.

"How old're you now? said Harvey. "Fifteen, goin' on fifty?"

They both snickered.

Dennis waved me into a folding chair. "Don't listen to that dummy, Cousin Alan."

I sat there. And tried hard not to stare. But gawked anyway at the tattoos covering Dennis's arms, chest, shoulders. They hadn't been there before he got sent up and they were a little like the hand-drawn numbers that my mother's friend Ruth—who'd been in Auschwitz—had on her arm. But the tats on Dennis were even more jagged looking, crudely drawn.

Dennis, noticing my stare said, pleased: "You checking these out? I got 'em in the joint."

"Them's tattoos," I said.

"Yeah," he said.

"But I thought Jews don't get those. My mom says Jews don't get buried Jewish if they get those."

"Yeah," said Dennis, glancing over at Harvey with a mischievous grin. "Well, I guess I'll worry about that when I'm dead." They both guffawed.

"Lemme see?" I said.

"Help yourself, Cuz."

"You got all those doing time?"

"And a couple on the outside."

Soon after, Dennis got into trouble again and tried to kill the DA's main witness during a trial for a jewelry heist and was sent upstate to Sing Sing. While Harvey, who kept up his end of the heroin trade, slipped a bag of smack to his brother Ivy, who OD'd and died in his mother's bathtub.

For Ivy's funeral, two police bulls brought Dennis down cuffed and dressed in a prison-issue brown suit to say goodbyes. They led him into the chapel by the elbows, a defiant sneer on his face as he peered into his brother's coffin, and then led him out, no chance to speak to anyone.

My Aunt Ray cried and screamed, and my Uncle Arnold looked lost, but out behind the chapel, Harvey, who'd slipped the hot shot to his brother, lounged with his crew, leaned up against a big two-toned, fin-tailed Chevy, and was passing a joint around, the smell of which wafted inside. My father said to me, "C'mon," and out back we went. Pop walked right up to Harvey and backhanded the joint from his mouth. None of Harvey's crew dared move against Pop. They kept their traps shut and I noted as I scanned their hate-filled gazes (my own hand on the K-55 knife in the side pocket of my jacket) that a lot of them had tats on their hands and arms. This was the late Sixties and ink was already common among gangs.

"C'mon, let's get the hell outta here," my father said in a tone of utter disdain, and we returned to the chapel.

At the burial, Arnie got the idea that the Kaufman men should take over from the gravediggers, bury our own, even though our own had killed our own. We each took hold of the balancing straps and, on Arnie's cue, eased the coffin down into the hole. Someone lowered too fast, the coffin dropped, my cousin, wrapped in his white burial shroud, spilled out.

Around the grave Aunt Ray, my mother, and other female relatives swooned, screaming, hands to foreheads. My Uncle Arnold ripped open his new silk shirt and howled like an animal. My father stood there, shaking his head, muttering, "Goddamned hopeless, all of 'em."

I jumped in, followed by my cousin Larry. Brushed the grave dirt from Ivy's eyes and scooped it from his mouth with two fingers. He felt like cold butchered meat. Then we rolled him into the box, sealed it, and I yelled up: "Goddamit! Bury 'im!" The gravediggers tossed in dirt fast and drumming on his coffin. But though I had stuck my very hand into the corpse mouth of a dead drug addict I did not think of it as a warning.

7

AROUND THIS TIME I FOUND WORK AS A FLOOR
sweep and general grease monkey in the Bronx Motorcycle Repair
shop on Soundview Avenue. It was the main custom shop for the
Angels' chapters of the Northeast, from NYC to Massachusetts, and
was run by this guy named Eddie, a gearhead genius who turned
cherry full-dress Harleys into chopped hogs with extended forks
and with flaming death's heads painted on the peanut gas tanks.

He paid me under the table and fed me take-out shrimp-salad
heroes and quarts of chocolate milk. I think he kept me out of pity,
because I wasn't much with a wrench, couldn't tell a lug nut from
a washer.

The gig was a get-around boon for a tenement-poor sewer rat
like me—gave me the bucks to take out my first girlfriend, Kathy, a
short, seventeen-year-old mixed Puerto Rican and Greek girl with
long black hair down to her waist. Kathy wore stilettos, miniskirts,
and tight sweaters with uplift bras that turned her breasts into milk
bottle torpedoes.

I belonged, with my brother, to a dead-end crew that had its own storefront clubhouse bankrolled by a nutjob bodybuilder named Paul, where we drank wine, smoked joints, planned trouble, listened to the Four Tops. When I had Kathy in back, on the cot, she'd moan, "Keeese me, Alan! Keeese me, my baby!" I loved rolling and sweating, grinding and upthrusting those breasts into my face. But she wouldn't let me get further than a copped feel, which gave me blue balls so bad I limped.

One day at the motorcycle shop I heard a ground-rumbling roar that sounded like a tank charge by Patton's Third Army and watched as the endless ranks of the Angels rolled up in waves of chrome and fire.

They dismounted, and Eddie, dressed in his usual ragged greasy jeans, black boots, and ripped T-shirt, stepped out to greet them, mopping his face with a sweat-soaked bandana. He led them into the cavernous shop, introduced me to everyone.

"This here kid's Alan," he said. "He's Jewish, right? So, his mother was hunted by Nazis in the war. And she survived. Ain't that right, Alan?"

"That's right." I nodded shyly, avoiding eyes, hands jammed in pockets, shoulders slouched: a big proud strong kid planning to go out for varsity football that fall.

The bikers, fearsome, wild, studied me with interest. Then they parted ranks and up stepped an Angel with long black stringy hair, a grizzled face, and a certain familiar look of intense and torturous intelligence.

He pointed at the armada of hogs parked in neat rows outside. "My name is Jewish Bob," he said. "That's my bike. You see the sissy bar?" I followed his pointing arm to an iron Star of David welded atop the sissy seat of the baddest chopped Roadster I'd ever seen. It had giant monkey handlebars and chrome everything;

sat so low that cockroaches had to detour around it.

He pulled up the sleeve of his striped jersey and showed me a Star of David tattoo. "You been circumcised, kid?" he asked.

"Yeah," I said.

"No, you ain't. You see this knife?" He slipped one from an ivory scabbard slung on a black garrison belt with a grinning skull buckle. "Look at it. Genuine SS battle blade. My own father took it off a Nazi in World War Two after he shoved a bayonet up his ass. See that swastika on the handle?"

I saw it.

Balancing the knife in one hand, he took hold of the loose hanging tongue of my belt, sliced it off with a lightning stroke, and held it up for all to see.

"Check out this fuggin' foreskin!" he shouted, and the bikers laughed and cheered. "Today he's just got a circumcision, Angel style! Now he's really a man!" And he shouted the Hebrew toast to life: "L'chaim!"

All the grinning bikers pounded me on the back and jostled and made me feel like I belonged. I'd never seen a Jew like Jewish Bob. He seemed like the toughest, craziest Angel. As the day wore on he stripped off his shirt and colors and walked around bare-chested. He danced drunk, dropped some acid, and careened laughing into doors. Back and front he was a roped muscle wall of black tattoos, including what I recognized as the Hebrew word for God, YHWH.

From then on, I had friends among the clubs. One, a sergeant of arms for the New York chapter of the Angels, drove a Dad's Root Beer truck to make ends meet and worked the door as a bouncer for the Fillmore East. Every so often he would pull up in the truck, drop off a few cases of root beer, and hand down guest passes for shows.

One night, I showed up at the concert hall with Kathy and was greeted by a cheerful "What's going on, Alan!" from the Angel bouncer, who let us in for free. This so impressed Kathy that later, at the club, she almost let me go all the way, but not quite, which swelled my nuts so bad I howled.

8

SUMMER ENDED, I MADE FOOTBALL SQUAD AT A
sports powerhouse, the biggest all-boys high in NY, a state peniten-
tiary posing as a school, and eventually became offensive tackle and
defensive end on a team heading for the city crown.

One night out with a couple of schoolyard guys in Van Cort-
landt Park, passing big gallon jugs of Gallo port back and forth, I
felt the universe snap into view. I stumbled, drunk, to the grass
and lay with arms and legs akimbo, like an altar sacrifice, smiling
at the blazing stars. For the first time in my life, I felt connected,
happy, sure that life belonged to me and I to it. And I drank myself
unconscious.

From then on, my life's game plan became to someday live by
myself in a room stocked to the rafters with bottles of Gallo and
books by famous writers.

Once, I met up with a few players from the team at the
Killarney Rose, near Fordham Road; guzzled pitchers, and then
shots. Completely sloshed, I picked a fight with someone's face and

broke the place up. It was my first drunken brawl. The last thing I recall before passing out was lying with a swollen eye atop an Irish barfly dressed in a brassiere, in her upstairs bedroom, the feel of her stubbly upper lip as I tried to plant a kiss. The next day, sick as a dog, I learned from the others, who'd waited a turn with her, that I'd puked up on her neck as I passed out.

Finally, when my sexual threshold had grown explosive, I sought relief from a Delancey Street whore named Michelle, who worked for a cathouse on the Lower East Side and charged me ten bucks for a half-and-half—a bang and a blow job. My first real try at sex, I could barely get it up. The old nightmares roared back. "Are you tense? Is this your first time?" she asked. I nodded that it was. "Just relax," she cooed. But I began to obsess about human sacrifice, blonde virgin brides. The obsession with human sacrifice had nothing to do with the act of being blown; it was what my mind threw on the screen as sex occurred—an old obsessive way to buffer reality with twistedness. Still, the anguish it brought was sharp, real. I focused obsessively on a crumb-encrusted fork jammed into a butt-heaped ashtray on the nightstand, overcome by panic that if she saw me staring at it she would apprehend my sudden urge to thrust it into her chest.

Now ensued an unspoken game of eyes. If I happened to glimpse the fork as she performed oral sex, she'd snap my eyes away by stopping and asking how it felt.

I was sure that she had seen my eyes make contact with the utensil; knew, fathomed, my homicidal phobia. It made me so ashamed. I just wanted to crawl away from my skin and die.

After I came, I skulked out ashamed as Michelle looked on sadly. I felt that I barely deserved to live, so filled with nightmares that I could not even enjoy sex with a beautiful woman.

My response to this strange fork-stabbing fear in the weeks and months ahead was to drive my fist into another man's face, a kind of surrogate stabbing, I suppose, the wrestling, the spurting blood, the furious rush. In the Bronx, fights always had a manslaughter element. And football was like that, a kind of stabbing sex. All of me came to play. I slammed my opponent with everything I had, tumbled like a pit bull locked in a grunting death bout. But at the end of day, there was only loneliness, and the sore trek home under seagull-haunted skies, and the weight of an equipment-laden duffel bag, home to a family who hated my guts. I wanted so badly to entangle my legs with a woman's, cradle my head on her soft shoulder, lips at her breast, listening to her heartbeat, touching her pussy possessively— and reaching wholeness with a bottle of Gallo port.

9

LINDA WAS THE FIRST REAL GIRLFRIEND WITH whom I had serious sex. I was seventeen, a high school junior; she, nineteen, a miniskirted, blonde Bronx Community College sophomore with long legs, sweet tits, and blue, defiant eyes.

Her father, Fred, like mine, worked night shifts in the PO, different branch. Her mom, Raz, was a cripple laid up with MS.

I would go to her house when Fred had left for work, slide into her bed, spend the night. My first time with her I got so excited I couldn't get it up; delirious, pardoned myself, went to the bathroom, sat on the toilet, jerked off. When I emerged, she saw a spot of sperm on my thigh and said with a witchy laugh: "What's that?"

"Snot," I said. "I blew my nose."

"That's not snot. That's sperm." She grinned and, leaning over, kissed me.

After that, I had no problem with sex, though once in a while I wrestled with stabbing nightmares.

Sometimes, leaving Linda's house, hunkered in my black varsity letter football jacket under bright blue autumn skies, I sat next to scarved old ladies gabbing on the projects benches, and smiled at how nice the world seemed.

I thought about her all the time, the way she looked, how she loved Laura Nyro, how devoted she was to her mother. I got a job working nights at Krum's, a big confectioners on Fordham Road, to save for a going-steady ankle bracelet engraved with our names.

When I presented it, she was so happy she cried.

It felt damned wonderful, so I bought her tickets to see Laura Nyro and she couldn't believe it. Also got her a beautiful sweater, Leonard Cohen albums, took her to a fancy-dress dinner restaurant with a foreign-sounding name.

Our parents got to know each other. My parents liked Linda. Everyone felt sure that someday we'd marry.

Then, one night, while she was attending to Raz, I happened across a telephone bill lying open on her white dresser and noted a long string of collect calls from Fort Lee, New Jersey, charges reversed.

When she slipped back into bed, I asked: "Who's in Fort Lee?"

"What?"

"All the collect calls from Fort Lee. Who's that?"

She froze. "A friend."

"Oh, yeah? Which?"

His name was Eddie, a former boyfriend now in the National Guard, who was lonely, had no dad, and had a lush for a mom. Linda felt sorry for him, accepted the charges when he called because of how broke he was.

"He calls a lot. There's like fifteen calls for this month."

"He's having a hard time. His mom's dying. Please don't be upset. It's nothing, really. I love you."

"Okay. I'm cool," I lied.

Then, over a period of several weekends—our usual hang-out times—she became ever less available, due, she said, to end-term exams; kept canceling, last minute.

And then one day, on a park bench, she said, "Things have an order. Romance can't be number one!"

I thought, She has to study: no sweat. "You do what you gotta do, baby," I told her. "I'll get the hell out of your hair for a while."

She smiled, nodding somberly, in this very adult way, asserting, as never before, her emotional leverage over me, as if I were some delinquent little crud grounded until I'd learned some pointless lesson.

Pride stung, I left without goodbye, no embrace, hands jammed in pockets—shuffled out of there, dismissed, bewildered, ashamed, sauntering through the Pepto Bismol–pink brick housing complex, feeling a faint draft of the old unbearable loneliness.

10

I DIDN'T DRINK. AND TURNED DOWN OFFERS OF smack from friends as the drug spread like wildfire through the Bronx. When my parents were out, Puerto Rican friends locked themselves in the bedroom, cooked, tied up, and booted. Others sat around the kitchen, drinking wine, huffing glue. When some of the players fixed up in the locker room I looked the other way, played football, wrote poems, studied. I tried to avoid trouble. But my doubts about Linda had infected me.

One Saturday night, when she called to say that she couldn't see me—she and Shelly cramming for some important exam, the usual story—I sweetened my voice, told her no problem, you're my girl, do what you gotta. I'm here for you. Lotsa luck with the tests!

Off the phone, I dressed for combat—an old football jersey, jeans, black Cons, river rat hat, a bandana wrapped around my wrist, a short blackjack in my hip pocket, night's leaden weight in my soul. Palming my K-55, I headed out.

I rode the uptown IRT in a mood of grim resolve, like an animal with a bullet in its side, bleeding out, hiding in the bush, waiting to charge.

I had dreams of becoming a writer and had hoped Linda would share this life, and escape, with me, the blue-collar lack of options grinding down our parents' lives. I went to Shelly's. Pounded on the door. Heard hushed voices. Kool & The Gang on the stereo. Mazor, Shelly's boyfriend, dressed only in briefs, cracked the door a notch. "She's not here," he said and started to shut it on me. Behind him, I glimpsed Shelly in panties and bra. I blasted the door open. Shelly screamed as I bounded up the steps to the next landing, scanned the corridor, figuring that if Mazor had to ball her in the downstairs then someone must be in the upstairs. I kicked in Shelly's bedroom door.

She was naked on her back with him, I guessed it was Eddie, above her, between her legs, white ass muscles clenched, sliding his red horse-sized dick up and down inside her. She screamed. He jumped off comically, dick wagging. I reached for my K-55. Could have lopped it off. Stabbed her to death too.

But amazed, ashamed, embarrassed, I turned and left. I don't know if they called the police.

I found a liquor store. An old Irish guy stood outside. "Look," I said. "Here's two fins. Go in there, get me a jug of Gallo, keep the change."

Moments later he emerged with the medicine. I took the big green bottle with the blue-black contents up to the parkway lawn overlooking the columns of headlights barreling north. Unscrewed the cap, tilted the big jug, and took a long shuddering pull. Then another. Felt so hurt inside I thought it would kill me. Wanted to howl. The firm cold grass pricked my neck. I turned my head to drink more fortified wine, and I saw her, wrapped around his waist, her manicured red fingernails pulling him down by the shoulders into herself, to take him deeper, and on her leg, the ankle bracelet. She had not even had the decency to remove it before giving herself to him.

I thought: Fug it. The wine's sharp grape smelled pleasantly feverish, like a fatal wound. I shuddered and drank more.

BOOK THREE

11

THAT SUMMER, I FLEW TO EUROPE WITH THREE rock-and-roll heroin addicts named Barry, Jimmy, and Danny, who weighed a hundred pounds each and wore their hair in giant Jewfros. Their faces oozed with smack pimples. They all smoked Newport menthol cigarettes and were obsessed with the thought of either scoring methadone in Piccadilly—the Brits handed it out to addicts gratis—or else obtaining some large quantity of pure H in Marseille, a drug trade crossroads made famous by the film *The French Connection*.

Because they dealt smack, they lent me enough money for the summer, and then some. I purchased my ticket on a Freddie Laker flight for a ridiculously low sum, proud that they had let me come along.

In London, we headed over to Hyde Park and fell in with a band of hippies who offered us giant rolled cigars of cheap tobacco sprinkled with stingy pinches of pot. It didn't work well and we all began to jones. Barry and Jimmy went off, and in no time returned with bags of H, passed them around. I snorted too. Then we crashed with a hippie couple. Jackie Mod, with bangs and go-go boots, worked in a Chelsea boutique. Royal Richard drew amateur cartoons. He hadn't much patience, and after fiddling with pen and ink he'd sigh, slap his thighs, rise, and say: "It's all bollocks! Off to the pub!" We'd get hammered on pints of piss-warm bitters. Jackie Mod, coming home and finding us regularly smashed, grew understandably upset and left, she said, to go bang his best friend, Corey. Outraged, Royal Richard stalked off after her. Soon, my friends also melted away into the ulcerated underbelly of London, cruising for meth. They always found it and stumbled back to Royal Richard's and Jackie Mod's to boot up and nod.

I drank pints of bitters in a local pub and went to see my first play by Samuel Beckett, *Endgame*, at the Young Vic. It affected me profoundly because his characters inhabited the same lonely madness that I felt.

Often, I dropped in on Granny Takes a Trip, His Majesty's clothiers to the Who and the Rolling Stones, Rod Stewart and the James Gang. The Gang happened to drop by one day. There we were, sitting side by side on little Shanghai stools, as long-legged SoHo girls in hot pants and teensy sweaters helped us try on patch-work leather kicks and snakeskin shoes, velvet two-toned jackets and embroidered silk shirts. What are you doing tonight around two? the James Gang asked me. Nothing. Here's a pass to our after-hours club. They were some of the most ferocious rock-and-roll guitar gunfighters of all time, wielded their Gibsons like Colt .45s. Even the fearsome Winter Brothers, Johnny and Edgar, wouldn't draw on them. Two days later, eardrums stunned, I crawled out of that club on hand and knees, converted.

Not long after, we shot up north to Gloucester, to this commune I heard of, and there were sheep and foul communal stews and everything looked Dark Ages gray.

One night, I escaped to a pub with a single motorcycle parked
outside. Inside was a gang sporting patches on cutoff denims. I
sat down at their table and introduced myself as a visitor from the
Bronx. Impressed, they asked me what it was like. I told them about
working at Eddie's motorcycle shop. "So you met the Angels?!"
They fell over themselves to stand me drinks. "Where are your
bikes?" I asked. "I saw the BSA outside. What about the rest?"
They laughed. There were no others. Too poor. One bike between
the whole club is all they had. That night, I went back to their
clubhouse, a welfare flat on a crooked street in a dingy slum. We
drank cider, dropped mescaline, listened to the Rolling Stones.
We tripped, and told each other jokes that made us vomit out our
guts with mirth. Come morning, I joined a biker named Flash as
he followed a horse-drawn milk wagon, filching the bottles from
doorsteps and bringing them back for the club's breakfast. The rest
of the day was spent groaning in the crapper.

Back in London, reunited with my original group, we bought a
broken-down tiny green-and-white station wagon, which we registered using the Cornwall YMCA as our home residence, and headed
to France, where we drove around Paris tripping on acid. Slept in
an abandoned lot next to a Turkish camper overrun with rats, and
next morning, horrified, drove hell-bent for leather to Marseille,
a city of Africans with scarred cheeks, sunglassed Moroccans with
bronzed chests, and police officers in white kepis out of *Casablanca*.
But there was no one willing to peddle us smack. And no one could
really blame the Marseille dealers if the sight of three American
furry freak brothers with a long-haired brute Bronx bodyguard in
tow made them doubt our true intentions.

12

TIRED, BROKE, WE RETURNED STATESIDE. I WAS
now almost nineteen and went to a podunk college in Michigan on
a promise of a possible football scholarship. Long-haired, earringed,
brain corrupted by LSD, my chin ringed by a Mormon's beard,
twenty pounds under my playing weight, unwashed, pasty-faced,
stoned, I stood insolently in front of the coaches with beer breath
and bloodshot eyes, and I got benched, and then dropped.

Began to cruise around with Goldie and Moondog, two local
Ann Arbor heads who hipped me to the White Panthers, a political
pot party formed to free rock activist John Sinclair (sentenced to ten
years for a single joint). I spent a month in their safe house, crashed
on a fold-out couch that contained a duffel bag packed with weed,
which I smoked the way others chew mints. One day, in walked the
Panthers' house band, the MC5. Their underground hit "Kick Out
the Jams, Motherfucker" became the prototype of punk. I recall
being backstage at one of their famous Ann Arbor gigs too, and
it may be that Beat legend Allen Ginsberg—whom someday I'd

perform with—was there. Hard to say, though. The memory is fuzzy because I was so zonked.

Done with sports for good, I was admitted as an undergraduate in American lit with a minor in Jewish studies at the City College of New York, still known, at the time, as the Harvard of the Proletariat.

I studied with Yitz Greenberg, a Jewish studies pioneer, in a course on Israel and the Superpowers, and enrolled in a seminar with Elie Wiesel, the dean of Holocaust literature.

Elie, as we called him, frail, refined, wore an air of somber courtesy. But underneath lay an invincible sadness that was like a reproach. Virtually everything he said accused the world and confirmed what my mother had tried to teach in her own crude way.

Another Holocaust was certain to come. Governments of any kind cannot be trusted. The world is and always will be against the Jews. The Holocaust was a civilizational crime, but in a very real sense, no one, yet, had truly paid for it. In fact, those most culpable were now prospering.

Once, Elie stood at the blackboard, elbow cradled in his hand, eyes wistful, and pronounced in that slow, sad, thoughtful way of his: "The Holocaust is not the end point. No. It is a new kind of beginning. For mankind, a singular sort of precedent. History has shown that once something unprecedented appears in this world,"—he scanned our transfixed eyes—"rather than go away, it sets the stage for future reenactments of the same, more genocides, but on an even larger and more criminal scale."

Inflamed with anxious visions of impending Holocaust, I dreamed of armed resistance. Tried to think of ways to acquire guns. Even called Elie once, at his home. He listened, appalled, as I ranted and raged, drunk on Gallo port, about the need to rise up. The Hit Man and the Angel warred in me. The Angel won. With virtually no resources, I launched a magazine called *Jewish Arts Quarterly*.

The first issue contained work by Wiesel as well as lesser-known scholars and poets. My way now seemed clear. I must become a Jewish writer. I launched myself on this course with prophetic gusto. After many months of determined effort, I decided to announce my career path to none other than the quintessential Jewish writer of all time: Isaac Bashevis Singer.

13

THE FUTURE NOBEL LAUREATE AND YIDDISH author, who situated many of his best short stories on Manhattan's Upper West Side, also made his home there. His phone number was listed. He was famous for permitting just about anyone to drop by.

It took me some time to screw up the courage to call. I did so in part because I was fast becoming aware that my plan to be a distinctly "Jewish writer" was considered to be something of a career hazard by not a few of my teachers, themselves Jews, who warned me on the sly to avoid the label "Jewish writer" by any and all means.

One I recall in particular, who advised me, face screwed up in distaste: "All the New York intellectuals are really Jewish writers, but none of them, not even Roth or Bellow, cop to it. Only Malamud—the third of that 'Hart, Shaffner, and Marx' of literature—proclaims it, and he's the weakest of the three! There's Ozick, of course: she's very out about it. But on the whole, publishers don't really like the 'Jewish shtick.' And the lit mags, well, they're all run by Wasps like George Plimpton. Want to get ahead as a writer? Don't be too Jewish in your work."

"What about I.B. Singer?" I said.

I remember the look I got. "Sing-er?" His voice dropped. "You want to end up like that?"

I kind of did.

After moving to the Upper West Side, I would often spot Singer, already old, dressed in a dignified blue suit, shuffling down the dingy Broadway sidewalks, careful of pigeons, fitting right in with the boulevard's rich stew of old Jews with numbered arms, young seedy hotshots loitering outside the Off-Track Betting Office, Puerto Ricans and blacks crowding the Chinese-Spanish restaurants, and aproned Italian hot dog vendors with cigars poking from their mugs. I wanted to be like him, a writer hidden among life's weeds, one who cared for ragged birds and conversed with everyday folks. I never dared approach Singer in the Four Brothers Restaurant, where he sometimes went to eat, or in Famous Dairy, his usual lunch spot. But I needed to speak with him, badly. I sensed that only he could help.

For all the well-meaning advice that I'd been handed, I was in fact now incurably cursed with Jewish Writeritis. In the wake of Wiesel's class, whenever I set pen to page, out popped some Jewish character anguishing over the Holocaust. I felt like a throwback to another age. It was the Seventies, but I wasn't hip: I was obsessed with Auschwitz. My fellow writers effulged in prose about smoking pot and free love, but I wrote about a lonely Jewish survivor who spoke to his parrot and a dreamy sculptor who perished in the gas chambers. To make matters worse, I had launched, with my own meager resources, the Jewish lit mag and it was how people most identified me. I had gone from a cool Kerouac type to a pathetic, outmoded Sholom Aleichem, on my way to committing professional suicide.

I felt that only Singer would understand, and so I called.

"Who is this?"

"Alan Kaufman," I said.

"How can I help you, Mr. Kaufman?"

"Mr. Singer," I began, heart racing, "I'm a college-aged writer, a novice. I publish a Jewish magazine. My mother was in the Holocaust."

There was a tired pause. "Your mother, she was in the war?"

"Yes," I said.

Another pause, this one kinder somehow. "I see. And so. I can help you with something?"

"Please, may I...come see you?"

He considered. Then: "So, come. The address you know?"

I read it off the telephone directory listing.

"Good. You'll be here soon?" He seemed almost concerned for me.

"Right now!"

"I'm the building on the left, off the courtyard. Goodbye."

I ran the thirty blocks, and when I reached his amazing building on West 86th Street, a giant wedding cake of a thing with a doorman in a booth, I gasped, "Here for Singer!" and was waved right through. By the gloomy lobby lights I searched the mailboxes, and there, incredibly, affixed to the dented brass lid, was the name—IB SINGER—and his apartment number.

He met me dressed in the white shirt, black tie, trousers, unsteady on his feet. "Come in," he said, and led the way into his bedroom, where an open valise lay on the bed. "Alma, my wife, is already down in Miami. I'm flying tonight to join her."

"I shouldn't be a pest," I said. "I can come another time."

"At my age, there is no other time," he said without a hint of jest. "Have a seat."

I sat on the edge of the bed, as often in childhood I would perch on my mother's bed.

"And so, what is your trouble?" he asked. I hadn't said anything about trouble, yet he knew. And so I told him about my obsession with the Holocaust. That I felt alone, not only as a writer but even among American Jews; like a ghost, separate, inhabiting a kingdom of the dead unseen by the living, one made up of the murdered Jewish communities of Europe. I said that in my prose I wrote more for the dead than for the living. He listened intently, while slowly folding and packing shirts.

When I finished, he looked at me carefully and said: "You were born here, in America?"

"Yes, in New York. But how I ended up among the living, I don't know. I really shouldn't be alive."

He nodded. "This is because your mother was a survivor. She felt guilty and you took this on yourself from her. You might be right. Perhaps you are a ghost. I, too, believe in spirits. This is something we both share. But you should also know that in Jewish lore, when a funeral meets a wedding in the road, the wedding has the right of way. Life comes first. So, you brought me something to see that you wrote? Most young writers do."

Ashamed, I nodded and handed him a copy of my magazine containing what I considered my best work, a trilogy of short stories about Jewish American immigrants. After all, the only reason for a broke young student to publish a mag is to feature one's favorite author: oneself.

14

I CONTINUED TO WRITE AND ENTERED ONE OF THE immigrant stories for City College's prestigious Samuel Goodman Short Story Award. It won second prize: fifty bucks.

Emboldened by success, I audited a seminar with Anthony Burgess, author of *A Clockwork Orange,* who provoked my immediate outrage by publishing an essay in the Sunday *New York Times Magazine* in which he characterized his students, which included me, as a bunch of long-haired pot-smoking drunken bongo-playing ignoramuses.

It was true enough, but my ire was provoked; he was rumored to have been paid two hundred thousand dollars for his services. Incensed by his lack of gratitude, I stormed into his office one day.

"What the hell do you mean by this?" I demanded, tossing the magazine article onto his desk.

He glanced down, recognized the piece. "What I mean is the work pays well, and the *Times* pays well. I'm in need of bucks. About your edification, or that of your cronies, I couldn't care less.

I regard you all as utterly hopeless orangutans."

He reached down, jerked open a heavy iron desk drawer, removed a bottle of gin with two tumblers, poured us each an ample helping, and offered up a toast, which I, standing there outraged, declined to join.

"Here's to bongo jungle. And your loss, by the way. This is better stuff than any of the crap you can afford." He belted it back, wiped his mouth. "But here's the trick," he said, gasping and pouring another while nudging my untouched tumbler closer to me. "If you stop protesting, start fugging writing, and if you stop worrying about what some old British arsehole thinks, you could someday afford to buy this kind of gin for yourself, and with money paid for by your own books instead of mine. Now, wouldn't that be nice?"

Watching him down the second drink, I had to admit: it would. Defeated, I hoisted my glass with a weak smile and savored its slow burning descent down my throat.

In 1977, two years out of college, I lived in a squalid boardinghouse room on the Upper West Side where I continued to slug whiskey and bang out short stories about the Holocaust and about Jewish immigrants, stories that only the rarest journal would lend space to.

One of these was *Shdemot*, magazine of the kibbutz movement, to which I sent a story about a Jewish sculptor who is betrayed by her Gentile lover and perishes at Auschwitz. The editor, David Twersky, fired off a letter of acceptance which arrived in an onion-skin-thin envelope with Israeli postage bearing the image of Theodore Herzl.

I couldn't have been more thrilled. Included was a handwritten note from Twersky himself inviting me to "drop in at the Shdemot offices" should I ever find myself in Tel Aviv.

To me, who had no link to Israel or to anyone who did, it was like receiving an invite from Ben-Gurion himself to hang out at the Knesset.

BOOK FOUR

15

GROANING, STRETCHED ON MY SHOULDER, I surveyed the scene with fuzzy hungover eyes, blinking in the harsh sunlight at sun-browned feet, then up to knees, then the hem of a summer dress, a string-net shopping bag dangling from the wrinkled hand of an old woman wearing tortoiseshell sunglasses, a face framed by a cloud of white hair.

Came to my feet, swaying, asked the senior: "Where am I?"

She didn't say.

"Ma'am? Ma'am? If you don't mind: where am I?"

Astonished, with a thick accent, she replied: "What do you mean, where am I? You are in ISRAEL!"

Pale-faced, clammy with sweat, overdressed in a sweater and a tan knee-length thrift-shop camel-hair coat, clutching in one hand a leather suitcase and in the other a typewriter, I asked, baffled: "Where? Where in Israel?"

She gaped back, annoyed. "Tel Aviv! The city. In the center!"

We stood on a traffic island on one of the busiest thoroughfares in Tel Aviv. I had no idea how I'd gotten here. The last I recalled, I was stumbling drunk through Piccadilly Circus in London; then remember vaguely passing somehow through customs at Ben-Gurion airport. After that, drew a blank. I concluded that how I got here didn't matter: I was here. Good enough! Now needed to situate myself. Twersky had suggested that I go to a kibbutz.

"Would you happen to know where I can find the offices of the kibbutz movement?"

"Which movement? Each is different."

I remembered. "Ihud Hakibbutzim. Ten Dubnov Street."

"Dubnov? Dubnov is near. Here is Dubnov." She pointed. The loose underskin of her browned arm swung. "You see this big antenna? A couple buildings down is a white building, yes? That is your place. You are from America?"

"New York," I answered, as though it were a separate nation.

"You don't look so good. Are you all right? Why are you sleeping here? You are poor? A poor American? I didn't know there is such a thing."

"No," I said, smiling. "Not poor. Drunk. A drunk New Yorker. There are plenty of us."

Stiffly, she shrugged and crossed at the light to get away from my leering insolence.

Looked around. Saw a sign in Hebrew. Oh, my Lord, I thought. I'm really here.

As dubious a prospect as I may have seemed, I was assigned to a first-rate kibbutz and given a bus ticket to get there. The kibbutz, Mishmar Hasharon, or "Guardian of the Sharon Valley," was a sprawling agricultural settlement in the central plain, orange grove country, near the coastal city of Netanya.

The proud land swept through my eyes like a vision. In January, the sun flashed out of somber rainy skies with blades of steely light that clarified the sky into a pale-blue watercolor wash. And the hills sparkled with new green life. Everywhere people in sleeveless shirts and shorts sauntered along happily. Lining the roads were hitch-hiking soldiers, and one could see in their faces that there was no meanness in them, that they were good men and women, serving the Jewish state with a sense of belief, of purpose. I was the stranger passing through, my cheek resting on my fist, leaning against a vibrating bus window, given up to an almost pleasant sense of unreality: In this realest of real places, I felt unreal.

The kibbutz was a kind of paradise, with little white red-roofed cottages, winding rose-lined paths, a swimming pool, horses, and long-legged bikini-clad volunteers from the Scandinavian countries. Swedes, Danes, Finns strolled around in flip-flops, laughing languidly, making eyes at me.

I was young, tall, broad-shouldered, Jewish, unfettered, single. Could hardly believe my luck.

The kibbutzniks, tough, browned, good-natured men and women in blue work clothes, took an immediate liking to me; hoped perhaps that I might someday marry one of the kibbutz daughters—mainly homely old maids in their late thirties.

The kibbutzniks' instantaneous and positive assessment of my attributes cheered me. In New York, no one had said anything nice about me in many years. It was interesting that the same person could seem so unpromising in one place yet appear so worthwhile in another. Perhaps a change of scene was all it took. But on the other hand, I harbored a gnawing unease that the kibbutzniks didn't really know me.

The most promising kibbutz daughters had moved to the major cities or left the country altogether to study at university or practice their trade or marry an urban professional, while the sons, on the whole, were less socially mobile, more apathetic, stayed behind.

Their chief goal was to serve in crack frontline commando units in the army, and when at home, on kibbutz, to man their tractors, perform the duties assigned them, and sleep with the bombshell Scandinavian volunteers.

The volunteers lay at poolside after the day's work, sunning themselves in skimpy outfits, slender, busty secretaries and stenographers with frost-blonde hair and ice-blue eyes. For them, kibbutz was the next best thing to Club Med.

Some liked it so much they stayed on year round, worked in exchange for free room, board, medical care, the frequent fun tours sponsored by the kibbutz. On these jaunts everyone piled into buses along with tents, oil drums, big gas burners, musical instruments, sacks of potatoes, vats of homemade salads, boxes of plastic-sealed chocolate pudding desserts, plus fresh baked breads, coffee, tea, sugar, blankets, flashlights, handguns, and assault rifles.

In a big caravan of buses, jeeps, and vans, we traveled to some remote spot of natural or historical interest—Masada, say, where in Roman times a handful of Jewish fighters made a valiant suicidal last stand against the Roman Empire. Piling out, we would set up camp for a big *kumsitz* or "come sit" gathering.

Everyone around a bonfire for days, singing songs, cuddling, necking, playing accordions and guitars, dancing, and gorging on huge plates of fresh-made French fries and other foodstuffs.

Later, newly paired hand-holding lovers disappeared into the harsh landscape for a few hours of naked coupling under the desert moon. At some ungodly hour, the kibbutz men shrugged off blankets, kissed their lovers' sleepy foreheads, roused everyone, and shouldering weapons prodded us forward for a quick march to the summit of Masada.

It was on such a trip that I met Helka, a Finnish girl with a pretty affect of bookishness belied by shockingly blue eyes, blonde hair, a tan, slender, long-legged body, and small perfect breasts. She had no bikini lines—she sunbathed nude at every possible chance: a real uninhibited free-swinger. Our bodies contrasted comically: me, New York Jewish, sun-starved, almost blue tinged, against her warm sweet apricot-colored silk.

But the contrast excited her, I suspect. We drew close to each other with knowing half smiles of wanton, intelligent, slightly churlish lust.

It also helped that she spoke great English. Our talk did not struggle, it flowed—a tone, a theme established immediately between us of personas cut whole cloth from urges, masks we could wear to hide from ourselves, or each other.

We were, we felt, rootless cosmopolitan expatriates on the make for escape, passion, whatever scraps of meaning we could salvage, whatever clues would yield us to ourselves, show us whatever the hell it was we were supposed to be doing in this world.

But clueless though we were about ourselves, we also thought ourselves better than everyone around us. Even in that first exchange, I sat a little removed from the singing kumsitz circle, recessed in shadow, alone, Byronic. She dropped beside me on her knees, in a pretty, sweetly submissive pose, and said: "All alone? Why? Are you not having fun?"

"No."

"May I please sit?"

I shrugged.

"I can tell: you're a thinker. What are you thinking?" She smiled.

"That I don't belong here. That I don't belong anywhere. Look at them." I nodded toward the noisy celebrants. "The normal world."

The smile vanished. "Everyone belongs somewhere," she said, but sounded unsure.

"Do you really believe that?" I asked disdainfully.

"No," she said with a sad smile. "Maybe. I don't know."

"You don't belong here either. Or wherever you come from."

"Finland. Helsinki. No. I don't feel at home there or here."

"That's why you're talking to me. You can see the stranger in my face. No one else looks familiar to you, except me."

She laughed. "Yes, in a way, that's true. You don't seem like anyone I've ever seen. Yet I feel I know you." She touched my face with her fingertips.

I kissed her, softly, gently. Then, looking into her eyes: "It's not that we're better than everyone else. We are. But it's got nothing to do with that."

"You're nice."

"Maybe. I'm sure only that I don't belong anywhere. And, I sense, neither do you. In fact, I'm sure of it."

"What's your name?"

"Alan."

"I'm Helka."

I didn't offer the usual pleasantry. We sat silent for a time, gazed at the fire-silhouetted partyers clapping and swaying, singing and dancing—normal ones with a sense of place, who felt they belonged wherever Fate put them.

Then I stood up, offered her my hand, pulled her to her feet, and went off with her to find a spot in the desert where we could merge, disappear from ourselves, our estrangement from everything, at least for a while.

16

SOON, THE KIBBUTZ WAS BUZZING ABOUT OUR affair. Everyone knew everything about each other. Privacy did not exist. The kibbutz men grinned suggestively and clapped my shoulder and said: "Hey, Alan. How's Helka?"

"Up yours," I'd say with a smile.

They'd laugh: "You're a good boy, Alan! A man who gets to the point!" A very high compliment in Israel.

She asked to read my published short stories, poems. Their content mattered less to her than the fact of their appearing in print, and she regarded me with unconcealed awe, submerged in her own world of delusions. "You're the first writer I've ever met."

"And the last, I hope." Adding: "For your sake."

She hesitated, unsure of how to respond. I didn't really know myself exactly what I meant. Was always blurting out dramatic-sounding, bitter, often cryptic or contradictory pronouncements from off the top of my head, trying to seem profound or bizarre but also hoping to accidentally hit on something that might ring true, about myself, about anything whatsoever. I was woven into a fabric of lies and illusions so long-standing that I couldn't tell where I began and the fabrications left off. In effect, I had become a living, walking, talking lie—my very existence an ambulatory falsehood.

When alone, I could detect nothing within myself that I could quantify as depth or substance. In private soundings of my innermost self I heard only echoes of ricocheting emptiness, a hollow nightmare of synaptic distress signals. Or else felt flat-out void, seemed to have the emotional and intellectual texture of a protozoan or a basic protein.

For this reason I read voraciously. Books filled my vacant psychic well with content: social codes, subtleties, perspectives. I had an aptitude for absorbing and regurgitating quantities of commentary, ideas, tastes, preferences, attitudes, drawn from whatever book I happened to be immersed in at the time. I would be Faulknerian one week, Hemingwayesque the next, and Hamsun-like the week after. Even my ways of speaking changed to reflect these shifts in reading.

I read not for amusement or even knowledge but to draw from language regiments of details with which to reconstruct myself from day to day. Should days go by when I read nothing, there was no me, no one home. Sat and said nothing, numb, for all intents and purposes dead. But the glue that held me together, cemented the details, was booze. And that was blessedly plentiful on kibbutz, easily obtained. The commissary sold brandy, vodka, beer, wine, as much as I needed.

I needed a lot. Chose vodka for its low-cost lethal efficiency. A fifth, diluted and imbibed by the glass at regular intervals, could get me through a couple of days. Vodka was the blackness that filled the vast interregnums between my dead star constellations. Without it, there was no one home. Nothing more terrifying than to find yourself alone at home with no one home.

In this regard, Helka, who was also a hodgepodge of self-invention—an emptiness with eyes assembled from mostly cliché sources—was like a figure from a familiar novel whose plot I knew by heart. She didn't have a reflex that I could not anticipate. I saw clearly what she chose to believe about me and could easily fill in the blanks with dialogue, attitudes, airs that perfectly fit the roles she had assigned me. I was the tragic gifted American writer experiencing foreign cultures for the first time—an important step in my personal and artistic development. She, the fascinating lover whom I met en route to fame and someday would write about, the beautiful and moody enchantress who taught me the true meaning of love in a foreign land rocked by war, a mirror in which I could now see myself as I never had before. I could practically write the jacket copy for this turgid and tiredly cliché narrative.

There was more. She was scheduled to return to Finland in three months. She could return home alone, back to her lonely twenty-nine-year old life as an anonymous secretary, or remain with me in Israel. Or, possibly, return in triumph to her hometown, Helsinki, with a handsome young American writer husband in tow. Who knew where it could lead? Finding Helsinki too much the backwater, we might decamp for New York. The way lay open to a big adventurous life, with moppet-haired little Jewish-Finnish tykes running about underfoot as she knitted scarves and mufflers for the clan and I hammered out my novelistic masterworks.

I lay on a cot in my cottage, whiling away yet another afternoon sipping vodka with a novel by August Strindberg spread on my chest. Outside the door, some faded tough stalks of grass poked through the dusty ground. The sound of work boots on gravel crunched past. The air smelled of cowshit. I sipped more vodka. Helka's dream was a pretty picture. But she didn't understand me. Pounding out whole books—that wasn't about to happen anytime soon. The way ahead would be longer and harder for me than for most. I was earmarked for cosmic martyrdom. Could not even count on a James Dean–like early victory and quick, legendary death. My bones moved slowly. My brain stuck on rutting. My writing, I knew, was immature. I was incapable of sustained effort. I sipped the vodka, let it dribble down my chin as a sign of my ingrained rugged bachelor independence. Wiped my mouth with the back of my hand, a free adventurer. Noted with satisfaction the vodka that had soaked, staining, into my T-shirt. Mingled with my unwashed skin, it made me reek like a Bowery hobo. Family with her? Fat chance.

Helka might have proved a perfect wife for a career, if only there were something to sacrifice oneself for. But there was nothing. An infrequent story or poem or article I cranked out on a whiskey high, because at dusk the light in my room turned a certain shade of blue or a line in a poem sent shivers down my back, caused me to pick up the pen in response. But there was no programmatic pursuit of my art, no particular theme I wished to express. Virtually everything I wrote was in some way Jewish or Holocaust-related, but there was no coherence in my approach. I still believed in the lie of inspiration—that one must be struck by holy fire. Keeping fixed hours, a set routine, something I'd read about in numerous interviews with famous authors, was, to me, repellent. That worked for them. I was different. God's messenger, a hidden genius, I'd show them.

The idea of pursuing a single task over an extended time filled me with gloom. In fact, I was loath to finish anything whatsoever. Stories or poems or jobs or relationships—the moment I could foresee the outcome, I lost interest. In this respect, I told myself, I was a true avant-gardist. It never occurred to me that my distaste for endings concealed a phobic fear of loss and death. So that even as I did all in my power to traduce love the moment I had it, the prospect of losing the woman inspired nightmare feelings of fatal abandonment. Endings equaled the grave. I did not want lines of existence to travel from point A to point B: preferred that they remain indeterminately fixed in limbo.

17

FOR THE NEXT FEW WEEKS HELKA AND I MADE
love with unhappy urgency anywhere we could grab some solitude.
Sex became our creative act, our cultural statement.

Once, after a tough day hauling fish in nets across the kibbutz
fishponds, naked and knee-deep in mud, I found Helka stretched out
lounging in a nearly invisible bikini beside the swimming pool. Stood
over her, reached down, pulled her to her feet and marched her off to
a spot behind the volunteer quarters. Was so excited that my hands
shook as I positioned her to take my thrusts, the crushed swimsuit
so flimsy that I pushed it aside and entered her with a groan of shuddering pleasure. "I love you," I whispered into her soft, curving ear.
She held me so tight. "I love you too, Alan!" she gasped.

We made love at night out near the orange groves and behind
the cowshed. We made love too in a piano practice room, after
which she took me home and fed me sandwiches of fresh-baked
challah bread and canned smoked reindeer meat sent to her in a
parcel by her parents.

We drank a lot. Even she, a heavy boozer, remarked on my intake, though now I drank less than usual, substituting sex for drink. She was my new drug, my martini on legs. All day I worked in the fishponds and in the afternoons banged Helka. The more we balled, the more I wanted. Once was not enough. Twice, three times a day, until I was not only spent but drunk on our bodies' chemicals. My eyes wore a fixed, listless look. Helka began to bore me. Or rather, I became sick of the roles I played around her—my affected personae of jaw-clenched existential torment, all-knowing silences. Didn't want to analyze Camus, Beckett, Hamsun, Strindberg—authors she had not only read in depth but had dreamed of someday discussing with an erudite lover, and here I was. But after a few weeks of nonstop lust, all literary pretense fell away. My tongue did not want to discourse on *A Doll's House*; craved, instead, to tease her clit.

No fool, Helka took note. In her residential cottage, on her cot, we were half clothed, wound tight around each other, my aroused member prodding and probing. Her hand reached up and gently stroked my cheek as she pulled away.

"What's the matter?" I asked.

She gazed up into my face, studied my eyes, smiled warmly, and said with undisguised sadness: "You make it very hard to get to know you. What are you afraid of?"

Felt a mild sense of panic. For the first time imagining that in my eyes she could sight tight ovals of depthless fear. And again had the experience that I'd had with every woman I'd known. As if the whole were fast-forwarded through a life of scenes, I could see clear through, right to the end: the two of us aging, white-haired, kinder, the lines around our mouths softening into the inevitable physical surrender to death.

But I didn't want to grow kinder. Wanted to become more

savage, pitiless, steely. Could see it all, every Kodak color page of the photo album of our wedded lives—the friends and holidays, special family dos, retirement trips abroad, honorific ceremonies for work well done. All of it sickeningly predictable. My heart fiercely protested, didn't want to know the end; begged to be shown album pages of an indecipherable sort, a book not of standard watershed moments but of inscrutable mysteries.

I could not bring myself ever to say to any woman that this is what I saw—an inexhaustible round of dinners and nature walks, doctor's visits and grocery runs. The classic smiling snapshots of heads touching before the Eiffel Tower, waves from a gondola, creeping up with Nikons on silverback gorillas, the whole boring khaki shorts-clad suburban bullshit that passes for meaningful experience sickened me. Smiling heads posed in bouquets of joy were a happiness that vanished one moment after the shutter clicks, as they all returned to their socially programmed preset flight patterns to the family-package funeral plot.

What else a life could be I didn't know: another reason for my sunken-hearted certainty that no woman would be mad enough to risk the ride. And yet I'd hope, though I bitterly knew love that is an adventure was not possible at a certain point, once the routines set in. At best, all I could do was get aboard the Van Gogh boat, sail away alone. But the loneliness was killing. And my response was to drink heavily.

At the heart of me there lay the soul-crushing example of my parents. Recalled how as a boy of eleven I sat on the edge of my bed, fist clenched, cheeks and arms covered in welts, eyes burning with tears and swearing to God that so long as I lived I would never marry.

Soon after our little chat, I went to a Purim bash with Helka. On Purim, the Jewish answer to Halloween, one is mandated, by

ALAN KAUFMAN 71

holy writ, to get riotously drunk. I did. Don't recall much except that I found myself behind a shed, atop Helka, her naked ass in dung-smelling mud and me blindly grunting away. "Alan," she kept saying. "Alan. Please. Alan." If she wanted me to stop, I couldn't tell. But it felt like rape in the dark. I finished off a bottle of vodka and left her there, passed out, undressed, and stumbled off. Don't recall the rest of the night.

The next day, her eyes accused. I loathed to be near her and, equally, despised myself. I withdrew. Some kind of mechanism asserted itself: an old familiar one. The more you loved me, the less I cared. The closer you came, the farther I ran. And why was she calling my name that Purim night, again and again, in such a tone of quiet urgency?

Even the other kibbutzniks noticed her blues. Remarked the cruelty of my smile when responding to their queries. What's up with you and Helka? She looks so sad. Did you two fight?

I studiously avoided her. She sent notes; I tore them up. In the communal dining room, I sat apart, and after a meal, hurried out. If she knocked on my cottage door, I didn't answer. If I saw her approach, I turned down another path. I avoided the pool where she often hung out.

She sent two Swedish girls as emissaries to plead with me on her behalf. I told them that I no longer loved her and that they should tell her so.

"You should tell her yourself, coward!" one of them spit.

Knowing that she was right, I didn't reply. Instead, accepted a friend's invite to stay in Jerusalem. There was an Israeli girl he wanted me to meet. She was, he said, his wife's best friend, filthy rich, single, artistic and beautiful. If I had any sense, my friend advised, I would marry her. After all, he said, I was a pauper. A girl like that could really set me on my feet.

18

HOW UTTERLY SOULLESS I HAD BECOME. WITH shame I remember how arrogantly, heartlessly, I exited the kibbutz to bus down to Jerusalem, dressed in freshly laundered and pressed clothes, as Helka stood watching mournfully, her sleepless face haggard. Made my way out through the main gate, past the armed sentry, my heart stiffened against her. Weak, with no core values and with a foolproof escape hatch—alcohol—I was willing to betray the possibility of real love with her in exchange for a free ride on another woman's back.

On the bus to Jerusalem, I hummed tunes to myself as the landscape whizzed by. Smoked cigarettes and dozed or dug into my bag of kibbutz bakery cookies and chewed contentedly. Helka really loved me—in my book, a fatal error. My conscience, I told myself, could turn itself off at the first hint of real intimacy. She had come too close, wanted to ensnare me in her agenda. I wasn't having any of it, had other, bigger fish to fry. Heroics to perform. Books to write. Fame to gain. Also needed a place to crash where I wouldn't have to break my back in return for board. A place to unwind, write, produce masterpieces. Drink and not work. Justify shiftlessness and manipulation of women in the name of art.

The Israeli woman, Tsofnat, lived part of the time with her mother, Elia, and four very feral mutt dogs, in an old, sprawling, elegantly decrepit flat in Jerusalem's Katamon quarter, which had been a front line in the horrific battles for the city during the '67 war.

Tsofnat, not nearly as beautiful as my friend had claimed, was pretty in a peculiar, jaundiced sort of way. Had haunted eyes underscored with dark bags that showed bad nerves, and her body was slender but flaccid, her breasts droopy. Not only did she have a faint smudge of hair above her upper lip—for me, a deal breaker—but her legs were defiantly unshaven.

And yet, there was something morbidly appealing about her. A kind of nervous, aristocratic twinkling. A fallen naïveté reminiscent of Hollywood Southern belles, late-stage Scarlett O'Hara or Blanche Dubois hiding from the lightbulb's glare.

In an instant her look would change from darkly introspective, morosely inscrutable, to a very pretty, even charming kind of histrionic liveliness, replete with cheek-fracturing dimples, and her eyes grew big and bright with awe-filled gaiety.

She was very flattering, made you feel like a knight in shining armor, and it occurred to me that since she was purportedly rich, here was someone that I could manipulate at will. The idea of such dominance aroused me.

For my visit she wore a white chiffon party dress with a ridiculous red corsage: an outfit that confirmed for me her full-blown outright eccentricity, an immaturity bordering on psychosis.

Strangely, this awareness of her probable madness gave me further hope. I realized that only someone crazy could endure life with me. Also, she was rich. This would liberate me from the necessity to support myself, or her. My unwillingness to deal with money matters did not concern me overly. I was, I felt, engaged in a lifetime experiment to see the extent to which I could manage to evade money matters altogether.

All I required was cigarettes, whiskey, paper, pen, and boots. Foodwise, could live on whatever crap happened to be around, didn't really mind. Now and then, for lack of bucks, had even spooned dog food into my cakehole. As to clothes, skid-row thrift shops served me fine.

My reasoning went that given that she had dogs already, what mattered one more head to board, another mouth to feed? I thought myself no better than a feral hound, an opportunistic dog. To live comfortably I required little more than was needed to keep, say, a Great Dane. Surely one more mutt would not be too much.

Also, I liked her mother, Elia, who, it was evident, had once been, unlike her daughter, a very real beauty. She was fat but still hot: a former kibbutz potter of repute, with ceramic sculptures in such prestigious places as the Hebrew U and Hadassah Hospital.

Elia had jet-black hair, fierce, barbaric turquoise-blue eyes, perfect features, and a vivacious, keen intelligence that enfolded you in camaraderie and enthusiastic curiosity. She had big breasts that you wanted to rub your face in. Had she not allowed her once no doubt spectacular figure to go so completely and horribly to pot—with a huge belly and a behind that might need a wheel-barrow to transport around—I would have made my play for her instead, blown off the acrid daughter.

Elia and I were instant soul mates, two against the world. Tsofnat, who had that eerie, almost telepathic, insight typical of borderline schizos, grasped her exclusion. I had nothing to say to her. It was Elia I wanted to hang with.

When Tsofnat took me to see her penthouse in a building that she owned nearby, I couldn't wait to return to Elia's place, where the three of us sat all day in her lavish garden, eating grapes plucked from the overhead vines, as Elia regaled me with tales of her heroics as a fighter in the famed coed brigade known as "the Palmach."

She had fired weapons in battle, seen comrades fall, thrown Molotovs and hand grenades, gone on hair-raising raids. Here was a woman I could relate to. She had known heroes, she said, such as I could not even imagine, fearless kibbutzniks, moshavniks, Jewish farmer-soldiers who went about in shorts and sandals with a revolver and a knife on their belts and performed secret military feats of derring-do, ones that you'd never find in any history book.

Israel, she said, voice dropping, kept secret its most important resource. Israel's most important weapon was not those hidden-away atomic bombs—there "just in case"—but the people. Israelis were Israel's truest secret weapon. And the men—she fluttered her heavily mascaraed eyes and nibbled hungrily on a cookie—such men were both fatally irresistible and hopelessly unreliable.

"You men are butterflies," she said. "You live only for today. No yesterday. No tomorrow. A woman with her body, her need to breed and raise children, cannot afford to be so. But you men?" She shrugged and smiled. "You are a little like the men I knew. Though your life in America has made you soft, you have about you the splendid élan that they had in the early days, during the War of Independence. I'm sure that in the right circumstances you would make a brave soldier. I can already tell that you are a real heart-breaker with the ladies. Undependable. Irresistible. Come here."

I moved my chair closer. Elia kissed me on the cheek. Then reached up with her long, warm fingers and wiped the lipstick off. Tsofnat absorbed all this in silence, shifting uncomfortably in her chair. Now Elia took my hand, examined it. "You have calluses.

They make you work on your kibbutz, huh? Good for them! They are making you tough, hard, an Israeli! What do you do there?"

"I work in the fishponds."

"The fishponds!" She and Tsofnat exchanged quick looks, clearly impressed.

"You know," said Elia, "they only take the elite to work in the fishponds. The commando types. They must have a very high regard for you."

Later, Tsofnat took me to the summit of Mount Zion. As the sun descended I saw the entire ancient city of white stone turn a fiery gold. There and then I resolved, at all costs, to live in the seat of the ancient Jewish kingdoms and of the Bible, where David, the poet-ruler and outlaw, had bedded Beersheva, wrote his melancholic psalms, and wise Solomon composed his immortal proverbs as he bed-hopped among his thousand wives.

19

IN THE MANNER OF SUCH THINGS IN ISRAEL, AFTER hosting me over several weekend visits, Elia and Tsofnat decided, without any open discussion but by a kind of perfume-scented osmotic interchange of nods, sighing winks, moistening thighs, and trembling breasts, that I would leave the kibbutz, apply to study at the Hebrew University, and move in with them.

There was little ceremony about it, and I had the least say of all, one way or another. Besides, it perfectly suited me. Owned nothing but the clothes on my back, some notebooks and books, and the typewriter, my trusted old Smith Corona. Hadn't a cent to my name.

The prospect of living rent free in Jerusalem, the city of God, thrilled me. Of course, it was understood, if unstated, that their sole reason for housing me was as a marital prospect for Tsofnat, who had no suitors for miles in any direction and was drifting into misanthropy of a very real and chilling sort. Her suffering was there in her eyes, unmistakable: a dark stare of nightmarish childhood mental injury incurred by an upbringing on a borderland kibbutz where, every night, for fear of marauding robber bands and terrorists, the children were rousted from sleep and hurried, under fire, into dark, fetid bunkers to await the outcome of the night's battle, never knowing whether the figure appearing at the door to retrieve them would be a kibbutznik or a pistol-wielding killer poised for rape.

These experiences had calcified into dank mental crawlspaces into which she retreated and where no one could reach her. In all likelihood, she would go mad. Were she to, I couldn't possibly lose. I understood my advantage as perfectly as any gold-digging gigolo: Elia, a divorced woman without any illusions about the prospects for her increasingly strange old maid daughter; Tsofnat, a daughter living under the perpetual unspoken critique of her still beautiful, talented, and charismatically fiery mother; and me, an American Jewish boy, twenty-six years old, broke, needing to make his way in a new country. I would, could, provide endless amusement, not to speak of social, emotional, esthetic, and sexual relief—both directly and vicariously—to two brutally lonely single women trapped with each other.

Everything was understood, but unstated. The ostensible purpose of my "ingathering" into their home was patriotic. I was an immigrant Jew whose assimilation into the Jewish state they would jointly underwrite. I was a project. Obviously, I was too promising a prospect to have to endure the indignities and soul-bruisings of immigration in a war-embattled land.

My sacrifice for the homeland entailed eating vineyard grapes while seated at the feet of Mother Elia, learning the insider's history of Israel, while her mad daughter raced about the building she owned engaging in interminable, outraged lawsuits over plumbing fixture repairs, damaged walls, leaking roofs. At night, as Elia and I continued our conversational walk through history, Tsofnat, dressed in a horrific gray maid's dress with white trim, her hair stacked atop her head in a gruesome pyramid, cooked the standard household fare of turkey meatballs, falafel, salad, coffee, chocolate cookies, all topped off with filterless Selon cigarettes and Rishon LeZion brandy. At this juncture, they had no idea whatsoever about me and booze.

It didn't take them long to discover.

Elia was first to note how I seemed to down glassful after glassful of the brandy until none was left, whereupon I started on the wine. But she simply chalked it up to my bohemian temperament. The word *drunkard* was not yet assignable to me in their love-blinded eyes.

After a week on the sofa, I made my move. Crept into Tsofnat's bedroom. It was dark, but she was up. Lying there in a white nightgown, very still.

She said in a frank voice: "You have come for something?"

"Yes," I said, leaning over to plant a kiss. She jerked her face away, my kiss landing on her frizzy hair, which felt like steel wool.

"Not so fast," she said. "My mother will hear."

"She won't care. She likes me."

"You are so sure of yourself?"

"Yes," I said. And made to kiss her again. Again she jerked away. A part of me watched myself act like a cad yet felt helpless to stop.

"Look," I said. "You know why I'm here. Why play games? We're adults."

"I don't know what you mean."

"I mean"—I lied—"that I want you. I want to make love to you. I think you're beautiful."

"More beautiful than your Finnish whore?"

I paused to absorb this. "I knew that I should not have told Elia about that."

"Helky. Is that her name?"

"What does it matter?"

"A little slut with long legs and tits that lift like this?" With both hands, she clutched her sagging breasts and shoved them up so hard they almost bounced off her chin, which had begun to show signs of doubling.

I winced. "Tsofnat," I pleaded. "What's the point?"

Inside, I was panicking. Had ditched kibbutz and Helka for a free ride on this cash cow, and now she was refusing to give milk.

"She was ugly!" I blurted out. "Hideous, in fact!"

Tsofnat stopped, looked at me. "Liar," she said hopefully.

"I'm telling you, she was—I don't know just how you'll take this, because you have four of them yourself, but she was a dog. A complete dog." My hand made descriptive motions before my face. "Her eyes were small, her nose out to here, she had lips like a mule, the only thing pretty on her was her..."

I paused here. I knew that my lie would better persuade by avoiding undue exaggeration, that everything ugly has something beautiful about it, but whatever I chose to exalt mustn't be something that would throw Tsofnat into a permanent tailspin of self-loathing, some body part which she despised in herself, but rather should be a part of her physiognomy of which she could be proud, a competition category in which she felt unthreatened.

"Her neck," I said. "She had a long, slender neck, like yours."

Neck, after all, was not so important. Face, breasts, ass were the real minefields.

I took Tsofnat's hand in mine. "And she had pretty tapering fingers like yours."

"Oh," said Tsofnat, withdrawing her hand a little but not completely.

"And her waist. She had a little wasp waist like you." Letting her hand go, I clasped my hands around her waist, drew her close. "I admit. That little waist of hers turned me on a lot. Those little hands. But she didn't have those eyes of yours to look into when—"

"Humping?" She pulled back, tried to get free.

"Talking," I said.

"Yes, sure," she spit with fascinated skepticism. "I bet you talked much with this Finn."

"Her English was very good."

"Better than mine?" Tsofnat snapped.

"No."

"I see. What else did this Finn not have?"

"Your amazing hair," I said, knowing it to be a stretch—she was fully aware of its tumbleweed coarseness. But there is that part of us that yet wants to believe against all evidence to the contrary that the painful fact is untrue, that even our own perception of reality lies—that what is ugly is in fact beautiful.

On the other hand, I knew that if she bought the lie about her hair, then I had her in my pocket.

One month later, in a private ceremony attended by a few friends and relations from her side, we were married.

20

IT AMAZES ME TO REALIZE THE EXTENT TO WHICH we alcoholics stake our illusory hopes on the flimsiest, most ill-conceived evidence, all the better to later tear them down so that, bottle in hand, we can wallow amid the rubble in an orgy of drunken bitterness, survey the carnage with a certain longing, confirmed in our suspicion that life is a cheat; that all along we were right to suspect existence itself of shortchanging deceptions.

But though all along we intuit, sense, *know*, that only ruin can ensue from a foolish strategy, yet we elect to proceed, wed someone sure to harm us, in order to be harmed—feel the disillusionment that has only one possible, immediate, and quite lethal antidote: booze.

Clearly, Tsofnat was a severe manic-depressive. In marrying her, I knew what I would get, and got it. The raging shut-in with haunted eyes and bride-of-Frankenstein hair stormed through my days and nights, locking herself behind closed doors, weeping, screaming, threatening suicide, just as my mother had. And in my darkly mounting sense of justification—given Tsofnat's abominable public displays—I could grab, in turn, for whatever little pleasures and leisure and momentary stays from life were obtainable, and with a sense that these were my due, these I deserved: look at the psychotic woman I'm married to. The Shrew Queen of Hell.

Under the pitying witness of Elia, with considerable heartbreak and disillusionment I watched Tsofnat's performances. My own theatrics were, I thought, Emmy-level—so much so that I even believed them myself. At such times, I wept like a man lost. Elia, unable to bear this spectacle of a good-looking young new husband heartbroken by an insane wife, poured me tall tumblers of brandy and once even broke out a fifth of some very old British Mandate–era scotch and said: "Here, poor boy. I was saving this for a special occasion. But with a wife like that, you deserve it." I made quick business of the bottle. And then of the brandy too.

Under their name I ran up a tab with a local grocer for cigarettes and booze. By now I had little left of common decency and knew it, but I couldn't bear to dwell on that for very long. To kill the pain, I drank increasing amounts of liquor in the space that Elia had cleared for me out back in her old pottery studio, an amazing giant wooden shed of cobwebs, flowers, potter's wheels, unfinished semiabstract ceramic figures writhing from the workbenches and shadows. I loved it in there. Set up shop quite nicely. Want only to write, I told myself. Just leave me in here alone long enough, keep the cigarettes and booze coming, and one day I'll emerge with a masterpiece in hand.

But there was the painful shame of my treatment of these two women. It choked the language in me, blocked my ability to write. Often I woke from a blackout slumped over my typewriter. I read ferociously for escape from my despair: Dostoyevsky and Coetzee, Babel and Hemingway, Conrad and Borges. Occasionally, encouraged by booze, I sipped brandy, dragged deep on Time cigarettes, and sketched down the scenes humming through my head, a disjointed narrative of fragmentary nightmarish recollections that yet might have built to something, though probably not much. Inevitably, Tsofnat would crash into my redoubt and stand there, horn-rimmed, horrified, to remind me of my crimes against her: "Look at you! Happy as a cat! You've got it all! Lucky boy! Lucky American boy! Stupid Israeli women pay the rent, make the food, eh? Keep you in liquor and tobacco, huh? Give you where to write. Nice deal you got here! No job. All the time you please. At least if you were writing something worthwhile— that made money—but what do you got here, eh?"

Pinched between thumb and forefinger she held up a nearly blank page containing a single typed sentence with several cross-outs running through the words. "Today's output?" she smirked. "Or maybe this week's?"

"I need time. I'm just getting my sea legs."

"Sea legs! What sea legs? What sea? A sailor works! You are a lazy, lying thief! You think we are all stupid little chess pieces you can move around your board while you drink and smoke away the days, don't you!"

Yes, I did.

"Please," I said. "I'm just sitting here confused and scared because the woman I'm married to seems to be having a nonstop nervous breakdown." Made myself look as pathetic as I could. Which worked on Elia, never on Tsofnat. By now, she saw right through me; knew she had landed a drunken predator who right before your eyes, in the midst of your life, drained your resources and vanished. Now I was here, then not, liquor-transported to a realm of ground-less hope and tireless fantasy where she held no citizenship, was stamped an "undesirable," ridiculed as a nag, a slag, a drudge, and unceremoniously expelled.

Day followed night. The explosive pressure built. Anyone could have seen what lay ahead. But Elia and Tsofnat were clueless. I had chosen my prey well. They were vulnerable, naïve, too inexperienced to guess what lay in store.

One day, Tsofnat locked herself in her bedroom, raged loudly about my refusal to work. As Elia stirred a cauldron of soup and peered down at me with heavily mascaraed mournful eyes, concerned (perhaps intuiting some shift in my normally pleasant mien), I pocketed my nearly full pack of Selon cigarettes, picked up the bottle of Rishon LeZion, stood, and said: "What Tsofnat doesn't seem to understand is that there are no barriers, no fences, no walls."

I moved a step and waved a hand before my face to show its unchecked passage. "She can fill the air with her voice, her threats, her craziness, but none of that impedes my body's travel through space. I am free. Doesn't she know? I am always at point A. Wherever I decide is point B, I just get up and go to it. Nothing's in my way." I walked to the door. "I'm no mathematician, but this much I know: from point A to point B is a straight line, with nothing in between." I looked at her astonished face and repeated: "Nothing, Elia. Nothing."

"What are you talking about?"

"I'm out. Gone. Right now. I'll be filing for divorce."

She looked at me, incredulous. "Pish posh. Sit down. Don't get all worked up. She's just in a mood. She has her monthlies. You know how sensitive she is."

"I like you very much, Elia. You are the kind of person I hoped to find when I came to Israel. But she is insane. You recognize that, don't you?"

Elia's face hardened. "She's not well. But you knew that too, didn't you, when you married her. But you went ahead anyway. Let's not play games with each other."

"No games. Yes, I knew. I knew what I was getting into. And I also know what I'm getting out of."

"So, she's right. You only married her for the free rent and board."

Her words stung. The ugly truth hung there between us, and at that moment I could have cried for what I had done to this woman, who had been so kind to me, to her daughter, who had trusted me enough to wed. I was a complete scoundrel, unrecognizable to myself. As I stood in the doorway, about to leave, my eyes sought for hers, to say: Please forgive me. I don't know what I'm doing on this earth. But instead I shut the door quietly behind me. Hurried away into the unknown, chased by the thought of Tsofnat in her white nightie, banshee-barefoot behind me, howling.

But no one followed.

21

THE BATTERY OF GOVERNMENT BENEFITS DESIGNED
to encourage immigration included payment for food and board
and free university education. I rented a small cottage in a quarter
known as Nachlaot—a quaint working-class slum populated
by artists and laborers—and applied for and got into the masters
program in English literature at Hebrew University.

Studied Melville, Herzl, Freud, Sylvia Plath, Marx, and Edmund
Wilson. The days passed in boozy boredom. In a class on Charles
Dickens it struck me that to be the son of a Holocaust survivor, resident in Jerusalem, first in my family to breathe free air in a Jewish state
in two thousand years, and pissing away my days analyzing semiotics
of late Victorian British novels was an absurdly wasted opportunity.

The next day, reported to the Ministry of the Interior to change
my status from Temporary Resident to New Immigrant. Within a
month full Israeli citizenship was conferred upon me, and with it,
given my youth and single status, the mandate to report for immediate military service.

Soon to wear the uniform of an Israeli soldier, I skipped classes and wandered, elated, through Hebrew University campus in a kind of daze, my call-up papers folded in my shirt pocket, astonished to think that very soon, for the first time in millennia and only forty years after Hitler had chased my mother through the woods, I would serve in defense of the Jewish state. Was no longer an outside observer to history, passive and belt-whipped audience to its anecdotes and tales. Now, armed, I would write my own legends.

22

I CARRIED THE MAG, A BELGIAN FIELD MACHINE
gun, along with 250 rounds of ammunition on my back. My
combat infantry unit trained to the point of delirium, the effort so
strenuous that one kid named Claudio, nineteen, from Argentina,
stepped outside his tent and died of a heart attack. We stood around
an Israeli flag, in a U-shaped formation, crying.

There were frequent injuries. Once I hurt my arm so bad that
it swelled to football size and I ran a fever. Eyes bright, flushed face
burning, I showed the arm to the sergeant as we stood in a pouring
rain, about to embark on a night patrol. "So what," he said. "Army
is not where you get healthy." Through hostile villages we passed,
moved as one body. You couldn't hear us. Before starting out the
sergeant had us hop up and down, just once, listening to hear if
buckles jiggled, canteens blooped. Everything on us was taped
down, tied. "You are panthers," he told us, "Indian braves! No one
hears you. No one sees you." Then set out at forced march pace,
each loaded down with gear, into the night, for fifteen, twenty

kilometers, over hills, into wadis, and slipped so quietly along that not even the pariah dogs barked.

Once, on a trip to the Golan, we climbed in full gear a steep, nearly vertical butte overlooking an abysslike wadi where wild eagles circled with echoing cries, and as I fought for handholds and the boot heels of the soldier just above me kicked gravel in my face, had the eerie sense of having been here before, two thousand years ago, with a sword and shield, bearing the Star of David strapped to my back.

After several months of rigorous training, was sent north to guard and patrol along the Lebanese border. Cringed during artillery barrages in tiny outposts with night vision scope trained on the sky, watching for hang gliding terrorists slipping in quietly on wind currents.

One night, on a march through hostile territory, while attempting to assist a fellow soldier who had collapsed from fatigue, my elbow was smashed and I rode to the hospital in an ambulance with a soldier profusely bleeding from a gun wound. For the next few weeks drifted in a fever from ward to ward, shot full of antibiotics and bandaged and rebandaged. Then, because the wrong kind of soft cast was plastered to my arm, forming calcium deposits, the attending doctor, a major, ordered me held down as he snapped the arm straight and shattered the deposits. I fainted.

I was disqualified from combat duty for nine months—the duration of my regular service—and told I'd be reinstated with a combat unit once in the Reserves. The fact that I knew perfect English, held a BA in lit, and could write with professional proficiency got me temporarily reassigned to the army press corps, first in Tel Aviv at General Headquarters and later in the choicest and cushiest spot in the entire Israeli Army: the IDF press corps office in Jerusalem.

Nattily wounded, fashionable in my jaunty infantry beret, and wearing an old .38 Webly British revolver on my hip, I resurrected Hemingway's ghost in my cocky strut. Often, my assignments involved escorting foreign correspondents and combat photogs into "hot zones" in Lebanon or the West Bank, which entitled me to wear temporary officer tags, though in rank but a private. Entire companies on parade, thinking a general approached, came to attention with a snappy presentation of arms. Smartly, I saluted back.

After a day out in the field with the correspondents, we repaired to some local bar to get wasted. I drank with them in Jerusalem, Tel Aviv, and in Nahariya, in a little bistro just off the military checkpoint to Lebanon. The reporters and photogs swilled like pros and we all got blasted. Sometimes I led them into Lebanon, to meet Major Haddad, commander of the South Lebanese militia, a smart, pencil-mustached gentleman in pressed green fatigues, who hopped from jeeps like a cowboy and was escorted everywhere by gunfighter bodyguards wearing bullet-lined holsters with white-handled six-shooters. Other times, I took them into zones where Katyusha rockets spiraled black streaks through the sky, the photogs' shutters clicking to freeze-frame the explosions.

Back in the corridors of Beit Agron, I strolled the press building with the air of a military legend. My commander, a lieutenant colonel named Amir, didn't share my admiration for myself. He had me emptying wastebaskets and washing coffee cups. Or he'd call me on the carpet and, tilting back on the hind legs of his chair, eye me with the cruel scorn of a Turkish sultan. "So, here he is. And what is he? I'm not sure."

"At your service, commander," I'd say, grinning.

"I didn't tell you to speak! Why do you speak? Shut it! I don't like the way you're performing!"

"I don't hear any complaints. Gabe Pressman from NBC and I get along like a house on fire. And Bill Claiborne from the

Washington Post thinks I'm the most knowledgeable person he's ever met in the Israeli Army."

"Claiborne is a whore! He takes money from the Arabs. And this other dummy from NBC is an idiot. Did you see him when he picked up the Klatch? How many times did you have to tell him: 'It's not a Russian AK-47, Gabe. It's a Chinese Kalashnikov!' But how many times did Mr. Gabe still crap it up and they had to reshoot it, over and over, what, how many times? This Pressman has hummus for brains! No wonder you two get along."

"Amir, why are you so mad at me today, huh? I said something you don't like?"

"You're insolent! And you drink too much! You could be something in this army. Why do you think I had you brought down from Tel Aviv, huh?" He reached into a drawer and tossed out a copy of the *IDF Journal*, the army's first English-language information journal, which I had started while serving in Tel Aviv. "Everyone up to the chief of staff is impressed with this thing. I know you have talent. But you will amount to nothing."

Caught off guard, voice trembling, I asked, "What makes you say that?"

"What do you think, your commander is an idiot? I don't smell it when you come back from your little field trips? I tell you, next time liquor is on you, you go to court martial and I'll have you thrown in jail! I swear it!"

I never copped to drinking. And certainly didn't mention the joints passed between me and the photogs from Agence France Presse and Reuters. Nor did I try to stop. There was no stopping. I liked drinking far too much. It was by far the most rewarding thing I knew to do. Drinking in uniform made me feel tragic and heroic, though, in truth, I felt lonely and often scared. To throw Amir off my scent, I stuck strictly to odorless vodka and ate heavy foods before I imbibed, but nothing helped. Vodka still reeked and the food had no effect. I staggered into the office hungover, and as I'd correctly assumed, Amir had to turn a blind eye because very soon I'd muster out—just a matter of months. Until then the Israeli Army had far more serious things to worry about than a drunken immigrant with little time left to serve.

23

I MET EDNA AT THE SECRETARIAL POOL. SHE WAS at her desk, looking quite pretty, I thought, a touch less dour than usual.

"Hi, there!" I said. "Can I drop in on you this evening for a drink and a little conversation? It's been really lonely."

"No!" she snapped without looking up from her keyboard.

"Oh!" I said, acting surprised.

I obtained her address and that night went over to her place, uninvited, without knowing what I might be interrupting. Knew absolutely nothing about her.

When she opened the door, wearing a beltless kimono and nothing underneath, she said: "I'm not going to ask what you're doing here. I know exactly what you want. What I'd like to know is, are you on some sort of wager among the soldiers or reporters to see if you can screw all the government press office secretaries in a row? Is that what this is about?"

She stood there with her breasts, belly, and legs fully expressed,

her womanhood covered with a torn black panty, dragging slut-
tishly on a cigarette, completely unfazed by my hungry stare.

"May I come in?"

"What for?"

"How about a drink, to start? To be civilized."

"You don't strike me as civilized."

"Well, I'm lonely. I'm very, very lonely. That's a civilized
emotion."

She laughed with this slatternly laugh. "I see. And what does
lonely boy want?"

"Nothing! A drink. A little decent conversation."

"That sounds boring."

"Well, it will be fun. Depending on how things go."

"Things?" Her face contorted scornfully. "What 'things'?"

My face fell. "Look, the truth is," I lied, "I'm broke and don't
have what to eat. I'm ashamed to tell my commander. He'll know
what I've been spending my food allotment on. Out boozing with
the press boys. At first, they buy for you. Then you end up buying
for them. They're real pros. I got cleaned out knocking back a few
with the BBC guy."

"Cory?"

"Yes. Alex Cory. He wanted to go to Finks, the most expensive
joint in town. I'm so hungry, I feel my blood sugar plunging. Have
you got some bread or something lying around? A sandwich would
really stabilize my metabolism."

"GOD! You're something! Okay! A plate of food and a drink.
Then out with you, you bloody incorrigible scamp!"

"Scamp?" I smiled, crossing the threshold. "Do people actually
still use that word?"

"In South Africa."

"Is that where you're from?"

"Cape Town. Here's the noodle pot. It's real meat. And whiskey's over there, in the cabinet. Plates and glasses. Cutlery in that drawer."

I ate, drank like it was my last meal on earth. Then we smoked a joint and then another, and then drank more, and more again. She slurred her words, nearly slid off the couch. Had in her eye a leaden violence that I had seen in other drunks before. As though she really wasn't there. For that look I would have left, but she also wore the slatternly smile, irresistible. And looked like a Far Eastern hooker in that kimono.

"Lonely boy!" she slurred, hauling me to my feet. Said she had a little favor to ask. The lightbulb in her bedroom was out. Would I help?

"Show me."

In the bedroom, she grinned and said: "Those nylons on the floor? Pick them up. That's right, lonely boy, pick up my nylons. And now tie me to the bedposts. Hands here. Ankles there. Wait. I want to take this off." She shrugged off the robe and spread-eagled herself on the bed. Then instructed me to blindfold her with a curtain sash, which I did.

"And there you are," I said when done, scrutinizing my handiwork.

She writhed. "Anything you like," she said.

"Yes, of course," I said, abstracted. "I did a good job on those knots, didn't I? You're completely at my mercy."

She moaned.

It lasted for hours, most exciting sex I'd ever had. My trussed and blindfolded stag-mag girl, a little virgin sacrifice writhing on the newsprint alter of my garish libido. Cared nothing about her and could do anything I wished. Didn't need alcohol to keep it up. In fact, if anything, might need some to keep it down. Still, I drank. Staggered around her, pouring booze on her belly, licking it off, splashing it on her nipples, suckling them, jamming myself into any orifice I pleased, drinking as I liked—naked, wicked, young, feeling like a god. Passed out with head cradled on her whiskey-soaked pubes.

24

IN THE MORNING, A SATURDAY, FRYING EGGS brought the urge to retch. My head pounded with pneumatic intensity. Edna came in wearing a pretty yellow sundress that made her seem country fresh. I felt aroused just by the sight of her, the memory of what we had done. But was too ill to offer more than a weak smile and "Hello" with barely any conviction. Felt sick enough to die.

"Knödelkopf," she said, a Yiddish endearment for "matzo ball head."

"Edna," I said. Sat up, cradling my hungover brain. "That was absolutely incredible."

"It was fun. First time you've done that?"

"Oh, yes. Most positively. Had fantasies about it but never dared to think that it was actually possible to find someone to do it with."

She started a cigarette, handed it to me. "It's my favorite thing."

I moved in with her one week later and remained with her through the end of my regular military service, after which I married her. Three hundred Jerusalem hipsters showed up for the wedding. As I helped Edna cut the cake I thought, I'll be out of this fiasco in six months.

After the ceremony, a band of about fifty of us staggered, stoned and drunk, to a nearby hotel where I'd rented a room for the after-party, stocked with cases of scotch. En route, Edna, blind drunk, still in wedding dress and veil, took off her white high heels and threw them into a ravine. She then removed her wedding ring—one that had belonged to every woman in her family for several genera-tions—and tossed that in. Whereupon she took a long pull from a bottle in someone's hand, flagged down a strange car, and tried to jump in. The bewildered driver drove several hundred meters down the road with Edna half hanging out in her wedding gown and train, screeching drunken curses in Afrikaans. During this little escapade she fractured her arm, and we made a brief detour to the hospital, where we dropped her off to have it set. The rest of us returned hotelward, got wasted, and passed out on the floor or with vomit-caked faces cradled on the toilet seat or propped against furniture. It was a good night: no one fell to death from a window or killed someone in his or her car.

The righteous Israel that I had come seeking existed, but elsewhere. I seemed only to find the deadbeat bohemian freaks and hard-core addicts of all kinds. The majority of Israelis, wholesome, stepped around us like a big puddle of dirty water. I couldn't find it within myself to connect with them, though I longed to. We had no common language. The average Israeli's conventionality scared me. In the shadow of perpetual war, they seemed so sickeningly content with life's simpler rewards: wanting only to wash the car in peace, have a backyard barbecue with no threat of interruption by a war, or eat out without a suicide bomber blowing up the joint.

Essentially, Edna and I were supported by her rich father, who had high hopes that we'd make him a grandpa Zeder. Instead of grandchildren, though, we generated unpaid back rent and astronomical liquor tabs. Drug dealers slept on our floors, as well as Chilean refugees, radical leftists, neglected poets, South African exiles, out-of-work journalists, and hallucinating painters. Sometimes we all sat around with the political cartoonist Yaacov Kirschen of "Dry Bones" fame, and his partner, Sally Ariel, and got deliciously stoned, for though he was famously prone to paranoia—he had come to Israel as a young head from New York, convinced that he was under FBI surveillance—Kirschen liked his pot.

I perched on the sofa, with a stack of books on the floor and a bottle of Courvoisier VSOP on the table, along with an ashtray and several packs of Gitanes cigarettes. Often, in the months before mustering out of the service, I had stretched out here with Vivaldi's *Four Seasons* on the stereo, playing Russian roulette with my service revolver. When I mustered out, among the gear I returned was the gun, but the urge to kill myself remained, and grew and grew.

I could no longer pinpoint my reasons for wanting to die. It was simply there all the time, a part of me. Felt that there were no limitations, no rules or values in the free-for-all of the amoral world; that I could do anything, so nothing really mattered.

To some extent, I had always believed this, but I now realized that I was set on proving to myself as never before that anything goes. Once, Edna's sister, Ilana, came by, and while Edna lay blacked out on the bed, snoring, after a night bashing her wrists into broken glass strewn on the kitchen floor, I led her crying sister into an adjoining room, made to comfort her, but in no time we were tearing each other's clothes off. Another time, I balled her close friend, Angie, a Chilean girl and the wife of an artist.

Then I met Anna, wife of Itamar, leader of a small but important art collective, and my journey took a turn into heights and depths that I'd never thought possible.

25

THE COLLECTIVE'S STUDIO WAS A PUBLIC MUNICIPAL bomb shelter leased to them for a pittance by the city of Jerusalem. Here they made art, held exhibitions, threw receptions. Anna and Itamar's storybook two-story gingerbread house in Nachlaot was a nerve center for Jerusalem's cultural elite, and in no time Edna and I fell in among them, became in fact the couple's best friends.

We practically lived in each other's living rooms. Sat around from morning to night, putting away unbelievable quantities of booze, smoking cigarettes till our throats ran raw. We talked endlessly about literature, art, politics, film, music. Once a month, at the prestigious Israel Museum, under my direction, we mounted an Israeli version of the *Paris Review* literary and arts magazine as a staged theatrical production. Wildly successful, it placed us center stage in Israeli culture.

The program idea had come to me in the army, and in the way of timely ideas, took on its own life, quickly gathering volunteer talent and institutional sponsorship. Massive audiences came to the museum's newly built theater to see it. My influence was such that when the museum publicity department refused my request to print enormous posters to advertise the event all over town—claiming budgetary difficulties—it took me only a single phone conversation with Teddy Kolleck, then mayor of Jerusalem—a member of the museum's board and a vociferous champion of avant-garde culture—to have him pull up at the front gate the next morning in his chauffeured government vehicle, storm through the doors, hunt down the bureaucrats who had refused me, and send them flying in all directions, each outdoing the others to see who could get the posters printed and hung throughout Jerusalem first. We designed a logo depicting a female muse in blue robes, which soon became a familiar sight all over town.

The week when Yehuda Amichai, the country's greatest poet, won the coveted Israel Prize, he was scheduled to be interviewed on our stage by a prominent literary critic named Alex Zahavi.

Backstage in a dressing room, Amichai, a mistress cradled on his lap and surrounded by a retinue of mildly amused rough-looking literary cohorts, sat smoking, drinking, and in no great hurry to face his audience.

When finally he emerged, the crowd had been waiting for an hour. Amichai, bored, sank into his chair and sat there looking like an insolent truant forced to remain after school.

Zahavi asked him how he felt to have just received Israel's most prestigious accolade. Amichai shrugged. Lit up a cigarette, blew smoke into Zahavi's face. Whereupon Zahavi clutched his chest, tore at his shirt, struggling to breathe, and slid from his seat onto the stage, where he lay gasping for air. He seemed to be having a heart attack.

Amichai, the closest to him, looked away, bored.

Zahavi's wife leaped up in her seat and began to scream: "Yehuda, help him! It's Alex's heart!" but for whatever reason Amichai did nothing, seized by a spell of Amichaian torpor, an existential slug-gishness. Or maybe he had caught a good verse line in his head and didn't want to lose it. With the aid of an assistant, I got a nitroglyc-erine tablet under Zahavi's tongue and kept him comfortable until the ambulance arrived. Amichai, with bigger fish to fry, left.

Weeks later, in a Jerusalem bar, at a table with Ivan Schwebel, the painter, and the poets Natan Zach and Dennis Silk, we waited for Amichai to show, but he called the bar, said he couldn't make it. Schwebel, American born, was Amichai's favorite painter; one of his works adorns the cover of Amichai's selected poems. Schwebel boasted to Zach that I was a Bronx football player from the toughest high school in New York and could do more push-ups than anyone present. To prove it, Schwebel and some others hit the ground for fifty, their limit, and dared me to exceed it.

With lifted eyebrows, Zach, a portly man with a Faustian goatee, looked at me as if to say: So?

I jumped down, did sixty. Eyelids lowered, Zach nodded and smiled. To celebrate my victory we got good and smashed.

At Anna and Itamar's I held court, so to speak, said little, the mysterious, unapproachable, behind-the-scenes kingpin. But inside, I wallowed in a warm self-pity bath. Had an awful crush on Anna, could barely stand to look at Edna anymore. Though I planned, designed, and directed every aspect of every program singlehandedly, didn't really feel a part of it. There was me over here, the creative power and financial source, and them, the artists, over there, poor, disheveled, but in love, proud, working together. They were all so grateful. But what about me, I wondered bitterly.

As our gatherings grew to include more of Jerusalem's bohemian set, I sank deeper into a despair that I could not share with anyone, a surfacing undercurrent of frustration over the undeniable fact that I had fallen completely and hopelessly in love with Anna.

26

I LOVED HER SO MUCH THAT I DARED NOT EVEN sit close to her in the same room. Wherever she happened to be always found me at the farthest point opposite. Our group often went out dancing and drinking to little late-night gangster cafés along Agrippa Street, where everyone sat around in the yellowish electric light, smoking endless cigarettes, leaning against each other, drunk, looping limp arms around each other to stumble-dance, but Anna and I sat apart, exchanging terse pleasantries with others too drunk to stand, and always ignoring each other from opposite ends of the table.

I never for a moment fooled myself into believing that she loved me or harbored any reciprocal feeling except as colleague and familiar.

She seemed to be closest to Edna. They were together constantly, a commiserating female triumvirate of Anna, Edna, Debbie, always off somewhere, to the Turkish baths to steam up and put henna in each other's hair, or to lunch in workers' cafés and after, shop for clothes and personal care items in the cheap stalls of the Yehuda market. They were the kind of trio who turned heads, and when I saw them together, laughing with arms locked like mischievous sisters as they hoofed down the street, I felt even more hopelessly in love with her.

In the planning sessions for the museum shows, over which I presided with a firm but encouraging hand, I was all business—the entrepreneurial visionary who had roughed out each show's basic design, the go-to decision maker who marshaled resources from thin air, the miracle worker who made it possible for the creators to create.

At these meetings Anna was a consummate professional who stayed on point with her assignments and addressed only matters of concept, or if the conversation went deeper it was to better understand what I was attempting to stage in a particular show.

Dancers, singers, poets, authors, filmmakers, actors whirled around me, cyclonic. A wave of my hand could conjure a post-modern opera. The show mounted from astonishment to astonishment as I introduced innovations like computerized audiovisual stage sets and tightened presentations so they increasingly resembled actual holograms of a literary arts publication. At the program's height—and at the lowest depths of my inexpressible longing for Anna—audience and cast members alike had the eerie experience of watching the pages of an immense journal turn with each new presentation, and feeling that they were turning with it.

At show's end, a glut of Jerusalem hoi polloi and culturati poured from the theater and stood around to talk excitedly in the corridors, balustrades, lobby, and out in front of the giant institution. But if their eyes sought for me, I was nowhere around. Skulked alone in some backstage area, disconnecting cables and tossing soda cups into trash bins—anything to avoid the unbearable sight of her. For on such nights she wore her finest clothes, looked stunning. At the sight of her my throat would catch, I couldn't speak. This had happened to me after more than one program, to my mortification. I would find a way to angle in slowly on the group, but really, on her. Knew they were out there waiting for me to go party, celebrate. I would come around from a dark side door exiting onto the surrounding park, and for a time stand at a remove, in the shadows of trees, looking, smiling, tearful, shaking my head in wonder, hurting inside, and so dazzled—how could anyone be so beautiful? Then I thought, maybe some astronomer who has loved a certain planet or star since earliest memory feels that mingled pain and pleasure to see it through a telescope, and knows the same anguished wonder. Whereupon, drawing a deep breath, I'd come upon them, unsmiling, my usual no-nonsense self, and say something inane, like "Well. That was all right, huh?" and get hugged and backslapped and hand-pumped, and they probably would have carried me on their shoulders too were it not so plainly evident that I disliked any sort of appreciative horseplay.

We'd go out, to the music places, where liquor flowed. The hugging couples drifted over the dance floor or flailed around and spun and screeched with hilarity as the pounding music accelerated our pulses, and we drank, endlessly, while inside my head I watched, in a bubble, my anguish-frozen insides, unutterably alone, hopelessly solitary, like some freak fallen from space, green fluids dripping from eyes and noxious mouth agape, forming words in a language no one spoke.

Sat smoking cigarettes, polished off bottles of Rishon LeZion brandy. Sometimes wandered off unnoticed, or with some mumbled promise to return, and did not, slept it off in the streets.

Come morning, I'd stumble to my feet, let myself into the flat, knowing that Edna, drunk, had spent the night at Anna and Itamar's.

In a strange sense, I had become the hub of everyone's world, yet was nowhere to be found, and could not locate myself anywhere in it. And so had it been for most of my life, which seemed to have been lived in my absence.

27

THEN, THE WAR.

In response to ceaseless incoming rocket attacks from terrorist bases in Lebanon, the Israeli Air Force bombed Beirut. Then ground troops excursioned inland toward the Litani River, where, it was reported, they would establish a defense perimeter to hold as a preventive buffer against further cross-border shellings and raids.

Instead, under the direction of Defense Minister Arik Sharon, the army kept going into all-out full-scale surprise war.

But while the army went north, my unit went south, into the Gaza Strip, to conduct operations against groups infiltrating from Gaza and Egypt.

It was later called "the Secret War," small units holding down vast spans of territory, performing tasks that required ten times our numbers and that we were, by and large, completely unsuited for. And so while the big war raged northward our dirty little mission went unnoted in the south.

I know soldiers who during several tours in Lebanon were not fired upon once, but every night; on the border of Egypt, we were shot at by tired, disgruntled Egyptian soldiers, or else Muslim fanatics, or even Bedouin tribesmen. If patrolling in the West Bank, we were fired upon. This was supposed to be a "quiet" service, a "good" time. Our good time consisted of night operations in rank-smelling close-quarter market places where every door or alley concealed a possible assailant. Our "good" time involved leveling the homes of terrorists who had blown up Israeli buses or stalking wanted gunmen through labyrinthine housing complexes or making sudden, lightning raids on communities where we overturned the contents of bedrooms and living rooms, searching for Molotovs, and which, afterward, made us feel inhuman, dirty, morally bankrupt, despite whatever we might unearth.

We were not trained for such tasks. My reserve unit consisted of armored infantry attached to a tank battalion: of urban counter-insurgency we knew nothing whatsoever. Trained for the battle-field, we found ourselves conducting operations among populations seething with hatred, and we felt that hatred deep down in our very bellies, where it sickened us and sometimes made us want to get good and drunk.

I recall one operation where I and two others drove alone on patrol in a jeep to a far-distant Arab village on the frontier of the West Bank, at the very edge of Jordan, through a menacing market-place crowd in an area where several terrorist cells were known to be operating.

We had orders to make our presence felt, show ourselves publicly, with weapons held at the ready as we parted the crowd like surf, yet not to fire unless first fired upon. I remember the fear in my comrades' faces, the hypertense alertness as we scanned every eye, every wall crack, every changing rivulet of space appearing and disappearing between the amassed bodies of the marketgoers, knowing that in that shimmering interstice a handgun might appear, or a Kalashnikov, or a grenade. It felt unreal.

Experiencing a form of terror so brand-new changed the quality of fear, for me, into something like a hallucinogen. Moving through so much barely suppressed fury, hate condensed into a sea of staring, was akin to a religious experience. Felt myself transported out of my skin into a realm far beyond the reach of human enmity. There were constant house-to-house searches. Manhunts for infiltrators. But the worst of it was up in the West Bank, in Hebron, to which my unit was sent because, with the war in Lebanon going full-tilt, elements of the routed PLO had infiltrated the West Bank and were launching new operations there.

Locals were going at it nose to nose with the settlers, with the Israeli Army caught in the middle. It was here that we picked up two prisoners, infiltrators, whom we were told to escort to prison headquarters in the back of a truck. The men lay on the floor blind-folded, and as I looked at them I sensed the terror that they must have felt. Though they were potential killers sent on a mission of mass murder into an Israeli civilian population center, the sight of their captivity sickened me, made me want to puke.

I knew that were I in their place I could expect no mercy from their side. But it didn't help. They were killers, fanatics, prepared to slaughter us all. And yet, I could not bear to see them in restraints. There is a kind of blindfolding and binding—Edna's kind—that is erotic; another kind, this sort, that felt dehumanizing. Was there a link? We handed them over to their jailers and as I watched them led away, stumbling and falling, something inside of me fissured, a hairline crack.

From then on, I saw many blindfolded and wrist-bound men stumble down corridors into interrogation rooms, and each time, the crack widened. Realized that our foes had found the perfect way to destroy us: by placing us in the hopeless, impossible position of choosing between survival and moral disintegration, depriving us of any choice that would preserve both our bodies and souls. It would have to be one or the other, and of course I, like my fellow Israelis, chose life—what else could one do? But from that day on I lost the power of sleep.

Lay insomniac in my sleeping bag, fixated on one thing: Anna. Thought of her pale white feet with pink-nailed toes, the gummy-bear rubber sandals she bought in the Yehuda market, the dirty beige high heels she wore with a short black skirt, her slender legs, warm thighs, coltish knees.

I thought of her shoulders, how they tapered seamlessly into her arms, her arms into her electrifying hands, whose fingers, like spiders, seemed so effortlessly to spin solid matter into art. Thought of how she drew all the time, book in her lap, reddish-gold hair falling over her pale, aristocratic face, eyes full of longing. How she concealed disappointments. I had seen that there.

Stopped removing my uniform, slept alongside my weapon and ammo vest, head pillowed on my helmet, and when a mission needed someone, was the first up and on the armored car or jeep, face wrapped in a black kaffiyeh and goggles, gunstock wedged into my thigh, at the ready, a round chambered and didn't care who knew it—performing my tasks robotically.

Plunged down any hole ordered into, any darkness, berserking through hideouts, searching for weapon caches, gasoline bombs, rags, detonators, explosives, flags, propaganda tapes, uniforms, grenades, photographs, flyers, suspects—a writer without a book to my name, married to a woman for her money, dope, and apartment, in love with someone else's spouse, lonely, disgusted, badly needing a double.

Slowly, in the recesses of my ignored consciousness, my entombed emotions, a plan took shape, ill conceived, which acquired the momentum of a visionary religious conversion, until I felt almost as if I had been called upon by some god to execute it.

28

I HAD DECIDED THAT I MUST TELL ANNA THAT I loved her. If there was a God, or orbiting mother-ship aliens, ruling the earth, something greater-seeming than my little fears had commanded that on my next return home I must attempt, no matter how hopelessly, to persuade Anna to engage with me in adultery.

I would tell her how I felt, the whole painful truth, knowing that to do so would bring an end to everything that was my world. I didn't care. Craved Armageddon, despised myself, my lies: how the world paraded its wants and hopes but my shameful truths hid away in shadows.

For the first time in my life I was going to be nakedly honest about my feelings. Anna, I would say, I know that we are both married, but I love you and want to possess you, sexually, socially, intellectually, and in every way that one can possess another. Possess you and declare my feelings to the world.

Once I chose this course, it was as though I had been transported to another realm, a different dimension, where I saw life through eyes made fresh with regained innocence.

What was I doing in the Gaza Strip, a hellish place of incurable Jew-haters, religious and nationalist fanatics with guns? Far from home Anna was home. Lay on the ground near a fire in an oil drum, the dark, muttering silhouettes of other troops milling around. In uniform, ammo vest, hugging my weapon, helmet beside me, body stinking, filthy, face smudged with black camouflage stick, sweating, flies buzzing my face, tightroping on my earlobes, nibbling on bits of food and my peeling flesh. Dung beetles and scorpions scuttling over my abraded, scabby, black-knuckled hands, I had visions of walking with Anna through a town in Spain, wearing rope sandals, squirting endless wine down each other's throat from bloated goat-skins, staining her blouse, soaking through to the shape and hue of her satin breasts, how clearly they stood out, high and pert—and she and I dancing wistful drunken steps for smiling peasants in Basque berets, arms around each other's waist, shameless, wistful, intel-lectual, soulful, like Leonard Cohen and Joni Mitchell, two hoboes slumming in exile, gypsy moth bohemians far removed from inter-necine combat, hopeless battles, raging wars.

Soft music sadnesses and warm nights of gentle candlelit poverty, poetic simplicity would be ours, Anna. We'd have new friends, expatriates exiled from other exiles to pure white sand beaches, removed from clamorous ambitions, gossipy cultural scenes, the grubby lower depths of those struggling in the arts.

No more struggle. Love, sun, sex, writing, drawing, painting, food, wine, sleep, good conversation, chalk-white walls and doors painted red and blue, guitars strumming over little fishing harbors, the night tides twinkling with reflected stars. She yearned for it too. Could tell. Even as I knew that I was deluded.

When my leave came up I hitched a ride in the back of a police dog truck, curled up in the canine-reeking cage, still wearing fire-proof mud-caked combat overalls, half dead, sleepless, after days and nights of continuous operations, yet feeling more alive than I ever had. About to eject my false life, live a brand-new one of uncompromising personal truth, I drifted happily in and out of sleep, head rolling, dreaming of white flares pulsing through a pitch-black sky, camouflaged faces peering out over landscapes filled with wild field rats driven from their holes by the thunder of artillery duels, in the clap and flash of which I saw a terrorist I'd bound and blindfolded led away to interrogation, and I went outside, upset, to smoke—and woke, sweating, with a start, head bouncing on the jeep floor, tufts of dog hair stuck in my lips.

29

THREE P.M., WEDNESDAY AFTERNOON. AT THIS hour, she's at work. But Barry, her employer, told me that she took the day off to catch up in her studio.

Found her at her workbench in the bomb shelter, fashioning a little wire man with pliers. When she saw me she laid the pliers down, still holding the wire man, and said: "What are you doing here? Debbie and Laura are both at your place, keeping Edna company while she waits for you to come home. She's out of her mind with worry. We heard about some trouble down there. We were—are you all right?"

I descended to the base of the stairs, paused to look around. It was all in shadow but for Anna, who sat on the high stool at the work-table, an architect's lamp pooling light over her fidgeting hands.

"It was crazy," I said, leaning against the metal handrail.

"Itamar's in the north, getting shelled by the Syrians."

"At least he can still call himself a soldier. I'm just a morally debased policeman."

"Why don't you request a transfer?"

"Do you know why I'm here?"

"No," she said.

Could slip through a dark dank maze of suspects' rooms on a predawn search without so much as a flutter, but to tell this woman what I felt about her was...The room began to swim, frozen tears thawing at the corner of my eyes. "What if I told you that I love you?"

Without hesitation, she replied: "And what if I told you that I love you?"

Then we came to each other, breathless words tumbling out as we held each other close.

She: "When did you know?"

I: "The moment I saw you."

"The same for me. The night before your wedding I sewed mourning beads to my dress, the way Arab women do. That's when Itamar first suspected that I love you. Oh, my darling, I love you!" she said, wiping away tears.

We kissed every bare spot of warm skin. Crushed against each other, lips prayed to flesh with cardinal sincerity.

En route to her place, we stopped off at the grocer to pick up Rishon LeZion brandy, a few cartons of Time cigarettes, all on her nickel. "To unwind," I said. "I'm covered with bruises, inside and out." It was understood: I was broke. Bye-bye Edna's father's money.

"Darling."

At her place, we stripped, embraced. I wanted her. Was drowning. And no blindfolds, no spread-eagled binding to bedposts, but new saplings wanting only spring.

"All that shit that went down in Gaza, it's hard to make sense of. But it's making me insane. I think a lot of soldiers, secretly,

are going nuts down there. It's like a spreading mental illness, you
know? The other side wants to kill us, but the things we do to stop
them are killing us inside. I feel like a dirtbag. You don't remember
the danger, just the looks in people's faces. It makes you suicidally
incautious. As if that will make up for the sight of an old woman
curled up on her filthy pallet in a hovel we broke into, looking for
guns. The way she tossed and cried in the beams of our searchlights.
The sound of her voice. Or these kids I came across on a house-
to-house, lying there on a row of cots, eyes locked on the ceiling,
afraid to see me standing there. With my gun. Goddammit."

I couldn't tell her about the blindfolded suspect who haunted
my nights.

"My beautiful man," she said. "Do you know how happy I am
right now, just to have you here with me? I want to know everything about you."

Reached over for a bottle of brandy, screwed off the cap, took
a long pull. Then another. Wiped my mouth with the back of my
hand. Gasped. Couldn't tell her about the blindfolds—I don't know
why that detail. Pulled some more on the booze and once again felt
the warm spread and my insides calm. My medicine. I don't know
why blindfolds got to me. We passed a cigarette back and forth.

Then we reached to make love.

"We don't have to now...if you don't...want...to...now," she
said.

I rolled off, curled up into a fetal position, my back to her. "I'm
with the woman I've waited my whole life for and I can't get it up."

Anna clasped the back of my neck with her hand, pulled my
head forward, kissed me. "My poor darling. This is a lot, what we're
doing. It must be unreal for you. It is for me. But we have the rest
of our lives to get used to it."

The worst thing, I thought, was not the shot soldier with a bullet in the chest and blood all over, or the guy we picked out of the razor wire who'd been diced to ribbons trying to get himself out. It was the guy I'd blindfolded and tied with hands behind his back. Standard military procedure.

"I once blindfolded this guy. Tied his hands behind his back."

She looked at me, said nothing.

"You understand?"

"Well, who was he?"

"A suspect, maybe a terrorist. We had a photograph. This was a bad guy. And I caught him. The damned police came on the raid. Me and a police colonel went through the roof door. But when I looked around, the cop was back inside. I was out there alone, ducked with my gun behind a vent, and when I saw the suspect, crazily, I stood up, pointed my gun straight at his head, shouting 'DON'T MOVE! DON'T MOVE! I WILL KILL YOU IF YOU MOVE,' aware that on some adjoining roof or even on this one another crony of his might be waiting in a cross-fire ambush, but I went right up on him. Recognized him from the picture passed around by officers of military intelligence. He could have killed me. I didn't care. In fact, I think I hoped he'd open up on me. Just to kill him. But he was unarmed. I got him to come out. Threw him down, tied him up. And before I led him down, blindfolded him. Standard procedure. Then rode with him back to Gaza City, knee to knee, in back of a jeep, to the military barracks, and the whole time I watched his blindfolded face, thinking: What if that were me? And feeling sick."

"But darling, you were trying to prevent murders that he was sworn to commit."

"I know," I said. "But I can't make sense of it."

I drank more.

And then I said: "Enough!" And plucking the cigarette from her lips, turned her around, wrapped her hair in my fist, and penetrated her from behind, clasping my free hand over her breasts, fingertips grazing gently down over her breasts and belly, her clitoris, softly kissing her neck and shoulders for a long time, and then, when she was soaking wet, took her, forcefully and directly, selfishly, from behind, without thought or hesitation, wanting her, knowing that she was the mate life had fated me to love, of that no question—and though somehow our paths had led us away from ourselves right to each other, somehow, improbably, through self-betrayal, we had found each other, and clinging to each other now, rocking conjoined in ecstatic love, it seemed possible to say that I had come to Israel and gone through heaven and hell only in order to find her.

30

FOR A WEEK, I STAYED IN THE HOME OF MY
friend Itamar, banging his wife. Completely in love with Anna, I
felt justified in each delicious thrust. Thought of nothing else but
her. The moment I had her, feared losing her. Ran out of booze
often. Anna replaced it. Cigarettes, food, movies, restaurants, cafés,
a night's drunk in Finks, Jerusalem's swankiest bar—she paid for
everything, of which I felt deeply ashamed. Wanted to be a man for
her. Couldn't. Hadn't a dime to my name. It had all been Edna's and
now that she certainly knew about us, moneywise I was done for.
We drank all the time. Word had come from Laura and Debbie that
Edna was homicidal, suicidal, drunk, raging, smashing our home
to pieces.

That week, I did little but read, drink, and wait for Anna's return
from work. Checked out books from the British Library, where I
had a membership, and from the American Cultural Center, the
two best English-language libraries in town. Drank and read in
order to sustain a mood, an artificial mental landscape in which

committing calamitous adultery with your best friend's wife makes a certain heroic sense. But mostly lay on Anna and Itamar's marriage bed like an imbecilic child, feeling the slow bleeding away of my sanity and soul, mental images projecting through my mind at high speed, drab khaki-green visions of military hell alternating with the life, the world, that Anna and I were about to destroy: all-night drinking sessions downstairs, the nonstop excursions to dance in night cafés, dawns waking hungover on the Dead Sea's shores, the openings of new art shows, the happily chattering overflow parties, the adulatory museum crowds who came to their feet, show after show, in thunderous ovations. We were the cool set. People had wanted to be like us. Between shows we had engaged in constant banter, with a sense of doing something major. I thought of how all around me my vision of a collectivity rooted in intellectuality and art had wonderfully cohered—the equivalent of Twenties Paris, if on a smaller Israeli scale. But despite all that, always something had festered, threatening to explode and shatter everything: My loneliness. My drinking. My inability to form a bond with others. Had thought of it as the romantic Byronic solitude of the visionary whose paroxysms of imagination and fantastical initiatives sustain a network of artists—but in the end it was insupportable, a delusion. A lie. Along came a war like a great hand to sweep it all aside. And we were not writers and artists, directors and dancers, but angry or frightened or numbed engines of meat bombed on foreign roads or bursting into the dream sleep of old people and children and bearing off blindfolded men to ordeals. If we let down our guard, not only in the jeep, the armored car, the Noon Noon, the ambush wadi, the border tower, but now too, even here, on the love-stained sheets of adultery's bed, they, the foe, would never stop attacking and killing us. This was the simple truth at the heart of everything, which no international legislative body of diplomatic reconciliation could ever bear to countenance, no political lobby ever face or state aloud, no journalistic investigative organ ever unearth, no ruling administration ever vocally concede, so that futile peace initiatives ceaselessly rolled out by the brightest minds inevitably failed, collapsed, exploded, shot in the head. We were all rushing headlong in a murderous mounting momentum of bloodshed that could last for a thousand years. They would not stop and we knew it. And it was killing us, which was their intention.

I never tried so hard to be brave as in that first hectic week with Anna. At night her phone rang nonstop as Itamar tried to call home from his communications truck with the shells falling all around and we rolled clutching in the throes of ecstatic lovemaking, his frantic rings in our ears. In a way, he was blindfolded now, trapped in an armor-clad cell, unable to see or know who now occupied his home but no doubt could imagine as days passed without response from her. She didn't want to pick up, receive anything from him. Had picked up phones to nothing for years. Was now receiving from me all that she should have from him, and more. I had already replaced him.

Surely he must have sensed this, for it occurred on such a primal level that it could have traveled, I thought, kinetically telegrammed from our loins, our musk and heat, through the grasses and orchards, along the beach sands and into the rocks and forests and mountains—come to him on a breeze, or in the way the grass shifted in the lull between shellings, as if a great hand stroked what of the Lebanese earth was yet left unscorched by the perpetual fire and shrapnel of the Syrian bombardments. And told him, the stroked and moaning earth, that he had been replaced.

"He already knows that I love you," she said. "He'll put two and two together."

If a shell had struck and killed him, he would have died with a head full of pornographic mental images of Anna copulating with me. And he would think of the sweet moments when we lay belly to belly, and understand the war raging about us, of which he was part and forgotten; also the social and artistic scene that we had created and on which he had placed so much hope, now waiting to disintegrate.

"Who are you?" she asked ever so gently, tracing my face with fingertips. "I can't believe that you exist. But you do. Tell me you do."

"I do," I said, reaching for the bottle. Her hand touched my wrist, gently restraining. "Not yet. Wait."

I set the bottle down, but the ghost of my hand remained curled around it.

"Tell me the truest thing about yourself. Something you've never told anyone."

Closed my eyes. Said: "If you could see inside of me, here? Now?"

"Yes."

I waited. For some great truth about myself that I had borne since birth to be revealed. But only one appeared. "All my life I have known that I am a writer." In my ears, it sounded disappointing. I opened my eyes. She gazed at me with more love than I had ever seen in the eyes of anyone. It frightened me a little. Taking my face in her hands, she kissed my eyes, nose, and lips.

"I love you," she said.

"Aren't you disappointed?"

"No," she said. "I know who you are inside and I know that anything else you could have said would have been a lie to please me."

"Don't women like to have their men tell them pretty lies?"

"Not this woman. Lies are ugly. Only tell me the truth."

We lay there in silence. And only then I thought of something else that might be true, perhaps the truest thing, not only about me—about us.

"I feel as if you and I have entered a new world," I said, "where we can leave all our corrupt former lives and selves behind, our memories, and set out for some new frontier, new selves—reinvent ourselves, make a new world, in our own image."

"Precious one."

Our bodies felt like newborns, side by side, safely cradled by love, rocked by bottomless desire. When we made love it was a preverbal transmission from one to another, syntax of sensation and delicious orgasms. I emptied myself into her again and again, yet always there was more. To be inside her was my new home—this is what she wanted me to know; that never would I need another. By day, I would write the great books that I had always meant to; by night, come home to her embrace. Our love became my religion, the new god to which I pledged body, soul and myself.

But it was a jealous god, my love. Demanded perfection and complete fidelity. Chastity of purpose. Purity of heart. A god of quite clear absolutes that would broach no half-truths, no shades of gray. The color gray was banished from the realm of my love.

When Itamar returned home, though, I drowned in gray. Despite our paradisiacal week together, Anna felt that a ten-year marriage required a subtle, careful untangling of the life they had fashioned together. She decided to remain at home rather than join me in exile at Barry's, who offered us the use of his apartment.

I could not bear her decision. Saw it as treachery.

"But darling, I'm yours. The week we've just had together. Doesn't that prove something to you? I want you. You're my man now."

"You're going to let him touch you, aren't you?"

Her eyes grew elusive. "No. I couldn't. Not after this week. No. But I'm not going to treat him like some kind of fungus. We shared the same bed for ten years."

"What does that mean? You'll sleep with him?"

"I don't know. I don't know what it means. Or what's going to happen. But I won't give myself to him. That I swear. I'm yours."

"Whore!"

She flinched, no less than if I'd slapped her. Took the wound deep into herself and grew pale, shaken. "I love you. Please don't speak to me that way. I thought we're better than that."

"Yeah, me too. That's what I thought. And now you're all vague and might share a bed with him. I can't believe what an idiot I am! To have thought that we had something different, something special."

"We do, darling! We so much do! But be a little patient. There are practical details. We're going to have to get a divorce. So will you."

"I'm used to it. It's no big deal."

"Well, it is for me. I don't want to make an enemy of Itamar any more than I may have already. I've publicly humiliated him. Everyone knows. I haven't tried to hide. But we jointly own this house. Both our parents sank a lot of money into it. I can't just run off. We need to disengage by stages."

"Stages! I don't have time for stages! There's a war on out there. I'm getting sent into cesspools to look for I don't know what anymore. What am I looking for? Do *you* know? Does anyone in Israel know what I'm looking for in those holes I get sent to? I want to know! Because now I've lost what I was looking for in there, or here with you. I thought I knew. Now I'm confused. I need a fuggin' drink. I need a drink and a street to sleep in. That's the fuggin' truth! Women! You're all fugging liars!"

"No, darling. Don't say that. You know it's not true. Please,
Alan. If you love me. There are other reasons. I'm in my first one-
woman show at the Israel Museum, because of Itamar. It's the most
important thing that's ever happened to me as an artist. When the
war broke out, we were working on the installation together. I need
his help to mount it. And to liaison with the museum."

"Yeah. Sure. And will he be mounting you while you and he are
doing all this mounting?"

"Darling, please. What are you talking about? I'm going to spend
the rest of my life with you. I just need a little time to disengage.
My love!"

Her hand reached to stroke my cheek. I batted it away. But jealousy didn't make me the monster I became at that moment. It was
that I knew she was an adult and I just a child who couldn't bear
the pain of complex grown-up situations. She was a woman who
needed a man, but I was emotionally stunted and anything hinting
at shades of gray would unleash in me a howling sense of abandonment that only alcohol could numb. I saw the pain ahead and knew
I couldn't make it. Better to be alone. Better a blackout in the street
than share a bed of nuanced love—for me a bed of nails. Looked
at her as if to say, How could you do this to me? and stumbled out
of there, angry, to get myself a bottle of brandy. Then went to the
drugstore and bought a box of over-the-counter codeine tablets,
no prescription needed. Careened through Jerusalem, swallowing
handfuls of codeine washed down with brandy. The Old City, lit
up like a Walt Disney castle, perched at a tilted ledge overhanging
a black abyss, and then wobbled the other way back, and the whole
sky seesawed as I staggered from neighborhood to neighborhood,
moaning Anna's name, wanting to be held by her, consoled, apologized to, reassured that in fact she had changed her mind, would

stay, commence at once our Adam and Eve exodus to the beginning of time, where we would start over, undo all the mistakes made in the Garden, recalibrate the world.

But knew in the pit of my being that she would not reverse course, must proceed with her plan, driven by a personal code I didn't have, a sense of what was right to do. Told myself that I was to her but a piece, a part, not central, not the radiant core that she was to me. Without her, I was nothing inside and the world was only kiosks, parked cars, passing groups of laughing friends in sport clothes and dresses, smelling of aftershave and perfume, strangers immersed in their own unknowable trips. And what was all that to me? Nothing! What was Israel, what was the whole world, to me? One big fat death trip. A hamster wheel flying a flag. And the more I thought about it, the more disconnected from reality I became. Where was beauty, depth, intelligence, discussion, I wondered. I wanted Dostoyevsky! Van Gogh! Kerouac! Pollock! Tolstoy! *Meaning!* She wanted to sort through deeds of ownership, study columns of assets. I wanted pleasure and celebration, impudent rejoicing, heartless joy! Yes, as war raged and others perished ignobly in fire and shrapnel, guts spilled out and crying for their mothers, as those who returned to the soul-killing lairs of sidewalk terrorism strapped on their garbage-disposal apparatus, let Anna and me burrow deep into each other, extract pleasure by the bucket, and laugh wickedly, wolfishly, at the stupidity of life! And let us depart gracefully, slipping out the door of Israel, away from the whole giant ignominious world stew of woe, and go find ourselves a Dionysian island of nudity and privacy, sun, sand, and each other's lips.

But the Old City only tilted a little more, like an ocean liner sliding, with all its passengers aboard, down into bottomless ink-black depths.

31

FOR SEVERAL MORE MONTHS I REMAINED IN
Jerusalem, drinking, eating codeine, sleeping with Anna, furious,
fighting and accusing, unable to get over the initial shock of her
decision to ease away from Itamar rather than make a clear, clean
break. She was spending most nights with him. The pain for me
was insupportable, but I feared to let her go. And the combined
sense of rejection and offended pride made me vicious.

Our fights were bad. She wept and pleaded; I sneered and spat.
She begged me to see that she was true, that she had filed for divorce
and was slowly, carefully sorting out their joint interests, that it was
now more or less but a minor matter of settling the finances. She
didn't even sleep in the same bed with him anymore. He stayed on
the sofa. She swore to this.

But for me, it still wasn't enough. I needed her around to cling
to all the time. Couldn't stand to be alone, to drink alone with
myself on those nights she stayed with him. And I was drinking all
the time now.

"We don't need finances," I raged, standing with a bottle clasped in my fist. "We only need each other." I could as well have been speaking about the bottle. "But you're ruining everything. You don't even know how much or how badly. EVERYTHING is going to HELL! You've destroyed my TRUST! Betrayed my LOVE! You're STILL with him!! So, yeah, I still love you, but I don't TRUST you!"

"Precious one, I'm leaving him. You'll have me for the rest of your life. He only needs me now, while we split apart, which is so painful for him. I'm just trying to be decent. I love him as a good friend. I owe it. We built that house together. We have all the same friends."

"Friends!" I laughed. "Some friends!"

With the exception of David Twersky, the writer and editor, Roy Isacowitz, the playwright and financial columnist, and Robert Rosenberg, a reporter, a majority if not all of the "friends" I had made as a result of the museum melted away once they learned that not only had Anna left Itamar and I had dumped Edna but the museum program was as good as doomed.

I was widely denounced as a renegade and homewrecker, a drunken loner, an outlander who had invaded Jerusalem's cultural scene with commendable ingenuity but quickly showed his true colors. I was the vulgar, shallow American. Those who had hated me all along resented their exclusion from the museum programs, vigorously campaigned to besmirch my name. Others who envied my rapid rise applauded my decline. As the rumor mills raged and the war up north continued, I obtained a divorce from Edna. The three presiding rabbis were the very same who had divorced me from Tsofnat. One of them, an ancient graybeard, winced on seeing me and said: "You again?"

★ ★ ★

In a desperate bid for sanity I broke with Anna and left Jerusalem; moved into the home of a man named Yeheschel Ben-Hur who had once been incarcerated in a British Mandate prison, sentenced to hang, for an attack on an Arab bus that had left a boy dead.

Like me, he was a dour loner whom others steered clear of. I sat in the empty lower portion of his white frame house, sulking and drinking behind drawn shades, dropping codeine to fend off severe paranoid delusions, auditory hallucinations, but the codeine only multiplied them. Lost track of day and night, couldn't differentiate anymore. Finally, a call-up came from the army. I reported for yet one more tour of duty in Gaza.

Rode down in a reservist's bus, detoxing from months of drinking and drugging. My nerves, having grown centipede legs, crawled over walls and onto ceilings. I grew convinced that the members of my unit were out to kill me. More than once, put the barrel of my rifle in my mouth but hadn't the guts to pull the trigger. Would sit like that, at a remove from the others, in the desert dark, a hunched shape with a long protrusion extending from his mouth to the ground, a self-executing mosquito. Once, after an operation in which we razed the home of the family of a young man in his twenties who had thrown a grenade at commuters in the Central Bus Station, I experienced a mental break from reality so complete that the soldiers serving with me asked what I was on.

"What is it? Pot? Hash? Coke? C'mon, Kaufman. Share the wealth!"

But I hadn't taken anything, though I badly needed to. Simply put, I was losing my mind.

After my service, I announced to Anna by telephone that I was leaving the country, returning to New York after almost seven years away in Israel. She said she would follow. Do what you like, I told her. I didn't really care anymore. She was still living with him.

At the airport, tearful, she saw me off. I recall how, as she stood at the foot of the last escalator before the "Passengers Only" zone, mournfully watching me ascend, the low-hanging support beam slowly erased her, head to foot, until she was completely gone.

On the airplane I expelled a relieved breath. The whole nightmare of Gaza, my shattered social and professional life in Jerusalem, was behind me for good. Could now finally sit and nurse a civilized tumbler of watered-down airline scotch as I watched Israel fade behind a wall of unreal snowy white clouds, and when the tumbler was empty, lift two fingers and have a pretty attendant in a flight uniform bring another and then another—and pretend to myself that I did not love a woman or a country that I had waited my whole life to find, only to desert.

BOOK FIVE

32

GOOD FRIENDS OF ANNA, THE ISRAELI PAINTER Natan Nuchi and his wife, Smardar, daughter of the Hebrew-language novelist Aaron Megged and stepdaughter of the Abstraction Expressionist historian Dore Ashton, had obtained for me a small apartment on 5th Street, off First Avenue, in the East Village, just a few blocks from their home on 3rd Street. Their understanding was that I would feather this nest in anticipation of Anna's arrival. I did nothing to discourage this illusion.

They lived in the Wyoming Building, in a loft owned by Ellen Stewart, legendary founder of La MaMa, the avant-garde theater. Composer Philip Glass lived just down the street and Jean-Michel Basquiat painted close by. It was a heady time to be in the East Village.

Almost the entire district was on tenant strike, and I found that I didn't have to pay rent at all. Meant to be held in escrow, the rents had all been spent on parties. The entire neighborhood was rental outlaws living in arrears.

My experience working in both the Israel Museum and on kibbutz fishponds led an employment agency to find me suitable for work in the Department of Ichthyology at the Museum of Natural History, where my official title was "Scientific Secretary," Grade I, a civil service job with good pay and handsome benefits that required very little of me. Either I typed up scientific papers or tagged big muddy barrels of fish dredged from the Hudson as part of environmental impact statements.

To perform these tasks I kept a bottle stashed away in the leather satchel that I brought to work each day. Also quickly fell in with visual artists and taxidermists from the museum's exhibition department upstairs on the fifth floor—a hard-drinking bunch of unrulies who staggered back to work each afternoon after lunch, shirts unbuttoned to the waist and blind drunk after orgiastic two-hour lunches in the local bistro during which they threw up all over themselves and sometimes tangled—jeering and incoherent—with other outraged customers. In effect, the city paid us to get blasted. Since we were all unionized, we often charged overtime for this invaluable service.

For a week or two, things went fine. But memories of Anna lurked just beneath the surface. I still wanted her, still felt her in my core. My skin missed hers. And the nightmares of Gaza returned to me at night. Cracks began to show in my facade that not even a London Fog raincoat could camouflage.

It began on a weekend as I rode the subways. A girl with a pale face spoke to me on the platform. Couldn't tell what she was after, yet I seemed unable to disengage. She had me spellbound, locked in. Like some phantom figure born of guilt and repressed longing for Anna. Said that she needed help, would I go with her to a transient hotel to speak to the management on her behalf, stop them from throwing her out.

Inexplicably, almost helplessly, I went—unable to refuse. My heart beat fiercely in panic. Felt a pulse-racing shriek gather in my skull. In a trembling voice I attempted to ask questions: Where were we going? What is the problem? But she only looked solemnly at my trembling hands and said mournfully: "Soon we'll be there." She was beautiful but like an arisen corpse, her skin tone blue-white. We exited the subway at West 34th Street, hurried along to a strange-looking building that did not seem like a hotel, more a low-rent warren of office spaces leased to shadowy enterprises. I said, "I don't think I should be here," but she said, "You are very kind, very generous to help me." And witlessly, I followed along behind her though every nerve in my body begged me to stop. Finally, we came to a door with the name of a company stenciled on the opaque glass window. She knocked. A voice asked who it was. She said: "Me."

As the door opened, I turned and ran down the long institutional green corridor, to a flight of stairs, which I bounded down three steps at a time, and burst onto the street—it was April, very hot. Looked around in wild-eyed terror. Felt a stare burn my back and stumbled a few steps forward. A female voice snapped: "Move it, slowpoke!" Belonged to a woman in a business suit transporting a luggage carrier. Quickly, I began to walk downtown, glancing back to see if anyone followed. Stopped at a newsstand to buy cigarettes and as the vendor made change realized that he belonged to a PLO hit squad that had been sent from Gaza all the way to America to assassinate me. Tried to appear calm as he counted out change, which I shoveled into my hand and thrust into my pocket. Walked away rapidly, tears welling in my eyes, white-hot panic spreading throughout my chest and abdomen and a nonstop sequence of horrifying scenes of abduction and blindfolding, torture and humiliation, flipped through my brain.

Now grasped that everything about me was known to my foes. Where I lived, worked, who my friends were. Clearly, the girl was a terrorist operative. Ducked into an alley, cringed, forehead pressed to a brick wall, muttering: "Oh, my God, Elohim, Yahweh, oh my Lord, I am without a gun. I beg you, please, save me from this fearsome fate."

But, no go. Lifted my face, even more terrified. Realized that I was utterly alone, unarmed, without a single person in the world to tell about this, anyone who could help—a veteran of a foreign army with no veterans administration on hand to assist.

Walked ever farther downtown, to more familiar environs, to calm down. At a bar on Second Avenue, stopped in, resigned, waiting for hands to lay hold, drag me to a van. Ordered endless rounds of boilermakers, then cut out to a liquor store, bought a fifth of Cutty Sark, and staggered on, the fear still full-blown yet muffled now. Paused to tilt the bottle back for long pulls, swayed, and stumbled on, the fear shrinking into a grisly puppet play, a hallucinated farce in which I saw myself before my torturers, blottoed and ridiculous, bound dangling from ropes, jeering and spitting into their faces. How ridiculous you are, I shrieked, to want to kill someone who has known only suffering his entire life, only lovelessness. Why in the world would you want to kill, of all people, the world's loneliest man? A failed writer? Someone who couldn't keep the woman of his dreams even when she threw herself at him. Who went to pieces serving the Jewish state? A broken man who had left the United States in flight from the long history of his defeats. So, my torturer, what sort of agenda is it that must build on the debris of one so ruined?

But there was no answer from anywhere, though the sense of conspiring threat was all-pervasive, imbued the very air and fading light. As dusk fell I found a doorway to curl up in and mercifully blacked out.

33

THE AFTERSHOCK OF SUCH AN ATTACK LASTED
days, and the attacks occurred ever more frequently. Physically
exhausted, emotionally drained, I took frequent leaves from work,
infuriating my superiors at the museum, scientists who wanted as
little as possible to do with administrative worries. Now and then,
I was called onto the carpet, warned. Contrite, I promised to do
better. Days later, paranoid, delusional, and too afraid to leave the
flat, again I called in sick.

Ran out my sick days but didn't care. Had no rent to pay, few
necessities besides booze, cigarettes, and, now and then, food. By
my hobo calculations, were I fired, I'd still collect enough unemployment to keep me in hay for a good while more. Either way, stay
or go, I couldn't lose.

Now and then, I resolved to stop drinking; recognized its cruel
effect on my life. For a day or two would succeed either to ingest
no booze at all or just a few beers. Whereupon the global conspiracy
plot against me resumed with redoubled ferocity. In the eyes of

a co-worker, or some stranger's expression, or a question from a waiter about a menu choice or simply how the light fell across a room at a particular hour, irradiating a dust ball with corpse-blue death ray energy, again the plot against me would unfold, force me to take actions for relief which, though prompted by dread, only seemed to amplify it.

A passerby's glance would put me into evasion mode, though what exactly I sought to elude was never clear. Plots seemed to unfold in subtle hints that triggered in my head, chest, and abdomen anguished shrieking signals of alarm during which—for survival's sake—I must pretend to be unsuspecting, at ease, for any word or action or expression on my part, hinting at knowledge of the plot, would assure its success. So long as I played the game flawlessly, I would not die just yet. Trapped on a high wire over a volcano, I had to stroll as nonchalantly as a Sunday pedestrian out for a pleasant promenade. This, of course, was excruciating. Sometimes it occurred to me that the effort to appear sane, normal, while in the thick of such a horrible psychic state was the very torture that I sought to elude. But I would quickly lose the thread, plunge right back into my thin-ice dance over the mental lake of fire.

The only remedy I knew was to drink and then drink some more. Sometimes lay in bed fortressed as in childhood by surrounding walls of books. But now, along with Hemingway, Kerouac, Hubert Selby, there was VSOP and Gallo port and cartons of Camel cigarettes. Shades drawn, clock turned to the wall, telephone unhooked, I read my way forward, sailing on a fantasy barge of slow words downriver past black night terrors, until Thursday became Friday, turned into Saturday, and by Sunday, having drunk whatever lay at hand, I blacked out and awoke again into shuddering incomprehension and drank yet more to ward off the inevitable crushing hangover—an army of vengeance poised to attack.

Lay there, covers over head, drunk yet somehow not, the liquor's effect disappointing, flat. No matter how much I drank I seemed only to bloat and my sickness deepened, but the warm comfort that I sought for, the panic anesthetic, just wasn't there.

Had no other recourse, then, aware of none: experiment with different brands and combinations, drink yet more. That only worsened my condition. I sought return to a warm wet womb where I was loved and protected. (If only it could be! If only I could crawl from these clothes, this skin, return to my origins, even just for a bit, get some bearings, see where I had made the wrong turn, and then relaunch, navigate my life by correct coordinates.)

But it was not in the cards. My arms and legs ached, flesh leaden, swollen, listless, lifeless. Smelled bad. Didn't know, or want to, what time it was. There was nothing to this world, just cracked walls, unswept rooms, multiplying mirrors, and this great groaning sadness of a failed life that occupied my marrow like an alien being.

Anna called. Said she loved me. The room tilting. She had filed for divorce. Something crawling my way, shadows. Her affairs in order, she was coming. Was I glad?

She did not know that she had called into a green-glowing bunker sandbagged with hand-grenade hallucinations. Anything that could lift the siege was welcome.

"Come" is all I could manage to croak.

One week later, Anna, my incarnated soul mate, slender and with cream-colored skin and red hair tied in a pony tail and intelligent eyes that by turns burned with creative fire and twinkled with erotic mischief, walked toward me down the passenger ramp at Kennedy, and all I could think of was escape through the bottle.

Up close, her looks showed signs of wear. Dark rings scored her eyes. She had a kind of stress-fractured smile. But I was so glad to see her. Held her in my arms, kissed her long and lovingly. Her body's contours fit mine perfectly. God proportioned us for each other.

In the East Village, we wasted no time—tore off our clothes and knocked each other into bed, where we made love for days and talked. I felt sanity's return. And with it, hope. A homesick longing for Jerusalem took hold. Head on my shoulder, she told me what that had happened when I left for New York. Crushed by her application for divorce, Itamar, called up again, had gone north to perform more of the same duty. All his friends had turned against her except Debbie and her husband, Menache. She had heard that David Twersky was back in Lebanon. The whole local cultural scene had evaporated. People either left the country or moved north to Tel Aviv. Jerusalem was a ghost town. It would never again be as we had known it. There had been a news report about the ugly little war going on unreported in the south.

"They said all the things that you had been telling us," Anna said. "How the war would now come down from Lebanon and erupt out of the West Bank and Gaza. Alan, you had already seen the signs. That all we had succeeded at doing in Lebanon was move our foes closer to our urban centers."

Come to make a quick, fresh start, in no time Anna had a job telemarketing for a dance company and proved great at it. Made fast friends in the East Village performance art scene and was soon at the heart of a multiplying network of parties, performances, art shows, and readings. Energized by all the activity, she went out almost every night while I chose to stay behind, drinking in local watering holes.

Abetted by the presence of Anna, her enthusiastic optimism, I felt the flood tides of insanity withdraw, and a renewed sense of confidence that I could, after all, with moderation, drink as I pleased. Soon slipped back into old patterns of chronic absenteeism at the museum, or else outright on-the-job drunkenness. En route home stopped at East Village bars and, bleary-eyed, speech slurred, knocked back rounds; stumbling out to a liquor store to get a bottle that I took over to Tompkins Square park, sat on a bench, peaceably drank. People walking by seemed so alive, animate, talkative—yet I felt like an unseen shade, a voyeur of emotions as they walked with arms around each other's necks, laughed, backslapped, gestured, humans who had each other, cared, sparked a love interest in one another. Tilting back the bottle, I swigged a mouthful, tilted some more, down the hatch, burning away the landscape inside, and later climbed the stairs to our place, let myself in, flowers behind my back, a surprise. But she wasn't there. Found a note. She had waited, waited, suffered and waited. No word or sign. Then had freaked out and gone to her friend Patty's, not to be alone. Please, please, please call there as soon as I got home.

I didn't. Drunk, ripped up the note and flung it angrily around the room, shouting, "The hell with you" to no one in particular, and betrayal searing my chest.

How dare she leave me here alone? I needed to find her waiting to console me. Ran down, lingered on the stoop, the sky a cartoon-purplish black; passersby leered, looming from dark streets as if each possessed knowledge of my imminent and horrible fate. Buried my face in my hands. Only the bound and blindfolded victim has no idea of what awaits, stretched upon the altar, beyond aid, unloved by those gathered to watch the bloody harvest, eviscerated intestines spilled from abdomens, breasts sliced off, torn-out tongues dangling from red-hot pincers, pliers gouging at a little wire man. O Lord God, save me, I prayed. Saw the sweat-soaked sinewy forearms of hooded men methodically exact suffering from innocents. Unable to stand more, bought a bottle of scotch, unscrewed the cap, and sluiced down several fierce swallows. Don't recall the rest. Another night of violations. Woke beside her with a sensation of mad dogs tearing at my jugular, a kind of mild seizure. Had a dim memory of garments rent, doors slammed, shoving, pleas, screams.

34

SHE TOO BEGAN TO DRINK. AND INCREASINGLY lost weight. The strain of all that I put Anna through told in ways that frightened even me. She grew gaunt. I flew into constant jealous rages over Itamar, or any man. Wanted to strictly control her. At work, a departmental process had begun to oust me from my post—no easy task. I was unionized, a civil servant. Written complaints were lodged, all justified. A case against me built. I got warnings. Offers of counseling. Tête-à-têtes with sympathetic members of the admin. I was observed, I noted, with a certain look of dismay, as if they knew something. Did they? What? Felt sure they were on to my impending annihilation. At times, considered killing them all, to protect myself. But would collapse into a little crying child without an ounce of willpower. Baffled, Anna clung to me. I could no more kill anyone than pretend not to know who plotted my imminent downfall. But other times my disdain for my invisible assassins was boundless. The look in my eye mocked. You are nothing without me. So, kill me. But when I'm gone, what will you be? The nothings that you are.

I just had no idea whom I was speaking to. Knew only that they were there.

And it was only then, in the depths of my drunkenness, that I could admit to myself the truth: *Anna, I love you, more than life itself. And it is because of love that I must remove you from harm's way. For there is no possibility of revealing to you the terrors working against me, against us. If I do, your life is endangered too. The thought of you suffering the same fate that awaits me is the worst torture of all.*

The work of eluding monsters was hard enough. To be effective, needed to move quickly, act on reflex; take spontaneous evasive measures in sudden ways that she would never fathom. Reversing course in alleys, spinning around, heading in the opposite direction; rushing down into random subway stations, boarding any train that happened along; riding arbitrary buses to Queens, Brooklyn, the Bronx, as I often did, making circuitous returns by illogical routes—such tasks might eat up entire days and nights, deployed at the first sign of something amiss.

To survive I needed unimpeded latitude. She, unaware of the threat, moved at the slow, purposeful gait of sanity, didn't see what lurked at the corners of sight. With her in tow, I was sure to die, and in the bargain, she as well. And so one day I called her father, Ben, in Toronto and said: "You'd better come get your daughter. I'm going crazy and can't take care of her anymore."

Three days later, Ben and Sally pulled up in an auto, come all the way from Toronto, and led her down, wrapped in a jacket, crying, as I followed behind with her bags. In the street, took her in my arms and said: "It's only temporary. See you soon, when I'm on my feet," which I knew would be never. As the car pulled out, I felt only relief.

35

I DROWNED THAT PART OF MYSELF THAT WOULD have hoped to ever hear from her again, vanished into someplace that I could never wish to find. All of me down that pit. A blue-black place of self-murdered heart. Like a fighter plane that bore all the armored decor and battle insignia of a savagely unstoppable war instrument but was in fact all balsa and house paint, planted on the runway, a decoy to fool the foe. My balsa life of blood, tears, silence, pilot in the cockpit dead and wings ablaze, a hollow burning facade tumbled from a sky where it never really flew in the first place, aflame, on the runway, never to take off.

Now was free to enter into the bunker. Monitor the sinister knowing looks in strangers' eyes, the expanding, unfolding mass plot, satanic clues overlying everything, from the sewers to the stars, in the hub of which I moved in a perpetual dodging dance that must not stop or else: death.

Now and then, thought of my dirty little war on behalf of the Jews. A malevolent dangerous war in which soldiers like myself had worked to hold back a rising tide of lethal violence, placed our bodies between our people and the bombers, along with horrors of the Holocaust, the mass graves and gas chambers, corpse incinerators and torturers, neo-Nazis, Aryan Supremacists, the Inquisition, White Russians, Islamic Fundamentalists, the Klan. Sometimes awoke in the morning facing an almost empty bottle of vodka or beer in which a cockroach navigated soaked cigarette butts, and smacking my dry, spittle-caked lips, blinking like a child in a cradle, wished as if upon a star that one day I'd wake to find that none of it had ever occurred. That no one had ever hated us Jews, hated me, that I inhabited another sort of world, a different kind of place, could have back my Annie, live a sane life.

But risen to my feet, the last of the cockroach-cigarette swill drunk, reentered the game to which there was no end, stalked by hostile, relentless, invisible killers, a dangerous match of camouflaged strategies, intuited moves, second-guessing faceless hunter-stalkers with the wiles of hyenas and jackals—my assaulted mental faculties collapsing under the sheer weight of constant hypervigilance, impossibly multiplying rules of the game—and in all of this, in the depths of my love, I had wished only to save Anna by putting her out of reach of the killing delusions bearing down so hard upon me without relent.

I was inexplicable. No one knew anymore what to make of me. Natan, the artist, furious at my abandonment of Anna, refused even to speak to me. I sat in my kitchen with a wet blank stare, the air amassed around like wooly dust. Watched a cockroach crawl up the cracked wall, a journey of hours, even years. Waited for nothing, except my inevitable slaughter. Was to be killed, of course. Sacrificed. To the furnace mouth's encyclopedic and incinerating prejudices. I was the contemptible Israeli, the despised Jew. Despite all PR to the contrary, I clearly saw: the world had changed little since it set the Gestapo on my mother. Now they followed me. If no other Jews yet saw what was coming, in my parallax view, I was living out the fate awaiting everyone, twenty, thirty years from now, say, in the future. Soon the human hunt for innocence would be global, with Jews first on the list of the wanted.

Some days, thought it best to offer my neck to the blade, just let them have me. Certainly, deserved death, I felt. My writing career a sham. True love ruined. Day passed into night, remained there, hostage. The door creaked, a hall draft, footsteps passed in the stairwell outside. Around me the East Village exploded with new galleries, magazines, poets, movements, art, bands, but here, in my private rat hole—always, in the end, alone—I drank and waited for something that never seemed to materialize but the approach of which was always imminent, anytime I stepped into the street.

So I rarely went out. After a week or month, I don't know, received a call from the museum requesting my appearance at a departmental hearing. Received, too, a summons in the mail. So, this was it. The execution. Drunk, I went, and after the heads of the department had each taken a turn detailing my derelictions, was advised of my termination with the full consent of the union and asked if I had anything I wished to say in my defense.

"Yes," I said, "I wish I had told you all sooner to go to hell."

Now I'd collect my unemployment. Now no need to rise, bathe, eat, dress, and mobilize myself. Now could lie on the floor cradling a bottle and watch dust motes dance in a pale blue beam piercing the filthy alley window. Now Oblivion was a country all my own, a mystic magical place that lay only just one bar away, one more drink ahead. Every night visiting there, my unconscious stormed through lunatic adventures that I could not recall except in hints and flashes. My road led through a forest of bar-stool thrones, a succession of neon kingdoms that began in leather and ended in duct-taped patched vinyl, with barflies whose torn stockings were not intentional punk affectations but lizard scales over unwaxed and varicose skin.

Into this void Anna called, her warm voice searching, wanting to draw me out from this evil mess. She searched blindly for me, but I was nowhere to be found. Left between us was only a superficial commonality of locations: Jerusalem, the East Village, and the Israel Museum.

"But, sweet one. I'm yours now." Her voice probing from a great distance, that other world she now inhabited.

She said, "I miss you, want you here with me. My husband. Precious one." Each word laden with a million-ton weight of shattered hope. Her voice lifted, but then stumbled and faded: "Come here, come home. To me. To Toronto." An echo of a whisper in a strange tongue. I pulled on my vodka. Vodka was cheap, did the trick just as well as scotch, even better. Slashed through all pretenses. Stormed my nerves with bare knuckles, pounded my blood like a thug. I pulled again. Had heard somewhere that because vodka was clear, the hangovers were milder. This, I had learned, was a lie.

Anna, hopefully: "Do you want to come?"

I laughed, softly, hoarsely. Could only imagine how it sounded. A cackling emanation from a black pit. "What'll I do there?" I slurred. "All I do is drink."

"My sweet, just come. I understand now like never before. Darling, you have PTSD, from what you went through in Gaza. What's preventing you from facing your PTSD is loyalty, the fear that doing so will make it seem like you're betraying your fellow soldiers. But darling, it's not a matter of politics. It's medical. I've got a job with the symphony. And I've found us a place on Queen

Street. It's like the East Village. I'll work to support us until you feel well enough to get on your feet. In the meantime, just rest. Let me feed and love you, my darling. And we'll have family here to help. We won't be so alone."

I took a train north, a railroad to life, hoping to be cared for and cured, healed by the only woman I'd ever loved and believed had ever truly, selflessly, loved me. A woman of high intelligence, profound depth, artistic brilliance—even, despite adultery, a kind of moral character. A woman so beautiful that every man in our Jerusalem milieu, married or single, had hankered after her. When we men were alone, she was all that we spoke of.

But what met me at the station had the pall of death. Anna had shrunk by some kind of eating disorder, anorexic, a near skeleton. Crazed as I was, her appearance shocked me. To make matters worse, Anna's sister, at the station to ferry us to our new Queen Street digs, addressed Anna and me in that high-pitched, wheedling, histrionic voice that people adopt when pretending that something horrible has not happened: the reduction of a superb specimen of femininity to a human broomstick, a wasted shadow.

"Alan! You look so great!" the sister exclaimed, lightly embracing me (we barely touched). Anna's stick form, swimming in a cherry-red satin jacket embroidered with the logo of the symphony, lurked into view. "Doesn't Anna look great?!" shrieked the sister.

I ignored this. Said nothing. Anna looked near death. Embraced her, fingers pressing through the satin down to the skin, bones. She looked the way I felt, like an X-ray, black and white, with a big tumor where once the heart had been.

Leaned close to her ear, felt her baby skin against my cheek. Her sweetness unchanged, just perishing. Felt a sharp stab of shame. I had done this. I; no one else. Reduced the most desired woman in

Jerusalem to a specter, a menial worker, a ghost searching for the life that I had taken from her. I was poison. The fiercer her determination to keep me, the sicker she got. I had only deeper graves to offer, darker, danker dungeons.

"I'm tired," I said. "Let's go home. Take me home."

"We can rest now, darling," she said, laying her skeletal head weightlessly against my shoulder. Her voice too sounded spectral. Neither of us belonged any longer to this world. "We both need rest," she whispered.

The sister dropped her public relations effort, grew as grim as the situation. Drove us silently to Queen Street. Anna and I in the back of the car swayed against each other like shocked survivors of an airplane crash.

The sister jumped out, helped Anna to her feet. Anna could barely stand. The sister handed me my bags, hugged Anna, and said, looking at me with dull pain in her eyes and little conviction, "You should consider yourself a part of our family now. We don't care what's happened before. It's a brand-new start." Then hugged Anna again, whispered something to her, kissed her, squeezed her lifeless hand, got back into the car, and sped off without looking back. We stood there on the sidewalk for a moment, unable to go backward or forward, two immobile monuments to insensible suffering and unquenchable love, looking down at our bags, then at each other, struck dumb by our wounds and inconsolable memories.

We shared a studio with a lesbian couple, the room partitioned by a curtain on the far side of which our alcove, barely large enough to fit a bed into, also contained two chairs and a hot plate. Anna had made it as homey as she could, given her limited funds and flagging energy. We were alone, the couple arranged to be out, and when we entered our space Anna drew the curtains, shrugged off her jacket, displayed herself on the bed as prettily as she could.

She looked like a concentration camp inmate. Perhaps her mother, Sally, who spent time in a death camp, a Holocaust survivor like my mother, looked this way when Allied forces liberated her. Perhaps for her all this had been in some unbidden way her unconscious effort to claim her mother's suffering for herself; the loss of every-thing, a terrible ordeal, and a long nightmarish journey home.

But no matter how seductive she tried to look, it didn't work. Thought of her not as a partner in pleasure but another medical case like me, in need of attention. Crawling onto the bed, stretching out on my back, I said: "Look, you know how much I love you. But I'm exhausted." Surveyed our little space. "Thank you for this. But tell me. Anna, what we've lost. Think of it. Was it worth it? What did we gain?"

"Each other."

"I gained you and you are wonderful, the woman of my dreams. But I don't know what to do with it. Tell me the truth. Isn't this about you wanting a kid?"

She blinked hard.

"I'm asking because I can't do that. I can't take care of you, let alone some kid. I can't even take care of myself."

"But you said...you once talked about a little Alan and Anna mixed together...a baby with our features and personalities combined. To make a new thing, a third 'us.' "

"Yeah, I know. But in the meantime us isn't doing so hot. And besides, you want to perpetuate me? Isn't one Alan Kaufman bad enough? One of me is enough for this world."

"No, it's not enough. You are a beautiful man. I think that you're a genius. But you don't know how to live. Let me teach you. You're like a boy who's been raised by wolves, thrown into situations you can't handle. But you won't have to. Let me deal with them. I know that you can do anything you set your mind to. I saw what you did at the museum. No one's ever done that before. You brought a whole new art scene to life in Jerusalem, one of the oldest cities in the world. You were a soldier. And a journalist. And a poet. And you wrote and published short stories. Whatever's happened to you can be cured with love and rest. Let me love you back to health. I want to. You're my soul mate. The man I want to have children with."

"How many?"

The question was like a slap, cold, logistical, a calculation, a position staked out in a desperate negotiation: not a response to her heartfelt call to love.

"I don't know. I thought, two..."

"Two," I said. And again: "Two." Then: "It's a good number. My brother and I were two. And Mommy and Daddy made four. And we all equaled one big fat nightmare."

"It can be different for us. We're not them."

"That's where you're wrong," I said. "I am them, in combination, the worst of both worlds. I'm their dream of what happens when you mix George with Marie. And look what we got. An adulterer. A drunk. A failure. A liar who reneges on his promises."

She cried.

I sat up and felt around for an ashtray, found one, lit a cigarette. Had caused so many to cry that I'd gotten rather used to it. Go have a drink when they're like this, I'd tell myself, and let them weep. It's the only really decent thing that you can do.

Her parents threw open her home to me, though Ben could barely conceal his hostility for what I'd done to destroy his beautiful and gifted little girl: wrecked her marriage and reduced her to a skeletal divorcée who'd stopped doing her art and was now working telephones to raise funds for other people's creative endeavors while she herself was remarried to a drunken freeloader. Others should have been manning phones to raise funds for her, one of the most gifted and original artists of her generation.

They gave me keys to their home when they were away on the little car excursions they liked to take. Anna joined them with my encouragement. I stayed behind. With them out of the way, I could raid Ben's considerable liquor cabinet. Often, they returned to find me blotto.

One day Ben sat me down to have a man-to-man. Bald, narrow-shouldered, with weak eyes and a trim mustache. I could have crushed him with one hand, which he sensed, and something inside me wanted to.

"Alan," he said, "I think that finding some sort of employment would help to raise your confidence."

"I'm not a citizen. I can't work," I said. "They have strict laws here."

"Anything. Do anything. There are jobs that don't require permits."

"Like what?"

"I don't know. But you should be willing to do anything for you and Anna to get on your feet."

I picked up a newspaper and flipped to the employment section. "Let's have a look-see," I said, smartly snapping open the pages. Brow furrowed theatrically, eyes narrowed in mock focus, I scanned the ads. "Well, here's something. WANTED. EARTHWORM DIGGERS—Graveyard Shifts Only. We get you there and back. Decent wage!"

His stiff smile faltered. He tried to appear upbeat. "Well, that would be a start. Honest employment is nothing to be ashamed of."

* * *

I answered an ad for a golf caddie, though I knew nothing about golf.
Was the only adult there, the other caddies aged twelve or thirteen.
I was attached to a cluster of four graying cardigan businessmen sans
golf cart, and carried their bags on my shoulders. When their poor
swings sent the ball vanishing into hedges, I scrambled downhill
like a fox terrier to fetch. This exhausting work dehydrated my
nauseated body. Badly needed a drink. Hadn't thought to bring
along a supply. At lunch break, followed on their heels like a good
dog into the clubhouse dining room, looking forward to some good
food, perhaps some beer and a little conversation with the congenial
gents. But one of them turned, with a cold smile: "Uh, no. You
take yourself around to the back, knock on the window. When it
opens, ask for the Caddie Special. Put it on my tab."

Mortified, circled back, knocked on the wooden gate. It snapped
up.

"Caddie Special," I said.

It slammed shut. A moment later, it snapped up and out slid a
tray with a single hot dog and a bottle of orange soda. The shutter
dropped like a guillotine.

At day's end, my employer said: "We all want to give you this
little something to express our gratitude for your great work." He
thrust into my palm a bill rolled as tightly as a piece of espionage, and
hurried off. It was a single Canadian dollar—seventy-five US cents.

36

ON THE BUS RIDE HOME THROUGH THE FREEZING
Toronto night—blacker and colder because that much closer than
New York to the polar icecap—I realized that certain passengers
were satanists who had singled out Anna and me for human sacrifice. They were following me home to her. Quickly, took evasive
action like a good military man who knows that one key to not
getting shot any sooner than your time is to change spots every
three seconds, too fast for the ambusher to draw a bead.

Cleverly, got off at the wrong stop, far from home, walked
down wrong streets and, doubling back, took others equally
wrong, circled around, got off at an alien stop, stood on an alien
sidewalk, where a young punk in Mohawk and leather whom I
knew, without doubt, to be a satanic operative passed me with
head ducked, hands thrust into pockets, clutching a knife probably.
He circled widely around me. I smirked in his wretched face as he
passed. Didn't he know who I was? A Bronx schoolyard battler. An
Israeli combat soldier. "I KNOW!" I screeched at his back as he

hurried past. "You HEAR ME, mother? I KNOW!!!"

Sure that there were others close behind (they never operated alone but always in numberless legions performing intricate deceptive maneuvers), I too moved, quickly, in a new direction home, sure that I had a brief reprieve for now, knowing that I had just succeeded in ducking a very large bullet, but an hour from now or in days to come, who knows? With Anna so intent on feathering a nest, making a home, successful evasive maneuvers were once more impossible. The problem that had haunted me in New York had followed me to Toronto. Her vision of happiness made us sitting ducks.

She could not grasp, nor could I explain, that in order to survive we must at all times stay mobile. Hadn't she learned anything from our mothers' wartime experiences—harrowing odysseys entailing a million intuitive twists and turns on improbable roads? *Move!* Staying in motion was the key to survival. Didn't she know that from Sally's experience, and after a decade in Israel? To enact normal rituals, pretenses of decency, in the face of Nazis, European Fascists, Arab terrorists, Islamic jihadists, White Supremacists, was an invitation to enter new, improved gas chambers. Constant vigilance and a willingness to instantly abandon all scruples in order to act with savage expediency in the face of overwhelming threat—this was key. But how to explain it to her? I knew: she was asleep, an ahistorical innocent. Could not see. Never would.

Up this street, down that alley, hour after hour, wait, knife out, all clear, hurry across the road. But could one ever be sure that one had succeeded? Everywhere lurked threat. Stood riveted to my spot, surrounded by snipers, expelling plumes of condensed breath, gloved fist to my mouth, teeth grinding on a knuckle. The pain felt good. Harder I bit. The fear abated. Looked up, searching the Canadian sky, the Toronto roofline, face anguished, head exploding, body sickened, craving a drink, spied on, overwhelmed by the sheer scale of threat which unfolded not only in this moment but extended from the ancient past into the unforeseeable future, an axis of dire suffering and unrelieved onslaught imbedded in my very DNA, and I its horrified and hapless prophet. The infinite calculations needed to elude my multiplying enemies for an hour, let alone a lifetime, was exhausting: an unmapped ceaseless calculus of intuited probabilities squared with the worst imaginable outcomes. It was too much. I was imploding. The whole house of cards collapsing. "Little Einstein" could not forever stay one step ahead of Fate. Inevitably, it must catch up, and when it did, what would it bring? The Unspeakable.

In an effort to show me how it felt to return from a day's honest labor to a real home with a loving wife, Anna had gone to great lengths, despite her own full day of work, to prepare a home-cooked meal, replete with candle setting and herself dolled up in what she knew I liked best to see her in: a skimpy halter top, short skirt, with high heels and the kind of earrings that made the heart stop when she walked in a certain way and set them jiggling.

But by the time I arrived, it was late, the food was cold, the candle low. Whatever weak glow she had fanned in herself was now squelched. "Sweet one," she said, weakly hugging me. Looked into my eyes, saw what she thought she knew was there. "What's wrong?" she asked timidly.

Couldn't bring myself to say. Still time to sit, pretend to enjoy the meal. But I couldn't. Not for a minute. Not with the shadow army gathering around our door. The lesbians on the other side of the partition, lying in bed, talking, would meet death too. I was in a studio in the run-down bohemian quarter of Toronto, with three women completely unaware of the slaughter about to ensue. Fear of this froze in my throat. I paced. Lit a cigarette. Leaned my forehead against a wall, eyes closed.

"Tell me, Alan. Sweet one. Tell me."

Nothing.

"Is it fear?"

Startled, I looked up at her. "What do you mean?"

"The fear," she said sheepishly.

"I don't have any fear."

Her eyes avoided mine, which blazed furiously.

"You do, though. You've had it ever since you came home from the Reserves in Hebron. Something happened to you."

"I don't know what you're talking about."

"I don't know either," she said. "But it's some kind of fear. Do you remember that trip we took down to the beach, to Ashdod, when you came back from Hebron?"

"So? Nice trip."

"On the beach you said that a group of bathers near us were criminals who wanted to rob and kill us. And that the old man in the postal cap who rode up on that skeletal nag was the Grim Reaper, a messenger from Hades."

"I was feeling poetic," I said, attempting a grin. "I'm a poet, no?"

"I thought it was just being that, yes. But then there were other times. We couldn't go to this grocer because of "things" you'd overheard. We couldn't sit through Pasolini's film *Salò* in the East Village because it was "satanic." I couldn't walk around dressed as I like because "it would attract dangerous killer types." We couldn't even list our telephone in the directory because the "wrong people" might see. Every day there was something else. Sweet one, you're hard to read. You don't say what's really going on with you. How am I to know? I don't care what it is, but you have to let me in, share it with me. That's why I'm here. Hebron triggered something in you. You've never been the same."

My eyes sought for a purchase. I debated whether to tell her the truth. She stood there, emaciated, face lit by love and concern, wasting away, the brightest and most caring woman I'd ever known, but I felt certain that she'd be unable to grasp the full extent of threat arrayed against us. Certain kinds of evil are beyond the imagining of innocents like her. Sally somehow succeeded in insulating her daughter from the poison that flowed in the veins of life, the savagery that lay in the hearts of human beings. Anna had not played chess against the Unknown. She had no idea of its moves. How, just out of bed, the pawn feet of your chess-piece life hit the floor and there she was, the mother of your existence, with a rolling pin or belt, waiting to beat you to a pulp, then tell you about the gas chamber. You hit the schoolyard at dusk for a half-court game and next found yourself rolling on the ground with someone twice your size and age, in a fight to the death. You entered a village where fleeing women and children led you into a maze where behind every corner might lurk a bullet or ignited gasoline, a hand grenade or knife. There was the dark in which your chess piece moved from square to square, in a cease-less match against kaleidoscopic variables whose endgame was your annihilation.

"Look," I said "Sit down. Okay? Here. At the table."

"Are you going to let me feed you?" she asked hopefully.

"Sit first."

She did. And I, facing her.

"You see," I began, voice weak, hesitant, unsure what to say, how to begin.

She retained a composed expression as I sought to explain, prefacing my assertions with "I know it sounds crazy, but…"

When done, we sat quietly for a long time.

"The food," I said guiltily, knowing it was long past edible.

She glanced over at it. "That's all right. Forget it."

I nodded. "Since we're being honest with each other, I need a drink."

"There's nothing here. We have to go out to get you something."

"Okay."

But we didn't move yet. Sat in more silence, Anna reflecting, I feeling a certain measure of relief but also a pinch of terror, for having brought her into this. Now they would know that she knew. Their surveillance was thorough. Now she was integral to their game. Her life was now in as much mortal danger as mine.

"Sweet one," she began, as she always did. "You've been under a lot of strain. I know you. You went to the army to be a hero, to do heroic things. But they threw you into a filthy job, and I think what you had to do...hurt your mind. But sweet one, you did it for us, even if I don't agree with it. I know that you did what you thought had to be done. And now, you need rest."

"Rest? You tell me I need rest and then send me out to chase golf balls all day? Your cheapskate father! I was a director in the Israel Museum. Ben is a nothing, a nonentity! With his little mustache and bald head. Adopting superior airs! If you recall, I gave you and that poor excuse of a dickless and impotent husband of yours the first real break of your careers! That waste of life who married you and for ten years couldn't find it in himself to make love to the most beautiful and interesting woman in all of creation!"

"It's not exactly like that. He had his little escapades."

This was the first I'd heard about philandering on the other side, and it came as quite the surprise. "He had someone for a few years. There at the art school where he teaches. I saw her once. A brunette. With a big bust. I guess he thought my tits were too small." She looked down forlornly at a bust so dear, so lovely, I wanted only to lay my face upon it for the rest of my life.

"I'm sorry to hear that. But it's beside the point. For me, there's no rest now. They're closing in. You're in danger too. And I can't carry all this responsibility, for you and myself. It's too much weight. I'm breaking apart and failing. I feel like such a loser."

She came over, wrapped her arms around me, but I pulled away, stood my ground.

"I have no money. Do you have any? I need a drink."

"Yes," she said with calm dignity, despite the agony in her eyes. Went to her shoulder bag, withdrew her purse, removed a few crisply folded singles; then, reluctantly, with slow, painful movements, removed a twenty-dollar bill and handed it over.

"I'm going to get my medicine."

"Let me come," she said.

"No!"

"Please!"

I couldn't stop her, but how to explain the white-hot anguish boiling in my chest and abdomen. Having to walk alongside her at an average pedestrian pace, unpresuming, in a street filled with sinister faces, mocking eyes in shifting combinations of lethal looks, ominous shadows, passing cars, windows slammed shut, others opened, curtains parted, a passing cyclist glancing at me through the slit of his ski mask. And she, unconcerned, unsuspecting, cocooned in a gigantic circus tent of denial, unaware of her designation for murder, or the malicious knowing looks thrown our way by passersby anticipating, almost gleefully, the disembowelments to come.

She took my hand, which perspired so heavily that I felt my fingers suffocate. Jerked away my hand. Hated her. Her simplistic nature. Her damned Bambi innocence! Goddamn you, Anna! Look at what's all around you. Pierce the veil of this benign, banal Toronto night and see the horrible malevolence lurking underneath.

Sensing my furious disgust, my dear love welled with tears.

But deep shame only stiffened my resolve. In this war, you must be hard, I told myself: her survival is at stake. You—well, you're as good as dead. But maybe you can yet save her. She will not understand. So it goes. Be a man! Take executive action. Go into EVASION MODE NOW!!!

At this, a bus pulled up. Grabbing her hand, I pulled her aboard. Astonished, she stared the length of the bus at the half-awake passengers, undead under the overhead ghoulish fluorescence. "What are you doing?" she cried.

"You don't understand, do you? We're being followed. And you don't suspect anything. We're being sought! And you mosey along nice as pie! I'm sick of your ignorance. Your refusal to face facts! Now, you listen and you listen good. You do what I say. Is that understood?"

"Yes," she said numbly.

I led her to the back, where I'd have a good view of the passengers, but no sooner got us seated than realized my fatal mistake. Here was a man with a crew cut and blue, homicidal eyes. A scar over his upper lip. Looked ready to rock and roll with a bowie knife or handgun. A killer, for sure. I froze. Never had I felt more certain of the plot against us. Anna felt the change.

"What?" she said.

"That guy."

"Which?"

"Don't tell me you don't see him. Crew cut. Cold blue eyes."

She glanced furtively his way. "What about him?"

Her question infuriated me. How could I detail here and now, as it unfolded, the subtle shifting deadly game afoot? A boundless chessboard of infinitely unfolding moves, the sole object of which was to butcher both the King and Queen.

Her sweet, sane, suffering face seemed insufferably stupid.

"You're sweating so much!" she murmured.

Yes, I was: with naked fear. At the next stop pulled her off and rushed her down the street, as fast as I could.

She cried, "Alan! Stop! You're hurting me!"

I howled back, "Just do what I say!"

"No! Please!"

"Listen! I'm trying to save us! Don't you see?"

So sadly, she said, softly: "Yes. I do see."

Our rescue path led to a liquor store where I bought a fifth of vodka, carton of smokes, and by twists and turns we found ourselves safely seated, huddled together, in the freezing dark, on a bench, where I cracked the bottle's seal, took long pulls, she too, until my nerves had calmed, the blackwater shadows retreated. Relaxing into the groove of the vodka kick, cigarettes burning down in our fingers, we kissed, our wet, warm vodka-dipped tongues thrusting desperately into each other's mouths, searching for something, not just peace, or even love, but for oblivion as the only way out of such hopelessness.

Some days later, a letter arrived informing me that I had been accepted to the prestigious Master of Fine Arts program at Columbia University—an improbability to equal the discovery of a second sun in our galaxy.

Just before coming to Toronto, I had read a cover essay by John Barth in the *New York Times Book Review* in which he identified the nation's four top programs, including Columbia. On sheer arrogant whim, as one who never purchases a lottery ticket decides to try once and wins the jackpot, I photocopied some of my published stories—violent and immature efforts all—and, dressed in a long blue thrift-shop overcoat with a torn pocket, trudged from East 5th Street to 116th and Broadway: Columbia University. Slogged up the steps of 404 Dodge Hall, the School of the Arts, to the second floor, the Writing Division, and found the department empty except for a single secretary: Lini Lehman, a pretty, pleasant woman who smiled and asked how she could help.

"I've come to apply," I said.

"Wonderful!" she said.

She gave me an application, which I filled out with a pencil stub and to which I appended the stories and twenty-five bucks in crumpled bills that stank of beer. Gave my forwarding address c/o Anna's parents in Toronto.

Looking over the application, Lini grinned and said: "I think it must be a first."

"What's that?"

"You have no idea to what lengths people go to get into this place. They send press kits, professionally produced videos that are like political campaign ads, letters from famous personages, the works. But you—a pencil, some stories, cash. I love it!"

"I walked here to save on carfare. That should give you some idea of where I'm at."

"Perfectly. Well, I wish you luck, Alan! We'll let you know."

I shrugged. "I know I ain't getting in."

That the letter came just then, at the bottom of my Toronto night, was an extraordinary stroke of fate. In one fell swoop I'd gone from mentally disintegrating drunken caddie/worm digger to Ivy League grad school writer.

Anna inspected the letter with a look of doom. "What are you going to do?"

I shrugged.

But she already knew.

37

THE UNIVERSITY DEPARTMENTAL STATIONERY FELT more real to me than the touch of Anna's flesh. Even as she spoke, her face, its expression, her voice, were receding into memory.

I did not understand what we had been through or to what I was now going. Once, she had been for me the lover and wife that God made from my own rib. I knew that anyone else was not creation's choice for my heart but only someone to mark time with until death brought life without Anna to a close.

"You know," I said, touching a cheek that at my very touch was disappearing, "I have never loved anyone but you. I will never love anyone but you."

"I'm your wife," she said.

My cheek cocked in an ironic half smile. "You are, aren't you? Sometimes I forget."

She laughed sadly. "Should we go on?"

"Why don't we let time decide. I'll go to school in New York. You stay up here. Let's get better, see how we feel. Anna—we've loved each other over three countries. Israel, the States, Canada. I want to say how sorry I am that I couldn't live up to partnership as beautiful as yours. I want you to know that I love you, though my love is sick and broken."

She didn't reply. What was there to say? We had dared the impossible, failed. We were an anomaly. Love like ours was not meant to survive, a kind of transgression, unreal, a dark beauty dreamed by night and slain by daylight. We had opposed too many forces beyond the power of so fragile a love, so tender a union—war, Jerusalem, adultery, angered friends, embittered colleagues, poverty, maybe even God. But deep down, I knew that the only real culprit was me: a truth so painful that I had to pretend not only to others but to myself that I didn't care, or see the wrong in it. Booze helped a great deal with that.

When the train arrived to bear me to New York, Anna slipped an envelope into my pocket. "To read later," she said.

"I can't say goodbye because it doesn't mean anything that I can understand right now," I said.

She stroked my cheek. "Precious one." She turned and walked off. I stood watching for as long as I could before boarding. In my seat, I opened the envelope. There was a note that read only "I love you" and $1,500 in cash, American.

I returned to 5th Street. Natan, amazingly, had kept it up. He turned the key back over but with the understanding that I would soon find other lodgings. He and Smardar had never really been my friends—had helped out only for Anna's sake.

I couldn't bear it there anyway, ghost-filled rooms, things of hers left behind all around, a comb, paper lantern, appointment calendar. Spent the first few nights on the floor, curled around bottle after bottle. Knew that if I were somehow going to pull off the Ivy

League, I would need to take myself in hand, and for a while at least, get health, cut back on booze, exercise, eat right. This would depend on whether or not new conspiracies appeared.

For the moment, though, something had shifted. Hope seeped into my soul. Perhaps all the horror and failure would vanish, disappear, just like that! And the nightmares, the operatives, the unfolding skein of sinister designs erupting from the skin of the world like my father's violent psoriasis would just dry up and blow away.

A shyster lawyer got me a divorce for a hundred and sixty-five dollars. I found a room in the Upper West Side apartment of a ninety-five-year-old former manufacturer of coat linings named Boris Gimpleman. For two hundred dollars a month and an agreement to keep an eye on him now and then, I could quarter in the study of his dead wife, Bella. The ad had been posted on the bulletin board of the Jewish Theological Seminary on a yellowing 3 x 5 index card that read, in shaky handwriting:

Gintelman to liv mit gintelman. Call Trafalgar 7-4011

It was a place of neglected elegance on West 79th Street. Boris and Bella had lived there for decades and raised a son, Kenneth, who died of cancer. Boris was now tragically alone. A Polish housekeeper came weekly to clean house and resupply the old man with meat cutlets, sliced tomatoes, Special K cereal, and orange juice. Now and then, he sent me down to D'Agostino's, a chichi local market, to purchase Stella D'oro Breakfast Treats, cookies that he liked to dip in his tea.

Each morning he dressed himself in handsome suits with tie and pocket square and spit-polished shoes. Then wandered from room to room, inconsolable, weeping, announcing to the walls and furniture and the heavy draperies: "I miss my vife! Oy, mein Gott! I miss my vife! Ver is my Bella?"

I avoided contact with him. His loss too closely echoed mine. His Bella was my Anna. Waited in the morning as his shambling figure trudged past my closed door before popping out my head, and if the coast was clear then hurried softly down the hall, ignoring the voice at my back calling: "Al! Al! Is that you, Al?" And slipped from the apartment with a soft closing click of the door.

His memory was so poor, minutes later he would forget that he'd seen me. Sometimes he failed to remember that I lived there at all and stood in his pajamas, alarmed, demanding: "Vot you vont? Vye you come to my house?" Other times he sat on the sofa watching *The Eight O'clock Movie,* and at the commercial break, when the program's logo appeared, he would grunt to himself: "Huh! Is eight o'clock?"

Other times, though it was a weekday evening, he thought it was eight o'clock on a Saturday morning, and, struggling to his feet, would announce to the television: "Is time to go to *shul!*"

At the Columbia departmental incoming student orientation a number of former alumni spoke about the importance of the program to their careers. These included Tom Jenks of Scribner's, who'd edited Hemingway's last posthumous novel; Tama Janowitz, the wunderkind author of *Slaves of New York,* who'd recently published an unprecedented four short stories in a single year in the *New Yorker;* and Mona Simpson, author of *Anywhere But Here,* a best-selling first novel.

Among my fellow students were some who would someday gain prominence, including novelist Rick Moody, then a scrawny kid in tees, jeans, and sneakers; the poet Campbell McGrath, who would win a MacArthur genius award; Jeff Goodell, author of a number of celebrated nonfiction works and feature writer for *Rolling Stone* and the *New York Times*; and Musa Meyer, already at work on her well-received memoir about her father, the painter Philip Guston. Two other fellow students who impressed me were Kim Wozencraft, future author of the best-selling novel *Rush*, and Joseph Ferrandino, who produced a novel, *Firefight,* based on his experiences in the Vietnam War. Kim and Ferrandino had met in the Federal Pen, where she served a term as a former rogue undercover narcotics agent who had played two ends against the middle and ripped off the drug dealers she was sent to infiltrate. The upshot was: the dealers sent a hit man to kill Kim and her husband, who was also a crooked narc. The shotgun-bearing hit man shot her husband and then turned the weapon on Kim, who wrestled the barrel away and just narrowly missed having her head blown off. In the ensuing investigation, she was arrested and imprisoned. About his own reasons for incarceration, Ferrandino never spoke. What little about him I knew is that after Vietnam he had served as a paratrooper against Central American drug cartels. He was a real Brooklyn Italian guy and I liked him right off.

But the fellow student I liked best was an affable poet named John Lane, a relation of Lincoln's vice president, who, despite an enormous gift for writing and ambition to succeed, would enter, following graduation, into a kind of self-imposed exile from all career moves. After a brief stint as a lecturer at UCLA, which he hated, he became a massage therapist and later a custodian at UC Berkeley to subsidize a life of writing, reading, and contemplation pursued at his own pace, in anonymity and exile, free from the compromise and pressures of professionalism.

He was, at the time, married to Kevi, a pretty pug-nosed warm-hearted woman with a first-rate mind and a touching determination to see John succeed in his dreams—little realizing, then, that one day he'd walk away from them to save his soul as a writer.

The last presentation of orientation day was made by Robert Towers, the head of the department, a tweedy portly Southern man of letters, ruddy-faced, clearly a heavy drinker, with graying hair, an amused smile, and glasses perched on the tip of his veiny bulbous nose. After surveying us with a degree of skepticism, he mumbled a few trifles of no import, but then closed with a remark—the real point of his brief talk—that cut right through us, for it best summed up the prevailing outlook of the program at that time.

"Here at Columbia," he drawled, "the world is divided into two kinds of folk." He scanned our faces with a sardonic twinkle in his bloodshot eyes. "Those who have published a book...and those who have not." That said, he turned and shuffled back to his office.

The message could not be clearer: bookless, you were dirt.

38

AT COLUMBIA, DISTINGUISHED AUTHORS WANDERED the halls like Madame Tussauds wax figures of the famous come tragically back to life. You might find yourself in the men's room assuming the urinary stance next to a legend with hungover eyes. Among the notables who most impressed me were Joseph Brodsky, Daniel Halpern, Richard Howard, William Mathews, and Stephen Koch.

I enrolled in a class with Ted Solotaroff, an editor at Harper & Row, who had produced the famed *New American Review*, a mass trade highbrow paperback of fine lit that brought to the public such notables as Gabriel García Márquez and Harold Brodkey. In one of the first classes, he had us form our chairs in a circle, create a kind of arena in which he prowled like a bull, snorting, murdering us with his eyes, daring us to push past our comfort zones, tap unsuspected inner resources, exceed our own infuriatingly dull limitations.

"Which of you dares to imagine attaining the stature of a Melville? The innovative daring of a Joyce? Can any of you see your name listed in the roll call of greatness? Faulkner, Hemingway, Fitzgerald..." and looking directly at me, he appended "Kaufman." Everyone glared jealously at me, as cold fear and wild hope shot through my chest. I chuckled nervously. He had set the bar, in no uncertain terms. Of course I must fail. Flattery and dread were a powerful concoction the only antidote for which was a West End Bar boilermaker: whiskey, with beer chaser.

He seemed to take a particular liking to me; invited me frequently to parties in his home where I met famous authors whose names I can't recall because I drank myself senseless, as did everyone else in attendance. It's safe to think that no one else attending those parties will ever recall anyone who also happened to be there.

My favorite teacher was the biographer, translator, and essayist Frank MacShane, a big Scots-looking gent with a rugged, ruddy face, skeptical blue eyes, and gray-brown Rudy Vallee hair. He wore heavy tweed suits, scotch plaid ties, and brogans. There was about him a quality of absolute integrity that I often imagined must have been like Orwell's. Whatever MacShane told you was forthrightly stated, honestly meant, and deeply felt.

He had produced several crisp biographies, including one about Raymond Chandler and another of Frank O'Hara, that were standards of their kind. He was also the head of *Translation*, a well-regarded campus-based magazine of international letters. There wasn't a trace of pretense in the man. He had no patience for cant. His one drawback as a teacher was the fury that he brought to his critiques of shoddy work. The culprit was torn to pieces with such mounting outrage that I cringed in the back of the room, struggling not to laugh. These gorings were so amusing that I invited friends from other departments to see. Once brought in John Lane to watch MacShane excoriate a bright young upper-class thing who had submitted to class an essayistic account of remodeling her kitchen.

It was a plodding sort of piece, fashioned after Tracy Kidder's best seller *House*, richly layered with pedantic details, and she was deep in a description of the struggles she had faced in choosing appropriate contact paper when MacShane exploded: "Who gives a bloody good god damn about which contact paper you chose for your bleeding kitchen!"

I nudged Lane, who nodded and grinned.

"Wars rage around the globe, whole peoples exterminated, children massacred, crime and poverty overtaking us, great undiscovered painters and starving writers breaking their hearts to produce ignored masterpieces, orphans molested, mental retardates rotting naked in their own filth in unmonitored state institutions, rockets going into space, new cures for murderous diseases just a rabbit's foot away, and this is the news you choose to bring? Your wallpaper?"

Lane and I choked laughing. MacShane was apoplectic. "Why would I give a damn for your kitchen cabinet, your butcher block cutting board?" and so on until the subject had been scourged of every last drop of preciousness.

If you were here to write for *Ladies' Home Journal*, you were in the wrong class. Here, in MacShane's class, you wrote to change the world.

39

IN MY SECOND YEAR, UNSURE OF HOW TO PAY FOR a semester's tuition, I read in a *New York Times* obituary for the poet and author Robert Graves that at university he had produced an anthology titled "Oxford Writers of 1921," which gave me the idea to assemble an anthology of the best student writing to appear from the four programs John Barth had named in his *New York Times* article: Columbia, Stanford, Iowa, and Johns Hopkins.

Ran the idea past MacShane, who was always available to students undeterred by his fearsome temper—close up, he was as gentle and pleasant a person as one could hope to know. He not only thought my antho idea great but offered his agent to represent me and even gave the book its title: *The New Generation*.

With John Lane's unflagging help, I assembled a manuscript that included authors like Ethan Canin, Gish Jen, Tama Janowitz, Susan Minot, Ehud Havazelet, Mona Simpson, Michelle Carter, and Bob Shacochis. Thanks to Lane, half the book comprised poets who one day would fill the top ranks of American letters. Lane even helped me type out dozens of inquiries to publishers, which went out on departmental stationery provided by the ever-helpful Lini Lehman. Several publishers responded with interest but Doubleday called the department directly, seeking me, to make an offer on the book, sight unseen.

When I met with the interested Doubleday editor, Jennifer Collins, a short, intense young woman, she enthused about the book and then handed me back the part of the manuscript—nearly half—that was poetry.

"We won't be needing that part," she said and smiled.

This was my first glimpse of the low regard in which trade publishers hold poets. It explained to me, somewhat, the sly unscrupulous personalities so typical of the poets I'd met at school. They behaved like embattled starvelings.

For example, when I contacted Iowa's Jorie Graham, a poet of some considerable repute who enjoyed every sort of professional advantage, and requested that she nominate a grad student to collect the contributions from Iowa writers, she tried, instead, to jockey herself into the post, thinking, perhaps, that it entailed some remuneration, no matter how small, or perhaps some slight prestige that would enlarge her hoard of accolades. Lane and I were amazed and disgusted.

Needing the money, I dropped the poets. Doubleday bought *The New Generation*, my first trade book. I now had enough for tuition and even for a belted London Fog raincoat and a leather satchel—coveted totems, to me, of literary New York.

Armed with these, I imagined myself as some sort of Brat Pack Saul Bellow rushing about campus and Manhattan on errands of earth-shattering importance. This was a time of publishers' lunches, meetings with my agent, Robin Strauss, and working late into the night in a loaned office at Doubleday, high up in a skyscraper's air-conditioned room in which I sat gazing out over virtually the whole of New York, feeling harshly unreal, but also tragic with distinction.

At one of the business lunches, held in a smart Italian bistro, Collins outlined the agreement for Robin Strauss, who changed, to my advantage, almost every key contract point. When Collins— who before coming to Doubleday had worked as marketer for Colgate toothpaste, or some such thing—asked me who my favorite author was, I promptly replied: "Herman Melville."

"Oh," said Collins, with a thoughtful look. "I never read him. Has he put out something new lately?"

Strauss and I shared a wide-eyed look of amazement.

"Uh, no." I smiled. "Nothing recent."

News of my anthology aspersed the department. Although many had received permission requests, those who didn't hated my guts. No one as yet knew who was in, who out. I held my cards close, even from Lane, couldn't bear to tell him that poetry had been bumped. I had put up no fight. Wanted the book, the money, the glory, even if it meant betraying one who had helped so much. Told myself, sitting on my West End Bar stool, knocking boilermakers back: I'll learn to live with it. This is what you gotta do to get ahead.

The West End Bar had been the first gathering spot for the early Beats. Now here I was, a book man in the flesh. Yet I felt heartsick, poisoned by my victory.

There were others too, fiction writers I wanted to include, believed in, but Collins, for one reason or another, adamantly refused to include. Jeff Goodell, one of the department's most gifted writers, a tall, lanky motorcycle racer from California, had sent in an amazing story about the races. It was perfect for the book, yet Collins said no. When I insisted, she took me to the editor in chief. The pleading look in her boss's eyes as he studied my face was enough: I complied. It was my first published book. I wasn't going to ruin it. But thereafter I avoided Jeff, too ashamed to face him.

On the other hand, other writers and poets, hearing of the book, drew close. I became popular. Sexual opportunities abounded.

The first was a tall, lanky blonde from Kansas City named Ginger, a girl with the flapper look of a gun moll, with whom I got reeling drunk and, returning to my room, stripped and balled on Bella's bed. The door flew open. There stood Boris, leaning on the doorknob like a cane, squinting half blind at the blurred pink Francis Bacon shapes wrestling on his dead wife's bed. "Vot is?" he called out. "Al? Is you?"

Ginger was tittering hysterically. I clamped a shushing hand over her mouth.

"AL! SOMEVON IS THERE!! WHO IS THAT MIT YOU???"

While the mattress under us slid to the floor, we rolled naked, clinging, over Bella's throw rugs. Ginger shrieked in glee and Boris cried out: "IS A VOMAN! AL!! YOU BRING HERE WHORES!?!? VOS IS DAT SMELL? IN MY HOUSE YOU DRINKING VODKA MIT A WHORE??"

What could I say?

I answered, seated there bare-assed on the ground: "Yes, Boris. I'm here with a woman—not a whore, Boris, a woman—and yes, we are drinking vodka. Not yours. Our own. And will you please get out of my room. I'm a grown man, Boris. You're not my poppa."

"IN MY HOUSE YOU MAKE HANKY-PANKY!" he howled. "SHAME MIT YOU!!"

I looked at Ginger, incredulous: "Hanky-panky?"

"That's so cute," she said.

"WHORE!" Boris raged. "PROSTITUTE! GET OUT FROM MINE HOUSE!!!"

Clutching our clothes, we ran out naked into the hall, where we hopped first on one foot, then the other, dressing hurriedly, and left. Adjourned to Ginger's place in a women's residence hotel down the street, where we continued our orgy.

Next was Carolyn Shaw. A poetry cowgirl from Montana, married to a former Navy Seal who now taught, weirdly, at a dance school and who, she claimed, tied her to a bed, spread-eagled, blindfolded, and beat her senseless as he raped her with whatever he could stick up in her. I shifted my legs uncomfortably, so that she wouldn't see how much the spread-eagled and blindfolded portion of her admission aroused me. The parallel with him was too close to home. His taste for violence sickened me. But in my darkness, I understood.

Necking nonstop, Carolyn and I took a bus ride to Nyack, New York, during which I committed myself, body and soul, to protect her from the blindfolding and sadistic Navy Seal. This was exactly what she wanted to hear. "I know you can too! You're the only one with balls enough to stand up to him. I'm terrified of the man. I heard you were an Israeli soldier. You won't be afraid."

"No," I boasted. "I'll kick his ass if he lays a hand on you."

Our first full-on sexual encounter was strangely lifeless. She was bone dry. Had a hard little unforgiving body. Without jelly it was like copulating with a hairbrush. Her nude body revealed the numberless beatings endured, the ghosts of old bruises. Her sickly skin and muscles cringed to the touch. Her eyes looked beaten down, puffed and evasive, with that hunted look that battered women get. I hardly knew what to make of it. But felt myself hooked, deeply, despite the complete absence of pleasure or even physical attraction. As though some deep sickness in her had entwined around some deep sickness in me and we were now umbilically bound by a taste for the psychotic.

40

DOUBLEDAY SENT OUT REVIEW COPIES OF *THE NEW Generation*, including one to Towers, who, impressed, invited me to a private party at his home attended by the novelist Russell Banks and others whose names greatly mattered in the literary game. Towers, quite drunk, approached me with a tall, wobbling glass of bourbon, handed it to me. Nose inflamed, words slurred, a real lush, he said: "Drink up, Alan! I liked your preface to *The New Generation*. This one is on me. Here's to your book!"

I easily drank it down. Towers studied me, amazed. "Well," he slurred. "That's…you can hold yours, can't you. Yes. Well."

When I excused myself to the bathroom to piss, he staggered right behind and as I urinated observed in his courtly Southern drawl, "Ernest Hemingway himself once peed in that very bowl!" Which so excited me to learn that I splashed my signature all over the seat, howling: "And now, by God, so has Alan Kaufman!"

As pub date approached, I found myself making manic late-night calls on Boris's phone to friends and relations from Israel to

Minnesota, all on the old man's dime. Drank constantly and saw as much of Carolyn as possible. She had decided to leave her husband for me. Thrilled, saw us as an ideal literary couple, she stretched blindfolded and spread-eagled on a bed, mouth gagged, as I read to her from the *New Yorker*.

At Towers's invitation, Bernard Malamud, whose novels and short stories I had admired since youth, even tried to emulate, came to Columbia to conduct a two-day seminar in fiction.

Slender, bald, with a sensible mustache and dressed in a conservative suit and tie, Malamud looked more like a CPA than a writer. Spoke at length of his association with the Italian existential sculptor Alberto Giacometti, from whom he'd learned formal techniques that he'd translated into prose and applied to his own literary art. He then announced importantly that he would read to us from a new work in progress, a novel whose central conceit was that Chief Joseph was really, secretly a Jew.

The room stirred.

When he finished, he asked for feedback.

I raised my hand.

"Yes."

"Mr. Malamud, Alan Kaufman here, and first want to say what a great admirer I am. I've read just about all your books. So it's with a sense of dismay that I must tell you that the Indians portrayed in your excerpt are not Malamudian."

He smiled coldly. "Malamudian. Well. What genus of Indian then do you assign to them?"

"TV Indians. Stereotypes."

Malamud's face shut down. Towers, his old colleague and close friend, looked furious. Hurriedly, the seminar was brought to a close.

The next day, I encountered Towers rushing down the hall, distressed.

"Hi, Bob!" I smiled. "Great seminar."

He stopped and spit in an accusing voice: "Malamud is dead!"

Said in such a way that seemed to suggest in no uncertain terms that I was directly responsible.

It was known that he had a weak heart, and the advisability of exerting himself in a seminar with a bunch of brash grad students was questionable at best. Apparently, he had felt unwell in the evening, died. Did my criticism of his Indians trigger stress resulting in heart failure? Evidently, Towers thought so.

Astonished, went to the men's room, leaned on the sink, peered into the mirror, and grinned in an evil Dorian Gray sort of way. "Kaufman," I informed my reflection, "you have just killed Bernard Malamud!"

My reflection seemed pleased.

But thereafter, my drinking accelerated to levels that in other times had driven me to the brink of nervous collapse. Sometimes I really did think that I had killed Malamud. Woke from horrified sleep, shaking my head in disbelief—no, it couldn't be. I loved the man's books! I'm just a dumb kid from the Bronx. Don't tell me I killed Bernard Malamud! And then Carolyn, with whom I was insanely obsessed, even though screwing her felt like getting a callus scraped, announced to me that she couldn't leave the old Navy Seal after all. Rambo needed her, poor thing. Strangely, she needed him too.

"The fact that he drove jeeps into your house and raised egg-sized knots on your forehead is beside the point," I said. "Those were just the things you shared. Yeah, most definitely, you deserve each other."

Insulted, she walked off.

This sudden abandonment reduced me to a squalling agonized knot. To kill the pain I drank scotch, in the course of which I decided that suicide was the best solution. Knew what was coming, the dehumanizing tsunami of pain, and couldn't bear the thought of living through that, past the limit of what anyone should have to endure.

Went to the bathroom, found one of Boris's razors, returned to Bella's study, seated myself at her desk, and stared at the thin blade pinched between thumb and forefinger. In a way, had always wanted this. All the army gun barrels in my mouth. Death had always been a wish. Considered the thick veins running under the white skin of my wrist. All you need to do is draw the blade down hard now, first across one wrist, slice, then the other, slice. Then drink some more. And wait. There. And there.

For a time, sat watching blood pour out with a sense of disbelief. Was that from me? Looked around. Was I really to die? What had I done? Blood everywhere. Unsteadily rising to my feet, wrists pressed tight against my shirt, I staggered to the bathroom, wrapped white towels around the bloody wounds, and with a sense of exhilaration, called 911.

41

POLICE ARRIVED, TWO PATROLMEN, ONE BURLY, one thin, sharp-edged. Boris was snoozing in his room. They looked around. The thin cop eyeballed my wrists as I explained to his partner that I had just cut them with a razor, intending to end my life.

"I tried to kill myself," I said with tingling joy.

"Uh-huh," said the burly cop, as if I'd just explained that I wasn't really a human being but an aardvark awakened somehow in a human body and trying to get back to aardvark world.

"It was," I said, " a suicide attempt."

When I said this, the thin cop winced and the burly cop seemed lost in calculations of some sort. Neither appeared to relish having to take me to the hospital.

"Are you going to call for an ambulance? I'm bleeding pretty bad."

"Well." Burly sighed. "I guess." Looked at his partner. "You want?"

Thin looked at me. "We'll take him in the squad car. But, uh, look, pal, don't get blood on the backseat, okay?"

"I won't."

In the squad car, I had a view of the backs of Thin and Burly's thinning wet-look razor cuts. Relaxed, heaved a relieved sigh: nothing more for me to decide. The authorities in charge now, me free to be as sick as I am and no excuse about it. I'd get help now. Proudly, sat up straight, held my towel-wrapped wrists flat against my abdomen, already the good patient, keeping my blood away from the black vinyl seat, bleeding all over myself.

"Officers. Which hospital are you taking me to?"

"St. Luke's," said Thin.

"That's a very good one," I said.

Burly and Thin glanced at each other. Then Burly, who drove, motioned to Thin with an up-and-down motion of his head and said: "Hey, uh...whatsit? Alan."

"Yes, officer."

"Listen, Alan. When you get there, um, they're gonna ask, like, in the intake, you know, how in the world, uh, you know—what happened? Where'd you get them cuts?"

"Yeah, they're gonna ask," Thin concurred, as though this was the worst possible development.

"When they ask," Burly continued, "If you tell them suicide—"

Thin spun around in his seat with a loud creaking of jacket leather and his eyes bored into mine: "You know what's gonna happen?"

"Tell 'im," said Burly. "Tell 'im what'll happen."

"It's gonna be a mess, okay? A mess. They're gonna have us *and* you there all night. They're gonna keep you for observation."

"All night we'll be there," said Burly. "Tell him why."

"I hate to say this, but legally, what you done is considered a sort of crime. Possibly a misdemeanor. No one'll call it that. But I heard of judges out there who want it brought to trial! Can you believe *that?*"

"Fuggin' psycho judges," confirmed Burly.

"But the likelihood is slim to none," said Thin.

"Slim to none," said Burly.

"But us there filling out the paperwork all night and having to hang out with you, *that* is real. That will happen."

"As real as it gets," confirmed Burly. "All night with the forms, and tell him what then."

"Book you, baby. Fingerprints. Mug shot. The whole shebang. You wanna be like John Dillinger?"

"Not just John Dillinger. Like a psycho John Dillinger. You tell 'em you tried to kill yourself, you got a record, forget about getting hired, forget about renting apartments, forget about meeting a nice girl and getting married. You're an official nutcase criminal for the rest of your life. Shit follows you around everywhere. They'll put you under locked observation. They'll use it against you in divorce court. You're an official bridge jumper, state certified. Watch how much alimony you end up paying. Child support?"

"HA!" laughed Thin.

"Fuggin' forget it!" said Burly. "And the paperwork. Whatsit? Alex?"

"Alan."

"The whole night."

"All night is right," confirmed Thin.

After a long pause in which I felt a hand tug murderously at the small frail hope that had taken root inside me, I asked: "So, what'll I do?"

They didn't answer right off. Pretended to consider. But I sensed that it was an answer they gave to every attempted suicide who was ambulatory. "Call it an accident," said Thin.

Both pretended to be excited by this, as though it were a sudden inspired revelation.

"Hell, yeah!" Burly enthused. "Tell 'em you had an accident!"

"There ya go!" said Thin with pleasure. "And you know what the beauty of it is? Nothing they can do about it. They gotta stitch you up and out you go. Home free! Long as no one uses the S word in that place, it never occurred."

"Never happened," Burly concurred.

"We don't even use the S word around the intake nurse. Or the go-get-'em intern that's gonna practice his stitches on you. We don't use that effin' S word nohow, no ways. Under any circumstance. And the beauty of it is—"

"Tell 'im! This is beautiful!" crowed Burly.

"We go our way, you go yours."

"And we'll all meet on the Great Highway," sang Burly.

"So whaddaya say?" said Thin.

Thin and Burly's little snapshot seminar on the protocols of municipal response to attempted suicide left me thirsting desperately for a drink. A drink that surely could not be had under psychiatric observation.

"Okay," I said.

At which Thin shifted, turned around, and faced the windshield. "Tell 'em you cut yourself by accident."

"Freak accident," said Burly.

"Capeesh?" said Thin.

"Capeesh," I said.

And neither said a word more until we pulled into the ambulance bay with the squad car lights spinning and Burly helped me out; leaning over, whispered: "No S word!"

I nodded that I understood.

As Thin and Burly stood by with encouraging winks, the intake nurse, a no-nonsense black woman in a winged white cap, inspected my wrists and asked: "What happened?"

I looked over at Thin and Burly.

"Go ahead. Tell her about it. Craziest thing," said Thin.

"Freaky one in a million," said Burly.

"I was up cutting a steak with this big butcher knife and it slipped, first this way, then that, and both my wrists got cut."

The nurse stared at me. "Both."

"Like you see."

She glanced up at the two officers.

"I couldn't hardly believe it myself when I heard. But he's telling the truth," said Burly.

"Wild," concurred Thin.

The nurse said: "That's what you want me to write?"

"Yes," I said.

She glanced inquiringly at the cops.

"His call," said Thin.

"Free country," said Burly.

She wrote it down.

"You're bleeding badly," she said. "We'll take you right in."

After the stitches and with big bandages taped around my wrists, marking me as an unmistakable failed suicide, I called Jeff Goodell, who came and got me from the hospital, though it was only 6:00 a.m. We returned to his place, where I had some wine and beer. From there we walked to John and Kevi's apartment. They took me in; let me lie on their floor with an ashtray, a bottle of whiskey, and a pack of cigarettes. I cried and got drunker and they tried to care for me with patient listening and offers of food, but I pushed it all away and blind drunk went stumbling out to look for Carolyn.

Talked my way past her anxious roommate, barged into Carolyn's room. Gone.

"Where is she?" I raged.

The mousey roommate stood there terrified, afraid to speak back to my six foot two inches tall, two hundred pounds of drunken bloodshot meanness with suicide bandages, my fist gripping a whiskey bottle.

"Where, goddammit?" I snarled.

She told me. Before I left, I jerked covers off Carolyn's bed, threw her clothes out of drawers, and scrawled obscenities in massive Magic Markered words over her bedroom's nice beige walls I rushed to the Columbia campus, where an English department reception for incoming teaching assistants was under way. Blew past the check-in desk, where a row of seated student registration aides all came to their feet, calling excitedly, "Wait! Stop!" as I entered the hall, swaggering like a nightmarish border rider come down out of the hills on a mission from hell, brimming with Byronic delusion and driven insane by loneliness. Scanned the room for Carolyn, saw her freeze as I approached. Two male grad school heroes blocked my path. I knocked them both down easily, first one, then the other. A hand tried to grab my wrist. My fist found its owner's face. More heroes appeared as I continued to advance through a gauntlet of bespectacled future literary critics, blowing by them easily, bobbing and weaving in the ring with Foucault and Derrida, connecting with jaws, eyes, taking an occasional solid shot on the side of the head or in the ribs from a postmodernist, reeling but never ceasing to advance, shouting "HERE I AM!" until standing directly before her, into her flinching, battered face I ranted: "I was gonna save you from him! HIM! The jerk who hit you! You wanted me to help you! And I did! I was willing to risk EVEN FUGGING DEATH!!!! And this is how you repay me? By going back to your batterer?"

She started to speak.

"WHORE!" I shrieked and belted her, once, hard, across the face.

Thereafter, I don't remember much. An army of hands laid hold of me, voices, men and women, screaming and raging, pushing my mannequin limpness out a door, down a hall, into the quad. I rode the hurricane of their outrage like a three-legged chair, a piece of broken furniture. In all this, never once lost my grip on the scotch bottle. Not a drop lost.

A week or so later, was called into Robert Towers's office, asked to sit. He was behind his desk, hands folded, strange smile on his lips as he observed me over glasses perched on the end of his inflamed nose.

"We have got a problem," he said. "And I think you must know what I'm referring to…"

I nodded.

"It's not only a problem of seriously violated house rules but a political one too. No one here in the Writing Division admires what you've done. We do not strike each other here. We do not do violence. We are writers, not thugs. But to strike a woman is especially onerous. We deplore it, and condemn it, each and every one. And I want you to know that." He let his unflinching blue eyes rest on me for a while to underscore this point. I felt it. My eyes dropped, ashamed.

"Your writing has its admirers among the faculty. You organized that amazing series of readings at La MaMa Theatre for our entire department, for which we are grateful. And you now have a book whose pub date is fast approaching. That book stands for everything that the Writing Division here at Columbia seeks to promote. And I anticipate, given the prominence of the publisher, Anchor/Doubleday, and that it's a book whose time has come, and that it has an introduction from John Knowles, it will earn you much prestige and honor this department, and all the writing programs involved."

Again I nodded.

"So, you represent us, in a sense. You see the problem?"

I nodded, ashamed.

"Look. I'm not trying to dig at you. We are writers here. We are different than others. Artists sometimes do crazy things. Literature is filled with crazy folks. Our social embarrassments are legend. But a student who, failing at suicide, goes with bandaged wrists and a whiskey bottle and in front of two hundred teaching assistants, and a considerable portion of the English Department faculty, screams obscenities, knocks people down, and then strikes a fellow student writer, a married woman, in the face..."

He leaned forward, brought his face as close as possible. "This is not an image of ourselves that we want to go public."

I nodded.

"And there's politics. The English Department, where you performed your actions, is this department's enemy. They feel that we divert important funds away from their coffers. That we are an unserious program and don't deserve autonomy. That we ought to be scaled down and folded into the English Department. They want you gone because they want us gone. And behind them stands the Student Senate, which also wants you out."

He leaned back, lifted a pencil, dropped it, sank down low in his swivel chair, studied my face. "It's a pickle. A real pickle."

I nodded. "Yes, sir."

"I say it is a pickle."

"It is a pickle, sir."

MacShane wants you to stay. Solotaroff thinks you have promise. So do I. Look—"

He came forward again. "No one here—we're writers. We're not distinguished for our mental health or social aptitude. Eccentricity—it's a given. But what you've done is an actual crime. We must draw the line at crime."

I nodded.

He fell back in his chair. Lifted the pencil. Dropped it.

"If Carolyn doesn't press charges, it's no crime. But it's still grounds for dismissal from Columbia. Is that clear? Do you understand why?"

"Yes, sir."

"Why, then? Let me hear it from you."

"Because we can't have our women students live in fear of violence from their fellow writers."

"That's exactly right!"

The way he said this made me feel like I'd scored an A-plus.

"I'm very glad," he said. "And relieved too! Hearing you put it that way, I believe we may still have a ball game. Here's our idea. The dean and me. You're to attend therapy with an alcohol treatment specialist at Columbia Presbyterian at our expense. We know you're broke. He's one of the best. If, at the end of treatment—ten weeks, say, the summer—he gives you a clean bill of health, well, then, far as we're concerned, it's all water under the bridge. On condition that you will have no further contact with Carolyn, not even so much as enrollment in the same classes, not even look her way when you pass in the halls. If you agree, we'll take you back."

"Agreed."

For ten weeks I visited the good doc, nice chap, who drew diagrams, gave articles to read, took an interest in my literary projects. When he spoke candidly to my drinking problem, I listened respectfully, nodding that I understood. Liked the man enormously, and after each session crossed Broadway to a nearby bar, ordered a double, and hoisted my glass in the good doc's honor.

Still, the Carolyn incident had shaken me somewhat. Resolved to grab hold of life's reins, take charge, straighten out. Joined a gym and got back in shape, purchased a new wardrobe, and sought a position befitting my background and firsthand knowledge of American Jewish and Israeli culture. I obtained high-paid employment as a fund-raiser with the New York office of an Israeli botanical garden.

Lastly, I moved out of the old man's flat and into a large room, with nonworking fireplace, on the top floor of a squalid but colorful hotel by the week—The Hotel California—just blocks from Columbia and, with my new regular salary, easily affordable.

Nattily attired, financially empowered, and muscle-bound, I appeared to my therapist to be in complete remission from drinking. Of course, he didn't know that I got regularly blasted five out of seven nights of the week, either in the West End, where I consorted, drunk, with fellow students who felt we were reincarnations of Kerouac and Ginsberg, or in Augie's, a jazz bar that stayed open after hours and where, to the tune of debilitated and washed-out former jazz greats, you could sit and get blotto with that big granddaddy sax scat-tatting in your ears.

Come fall, declared fit, I was readmitted to Columbia.

Far from alienating me from the other students, my little escapade, and the fact of imminent book publication, appeared to lend me an air of legend and tragic grandeur. People who normally never gave me the time of day now invited themselves to sit and talk, or approached with an increasingly familiar kind of hyena smile, hand extended, firing broadsides of trivial rubbish at my unreceptive face until I simply walked off, left them standing there—which, of course, only amplified the hype.

On the day of my book's appearance, I showered, shaved, splashed on cologne, dressed in my finest clothes, threw on a neck scarf and my London Fog, and grandly strolled twenty blocks down Broadway to Shakespeare & Co., one of the finest bookstores in New York, and stood, thrilling, on the pavement.

The front window displayed a tall pyramid of *The New Generation: Fiction for Our Time from America's Writing Programs,* edited by Alan Kaufman. It was, to then, hands down, the greatest moment of my life.

42

SOME MONTHS LATER I AWOKE CRUELLY HUNGOVER in my bed beside an attractive young woman with big crazy eyes and an animated British-inflected voice, who advised me as I listened, amazed, that she was my wife.

Her name, she said, was Esther, and she recounted with peals of laughter how we had tied the knot yesterday at city hall. When the justice of the peace had requested a ring put on her finger, I, having none, pulled a pack of Marlboro's from my coat pocket, removed the foil, fashioned a ring from it, and slipped it on her. She was still wearing it.

"Of course, I expect the real thing someday, but for now, this will do," she said.

I didn't dare tell her not only that I failed to recall any of this but had no idea who she was, period. A gentleman, I invited her out for honeymoon brunch at Tom's, a local luncheonette, where, in bits and pieces, I learned that she was an aspiring actress who worked as a waitress at Phoebe's, an East Village bistro, where I had met her.

Then, apparently, during the next four days I went out on a run with Esther and married her in a blackout.

Gradually, in the preceding months of continuous celebration and then mourning for the feeble rise and ignominious fall of my book's fortunes, my life had blurred into a resigned hallucination, a freak show of inevitable disappointments followed by incomprehensibly destructive drunken escapades. But this, waking up married to a total stranger, was beyond even my imagining.

The New Generation got poor reviews and was quickly remaindered. The reviews, which had appeared in such places as the *Atlanta Constitution* and the *Los Angeles Times*, had damned the book, railed against the soullessness and vapidity of the Brat Pack writers represented in its pages. Then Nelson Doubleday sold the venerable house to Bertelsmann, the West German company, and publicity for the book fizzled as staffers bailed "like rats off a sinking ship," as Robin Strauss sadly put it to me. With no one to promote it, my book sank from sight. In time, I would see piles of copies in the discount bins at Barnes and Noble, and I finally acquired the last few copies I could find, at a buck apiece, from the Strand Bookstore. It was heartbreak and my first hard lesson in the literary life. I just couldn't figure out what that lesson was.

As my lit star waned, my schmooze skills shined brighter every day. The world knows how to ruin you, and it will ruin you if you let it. I threw my arms around its neck and thrust my tongue into its ear.

One day, at work, I learned from the home office that the botanical garden didn't have outdoor toilet facilities and that consequently some 40,000 Israeli schoolkids annually had no place to crap while out there frolicking among the citrons and sabras. The home office had but one fund-raising lead to offer: Abe "Ace" Greenberg, CEO of Bear Stearns Associates, one of the most powerful men in the world of finance, an Oklahoma Jewish cowboy who had been knighted by Denmark for his service as head of the International Raoul Wallenberg Committee. Greenberg had once donated some quarter of a million dollars to have new restrooms built at the Israel Museum. "An unusual man," read the fax. "Has some sort of 'thing' for toilets." The garden's staff regretted that unfortunately they hadn't a clue about how one could get to speak to an individual so high up.

I did. Called Bear Stearns and asked the switchboard for Ace's secretary—and what, by the way, is her name? They told me and put me through. When she came on, I said: "Hey, _____! This is Alan. Let me speak to Abe."

"Hi, Alan!" she chirped uncertainly. "Just a sec. I'll put you right through."

A moment later a Minotaur-like voice came on. "This is Ace. Which Alan are you? I know about fifty."

"Alan Kaufman. And you don't know me. But I know that you understand what's important about forty thousand Israeli schoolkids with nowhere to take a crap. Each time they go to visit Neot Kedumin—Israel's famous botanical garden—they gotta hold it in."

"Never heard of it."

"That don't make it unimportant."

"Point for you. Go on."

"It's plain torture, Abe. There they are in the middle of the date palms and whatnot, jumping from leg to leg. No place to shit. Nowhere to piss. Imagine what that's like."

After a silence, he said: "That speaks more to me than you may know."

"I had a feeling it would. Tell me about it."

"You heard about the money I gave to the Israel Museum."

"I know they got a plaque up there on those toilets, engraved with your name."

"Know why I gave that money?"

"Tell me."

"Because when I was a kid, they took me on a school trip to this place that had no toilet. I told the teacher I must go. I begged: please, I gotta make! But there was nowhere to do it. I crapped myself. This was some embarrassment. I never forgot. So, how much do you need?"

"Seventy-five grand will cover it. We're talking outdoor facilities."

"You got blueprints, something for me to look at?"

"In your hands first thing tomorrow morning."

"All right. Send it."

He hung up.

I sat there in the office, trembling. The boss, a mother with kids, was out kissing ass, trying to raise a grand from some chintzy cheapskate philanthropist who made her sit through fifty hours of tea and chitchat, getting her money's worth in talk therapy, at a rate of about ten bucks per hour, before she'd hand over a check for $500 with regrets that her resources were overtaxed this year, sorry.

The boss wouldn't return to the office until Friday afternoon. I was holding down the fort.

It was perfect. I went out to a local bar, sat calmly sipping a whiskey neat, reflecting on the Greenberg blueprints. Of course, there were none. I'd have to make the whole thing up off the top of my head. Knew nothing whatever about architectural designs, construction budgets, etc. The figure I had thrown out was made up. For some reason fifty G's had seemed too little and 100 G's too much. Seventy-five had a nice doable ring. Anyone with millions can drop seventy-five grand on something they believe in.

I worked all night and through the morning. Kept myself up with coffee and No-Doze. By morning, had a six-page proposal with drawings, budget, history of the garden, nice things that famous people had said about the place (most of it I made up), and a cover letter requesting seventy-five grand. Short, sweet, to the point. I messengered it over, and that afternoon at about 4:30 p.m. another messenger came bearing a large envelope from Bear Stearns Associates. Mouth dry, heart pounding, I tore it open and removed a check for seventy-five grand from Abe Greenberg.

I lost no time. Called the president of the board and announced the gift, the largest ever received in the brief history of their US fund-raising efforts. I requested that I hand the check over personally to him and that I be appointed, effective immediately, as the new executive director, replacing my boss. He'd get back to me, he said. Then I called Israel, announced the gift. They were ecstatic. Explained my terms for continued employment. That they should consider that my boss had succeeded in raising less than four grand to date but I had just opened the door to a whole new world of donors. "I know Abe," I said. "I've got influence with him. He trusts me. There's endless water in that well. Plus, he'll lead me to his friends. But you've got to appoint me exec. In fact, to get the check I lied in my letter, said that I was the executive director. What if he finds out it's a lie? Goodbye, money."

When my boss returned to work on Friday, she was fired. I had taken her desk. Outraged, she sat in a chair in the corridor, making calls to the board, the garden. Everyone sympathized. But hard facts must be faced. The money Alan raised will keep the office open for another year, plus build the toilets (turns out they only needed about $20,000, but who's counting?) and pay for his salary. You, on the other hand, have brought less than nothing and are costing us. So, he stays and you must go.

And that was that.

In tears, she picked up her things, which I'd thoughtfully packed into two Zabar's shopping bags, and left, cursing my name.

To celebrate, I went out on a bender that lasted through Tuesday and from which I awoke in a doorway on Ninth Street, in the East Village—my Wuthering Heights place, where lately I always seemed to gravitate whenever blind drunk, perhaps to find Anna, vestiges of her, ghosts, an East Village Heathcliff roaming a pigeon-dotted moor strewn with shattered glass, kicking at rats, shrugging off addicts, bumping muggers, drunks, freaks with my powerful shoulders, howling for my Anna/Catherine, who was in Toronto, nursing her own shattered heart.

I didn't know what to do about Esther, felt so alone in that hotel room with her, had no connection to anyone I could ask for advice. What would I say? "Hey, guess what I did. Married a complete stranger in a blackout and now I can't stand to be with her! What do you think I should do?" I didn't know the woman even well enough to feel contrite for this awful thing I'd done, felt only fear and a kind of disgusted amazement and couldn't quite connect the misdeed to myself, as if someone else had done it and I had been falsely implicated, an unwitting accomplice informed of the crime only after the fact. I couldn't recall a single detail of the city hall ceremony or the days preceding it. It never even occurred to me to have the marriage annulled. Instead, I pretended to be aloof, tolerant, smiled when she spoke, thinking only of my next drink. I tried to put a brave face on the fact that I was now legally bound to one I'd injured and about whom I knew less than I might know about a random person standing next to me on a subway platform. I avoided home and my blackout bride as much as possible. But sometimes we had sex and were nice to each other for a little while, as if to prove that at least basic civility was possible. This would last only until I rose to dress and go to the bar, whereupon, outraged, she would shriek that I was an abandoning monster and a sadist. The fact that I readily agreed with her only seemed to make it worse.

Now and then, to impress my employers, I pulled off some utterly pointless stunt. Once, I arranged to have the West Point Military Academy mascot mule brought under police motorcade escort all the way across the George Washington Bridge and led out into the rotunda of the Abraham Joshua Heshel School, where my office was located. Requested the city to close off the street while the kids in yarmulkes took rides on the mule's back. Nonetheless, the board president, a vain oil tycoon who was on hand to shake hands before cameras with the Parks Commissioner, was pleased by my flim-flamming puffery and praised me warmly. Mission accomplished. I could go back to drinking myself out of my mind.

Things hummed along in a merry alcoholic haze, pierced occa-sionally by Esther's voice or a hurled piece of dishware exploding by my head. My loneliness and mental anguish were like mourners on a raft, drifting without paddles, in a great gray sea. I drank scotch, mainly, the better grades, and added pot to the mix. Little by little, I learned about Esther: that she was the outcast daughter of New Jersey–based British Jewish plastic manufacturers with factories all over; that Esther was their emotionally volcanic black sheep child; the others obedient Stepford children cookie-cut in the image of Mom and Dad, who lorded over them with iron fists, augmented by broken promises of future wealth.

All this filtered down to my indifference as a kind of remote static interference, an occasional white-noise alien transmission from an old crystal radio. Took it all in with little skull-crushing hangover headache nods and graveyard smiles to no one in partic-ular, and tippled some more.

43

I STOPPED WRITING. MY BOOK WAS A FLOP. DISGUSTED, I dropped out of Columbia.

My close friend and colleague from Israel days, David Twersky, asked me to take over from him as editor of *Jewish Frontier*, an old Labor Zionist journal that had once boasted contributions from David Ben-Gurion, Golda Meir, Albert Einstein, and the poet Charles Resnikoff but that had fallen, over time, into irrelevance.

Since it paid an extra annual ten G's and came with an office and staff, I accepted. I now had two offices in Manhattan.

The mag kept my writing hopes alive. I began to contribute essays, op-eds, met other writers. One day appeared a strange little bearded man in a vest and bowler hat, who introduced himself as Elazar Friefeld, an American-Israeli poet in town from Tel Aviv to offer me the post of American editorial coordinator for *Tel Aviv Review*, a prominent literary annual containing writing from the likes of Yehuda Amichai, Allen Ginsberg, Irving Howe, and Naguib Mahfouz. Of course I accepted, and was paid with the appearance in the next issue of six of my short stories. Felt back in the game. Took on a new book review editor, Ilan Stavans, who would someday become one of America's most prominent literary scholars. Ran cover graphics by Art Spiegelman and articles by Cynthia Ozick and William Philips. I interviewed Diana Trilling in her home, sat at Lionel's desk, held in my hands his copy of Isaac Babel's *Red Cavalry*, the one he famously wrote the introduction to, a volume I revered. Diana Trilling was as grand as I imagined she would be. Not self-important or grandiose but intellectually and socially rigorous: someone with high standards for herself, others, and who, most importantly, could live up to them. In her presence I felt at home, an equal, though I knew this to be an illusion: she was only being nice because of my interview.

Still, leaving the Trilling home was like stepping back, cultur- ally and socially, into a lightless sewer world. To return from this to Esther was simply horrible. She was frantic, manic, hysterical. A shrieker and laugher, a nonstop talker who snorted coke and became even crazier. I lived in the audio cesspool of her logorrhea monologues, delivered in a high stentorian faux-Victorian British stagecraft voice. She didn't know what to make of me. But there was something she wanted. I didn't know what. Whenever she tried to impress me or please me she sensed that she was only disgusting me more.

Even to attempt a divorce at this time would sic her father's lawyers on me, and slam me with an alimony rate that would crush me for the rest of my life. I would need to bide my time.

The next move, though, proved to be hers. And it was by all standards a masterstroke.

She announced that she was pregnant. We bought two different drugstore testing kits and each result confirmed that she now carried my child. She had no plan to abort. It was clear that this had been her intention all along, her reason for hooking up with a blackout drunk who gave no real thought to his life beyond doing whatever absurd tasks provided time to fiddle with writing, and enough cash for a steady supply of booze and cigarettes.

In all this, there was no room for fatherhood. Had no wish to be a parent. The very idea—especially as I had witnessed it in my parents—filled me with horror.

Parenthood was a guaranteed drain on one's dreams, something one sacrificed one's whole life to, with no payoff. Now that which I most feared had me by rights. There was no escape from DNA. This took some time to sink in. Life had caught me in its trap at last. I contemplated this with a grim smile. The consummate escape artist, who had succeeded at outwitting Bronx streets, poverty, crime, warfare, adultery, madness, was now ensnared by a baby. So be it, I told myself. I was a failed writer anyway. Failed husband. Failed Israeli. Failed student. Failed human. May as well add failed father to the list.

Yet something inside wouldn't let me. As though, from out of the flesh of this woman whom I absolutely loathed in every way, some magic force was compelling me to take actions and adopt attitudes that would formerly have been unthinkable.

Cut back on my drinking from hard liquor to only beer and wine, and then just beer. Began to hustle hard for more bucks— arranged to teach creative writing at the Brooklyn Botanic Garden, where one of my students was a young lady with haunting eyes named Alice Sebold, who would go on to write the international best seller *The Lovely Bones*. Already had the sinecure from *Jewish Frontier* and the editorial posting with *Tel Aviv Review* but abandoned the Israeli botanical garden to become New York director of development for a prominent Israeli University at a significantly higher wage and with good medical benefits. I moved us into a cozy apartment in Park Slope, Brooklyn, with hardwood floors and a garden out back.

My determination to do right by the child surprised even me. Anxiously, I awaited the arrival of Isadora Kaufman. On a hot July night in New York City, she was born. A tough experience for Esther, who screamed, shat, spit, kicked, and cursed like a panicking banshee, the doctor and nurses rolling their eyes at each other at how poorly she behaved. They spoke to her with barely concealed contempt. I felt ashamed to be associated with her.

But Isadora appeared on earth as pleasant and self-contained a little beauty as one could hope for.

"Mr. Kaufman," said the delivering doctor who had placed my swaddled daughter into my arms. He laughed. "Why are you crying?"

"Am I?" I sobbed, confused. "I don't know. I wasn't prepared for this. I can't believe how beautiful she is. I thought that newborns are supposed to be ugly."

"This is true. But sometimes," the doctor said, "there are special exceptions. It looks like your Isadora is extraordinary."

I would take the night shift, rising whenever Isadora woke up. At first, I would put on a CD of classical music or rap and, cradling her, dance around the room. Sometimes we waltzed. Other times, we boogied. She'd fall right asleep.

I was the only one able to quiet her. In Esther's arms, she squalled. But no sooner was she back in mine than she slept, little breaths puffing from her lips, a look of angelic intelligent peace lighting her face.

I adored her. Think that she adored me too. We shared an inexplicable link, an uncommon symbiosis. Had never felt such immediacy with anyone. The whole world snapped into view. Felt her in my heart, my bones, with joy that verged on tears. All through the day, even in her absence, dreamed of what she might grow into, become, whatever that may be, a mystery for me to bear privileged witness to.

We had named her for grandfathers on both sides but also for the great founder of modern dance, Isadora Duncan, a powerful and brilliant woman who had defied all conventions to express her imaginative gifts. Until now, I had chiefly used women for my own purposes, with arrogant hostility. Now dreamed daily of my daughter's empowerment. Fathering her made me see in the fullest light my wrongful actions. Were a man for any reason to strike her, I would kill him. Were one to exploit her money, make of her a mark, use her for sex, I would rope him to a fender and drive off with his skin.

Determined to provide for Isadora as best I could, I worked hard and was rarely home. When I was, Esther attacked. It was clear: near me, Izzy felt calm. But Esther terrified her. All former signs of mental illness seemed to have vanished from me with Izzy in her Snuggly, snoozing calmly against my chest.

Seeing this, Esther attacked. Returning from my two jobs, wanted to take Isadora out for a little evening stroll. Esther, shrieking wildly, hair every which way, forbade it. Would not even allow me, after a certain point, to hold her.

Others, consulted, said: "She's insane. Divorce her."

Once, when Esther screamed so loudly that neighbors called the police, one arriving patrolman looked at her, then me, and turning back to Esther, who screechingly accused me of violence, said: "Drop your voice. You're disturbing the peace. And I don't see what you're claiming. I see a quiet, reasonable guy who has just volunteered to leave the premises. I see you shouting and angry. I see you blaming. I haven't heard a single word of blame from your husband.

He looks pretty sad, pretty broken-hearted, to me. Like he loves his kid. So...okay? Think about that."

She told him to get the friggin' hell out.

We left. The patrolman said: "You want a lift somewhere?"

"Nearest subway stop is great."

"Get in."

As I rode in back, the other patrolman, who so far hadn't said a word, studied me in the rearview mirror for a time and then said to me: "Hey, chief?"

"Yeah?"

"Mind a word of advice from one who's seen these things?"

"Yeah?"

"That wife of yours?"

"Yeah?"

"Drop her."

Inside me, slow-motion disintegration set in. Helpless, I noted its appearance with a sense of dread. I knew this mounting chaos would crush the type of lifestyle that supported Isadora's well-being, her existence. Nevertheless, I simply could not fend off my resentment and despair, even though my baby's welfare was at stake. We could count on nothing from Esther's parents, and my own parents could barely support themselves. With me gone, Isadora's world would collapse.

During a routine pediatric examination, the doctor advised us that Isadora might have water on the brain, a potentially fatal condition.

My insides shut down, frozen. Numb, I worked frantically, shuttling from work to doctor's office, sent by my employers on fund-raising missions to Israel and then San Francisco, trying to raise large sums for the university, while also teaching, editing the

magazine, going to the doctor, calling pediatricians, X-ray techni-
cians, brain surgeons, pharmacologists, marathoning on the tread-
mill and all the while terrified of the peril facing Isadora. During
this time, liquor rarely passed my lips.

Once, in Tel Aviv on business for the university, I ran into my
old friend the writer Robert Rosenberg seated with wife Sylvie on
the veranda of the Café Picasso, along the boardwalk. Hadn't seen
him in years. He waved me over, said, "Sit." Turning out a chair,
"And have some of the most exquisite frozen Polish vodka. They
keep it here for me."

"No. I'm not drinking these days. Here strictly on business. You
know."

Rosenberg studied me with interest. Turned, signaled to the
waitress to bring the bottle. She fetched it from a freezer, brought it
over with a shot glass, which she set down in front of me. I looked
down at it. "No," I said, smiling weakly.

"Pour him one," Robert ordered.

She did. "Now, drink that and don't be a damned fool!"

"No, no, I can't," I said.

A minute later it went down my hatch and then a refill went
down, and Robert let me finish off the bottle. I stumbled off alone
and slept curled in a doorway somewhere, in a blackout.

If Esther had been crazy before, her madness now reached new levels
of operatic hysteria. Time and again, police came and I volunteered
for the baby's sake to leave the house, preserve the peace. Though
earning more money than ever before, I found myself after long
work days wandering homeless in my belted London Fog raincoat,
nowhere to go. Sat like a hobo on the neighborhood stoops with a
beer bottle jacketed in a brown paper bag. Only once did I really let
myself go—an afternoon after writing class at the garden. Two of

my lady students and I got righteously plastered on big jugs of cheap wine. We talked like crazy high school best friends and flirted and ranted: welcome release for me in a relentlessly dark time. At one point, we all wound up on the bed together, sloshed, but nothing sexual occurred—just a charged erotic juice sluicing through us of festering ambitions, frustrated dreams, wild hopes. We knew that whatever this life was, as we now lived it was not the answer. Something had to change for all of us.

The news that Isadora didn't have hydrocephalus released in me a strange new recklessness that caromed crazily through the soiled alleys of my life. She was healthy. What did money matter? Nothing I did was enough, anyhow. My wife was monstrous. Her parents hated me. My wagon was hitched to a dragon, the wheel spokes charred, the carriage bed heaped with ash. I couldn't face one more night of Esther violently wresting Isadora from my hands and screeching that I didn't understand parenthood or that I was trying to turn Isadora, now almost a toddler, against her.

"Her mo-ther! Her own mo-ther!" screamed Esther.

I smiled pensively. "And you really believe that Isadora, at less than a year old, understands all that, and is going along with my nefarious plot?"

"You've hypnotized her with your phony charm! Oh, yes! I know all about that charm of yours! You're smooth! Very smooth! Snaking your way into a woman's heart and then tearing it out, eating it!"

In her best stentorian stage voice—a bad mix of hyperbolic Dylan Thomas inflection and vaudeville tragedian—she snarled: "Yes, I DO believe that you HAVE turned my DAUGH-TER against her own MO-THER!!!!"

One could almost hear the sheet-metal lightning rumble offstage.

During all this, the subject in question snoozed in her crib, in the dark, little breaths puffing her lips, a self-contained cherub wanting when awake only to laugh and get around as much and as far as possible, with a pair of doting parents close by. No one wants to crawl alone in the dark.

44

ONE NIGHT, RETURNING FROM WORK, AFTER almost two months off the hard stuff, as I passed a high-end local tavern, I thought: I have done so well. Have a beautiful daughter. I've published a book. Though I found myself married to a madwoman, I managed to provide my kid with a decent home. I've been off the hooch for some time. Surely, just one…

Seated myself at the bar on a plush stool, took in the amber-colored luxuriance, and said to the clean-shaved well-mannered molelike bartender in a red waistcoat and black bow tie: "Give me a Chivas Regal," and as he turned, in a flush of expansive mood: "Make that a double!"

Held up the tumbler of caramel-colored whiskey against the warm, rosy light of an encased candle, inhaled its strong, virile aroma, knocked it back.

Warm, dilating my knots, imbuing me with an untrammeled sense of fresh starts, possibility, and power, it shuddered through me.

Another? Why not?

Which he brought, and I downed and ordered one more, and then another...

Heard thrashing, felt sharp stabs and scratches—balled up in hedges in a housing project in far western Chelsea, and with a post-nuclear apocalyptic aftermath hangover. Came to my feet at roughly four o'clock in the morning. Should have known exactly when, but my Rolex was gone from my wrist, and so guessed by the feel of night, color of darkness, a world in which every last inhabitant seemed to have died, except me, shivering, sick, head split by white-light frenetic high-pitched screaming headache, nose swollen and mouth puffed, as if pounded on by mobs of fists and baseball bats, stomach struggling not to heave out both my lungs and liver.

"God almighty," I groaned, standing up. Where was I? Realized. "How the hell...?" Looked around wildly for my leather satchel containing my wallet, valuables, take-home work. There it was, unmolested. Blood stained my shirt. Smelled vomit from my trousers, saw it caked on my shoes.

I staggered across town, pausing to lean against walls privately, out of sight, closed eyes, stabilizing, and trudged on, nauseated, desperate to reach my Fifth Avenue office near the Flatiron Building, where I let myself in, found the bottle of unopened scotch that we kept for special visitors, dignitaries and such, poured myself a tall glass, hands shaking. I downed it so fast the liquor splashed my chin and shirt. Luckily, I always kept a fresh suit in my closet. I cleaned myself up so well that when the secretary came at her usual hour, 8:00 a.m., she found only Mr. Kaufman, quietly poring over some files, looking up with a cordial business smile, bidding her good morning.

Another night, soon after. Went out for sushi with Rick, a friend. Ordered warm sake with our food, several cups. At meal's end, I proposed that we adjourn across the street to a place I'd spotted called "Downtown Beirut 2."

"I can see why," said my friend, "with your Israeli Army background, you might have an interest in such a dump. But I happen to know that place. It's a skinhead dive. I'd pass on it if I were you."

I grinned. "I'm going in."

"You and Arik Sharon. Well, good luck with that."

It was packed five deep with warlike skinheads wearing white-laced boots—Nazi supremacists. There must have been fifty in there tightly packed. And me. Jewish fund-raiser in a sports jacket. But inside, coiled for violence, triggered to explode. Had noted of late when I drank the frequent appearance of a grenadelike blasting rage in my midriff, strapped-on emotional plastique that boiled through my musculature, ached for detonation. The bar sold only warm beers, buck apiece. Put away about thirty. Looked at my new replacement watch, a cheap Rolex knockoff bought off a Jamaican street vendor on West Broadway. Two a.m. The barmaid, a bottle brunette with Bettie Page hair, dressed in low-cut sweater, tiny pleated scotch-plaid skirt, and high-laced Warlock boots, locked the doors, dumped coins into the jukebox, and as Mick and the Stones played "Street Fighting Man" climbed onto the bar, pulled her blouse over her head, tossed it, undid her bra, tossed that, and with proud breasts jutting did a strutting street-fighting go-go war dance down the bar, kicking beer cans aside with her boots, arms raised above her head.

The skinheads shouted and started body-slamming. Fists flew. Blood spurted. Something struck my head, and as I turned to swing hands from all sides laid hold. Went down in a volcano of kicking, stomping boots. Though blind drunk, knew this was "Crackin'," as they called it, could result in homicide. Came to my feet somehow, swung, connected. But too many fists replied.

And down I went, too booze-numbed even to feel my own body.

Was dragged out by my feet, dumped on the sidewalk. Heard distant enraged voices, felt the thud of more boots to ribs and back. Then someone said: "Kill him!" and something hard-edged smashed my forehead. Insensate, yet I felt this was no ordinary blow. Bystanders screamed: He needs an ambulance. Hurry! Please, help. Someone call! A woman's voice leaned close, out of the pandemonium. "Hello! Sir. Can you hear me? We've called for help. You're safe now. Can you hear me?"

This bounced off consciousness, weightless.

"No," I muttered. "No ambulance..."

"What? Sir? What's that?"

Another voice: "Did you hear what he said?"

Crawling on hands and knees, I reached a lamppost and used it to find my feet.

Concerned voices urged me to stop. Mentioned vast amounts of blood loss. Begged me to stay put. I could hear sirens in the distance and staggered away in escape, down a street, to a doorway, then another. Glancing back, wiping sticky blood from my face, I could see red and orange lights pulsing nearby. In the doorway, I slumped to the ground. Huddled there. Darkness-enshrouded. Collar turned up. Face hidden. Hiding white skin. Just make me a shadow. Oh, please, make me invisible now. And after a time, night buzzing and anonymous again, and gone the pulsing lights, the crowds closed over my near murder, I shuffled hurriedly to the nearest subway station, the one on Astor Place, at the intersection of the East and West Village, and purchased admission from a token booth vendor who studied me with sleepy-lidded interest. I pushed through the turnstile just as, thank God, a near-empty Brooklyn-bound local pulled up.

I boarded a car with a single passenger aboard, a middle-aged lady, who shrieked as if in a poorly made, badly acted horror flick. Catching my reflection in the tunnel-blackened window: my face completely masked with blood, and shirtfront and trousers black with it.

"Itttsssuright ma'am." I smiled reassuringly. Figure of grinning madness. Took a seat. Passed out.

45

ESTHER GAVE UP. I SIMPLY STOPPED COMING HOME. To me, the world was new. A fresh graveyard. I showed up only to put money into a kitchen measuring cup, mostly for Isadora and something for the witch.

I took a mistress, an art student named Eileen, who, one night, in the Ludlow Street bar Max Fish, sidled up to me and said that more than anything on earth she wanted to punch a hole in my earlobe with a safety pin and stick a ring through it. "Go ahead," I said indifferently, belting back a shot. Straddling my leg, she dipped her finger in my booze, rubbed it on my earlobe, and with sweater-molded nipples brushing my arm, punched the pin through the lobe and inserted one of her own earrings through the bleeding hole. I was too drunk to feel any of it.

That night we went to her place, an East Village dump, and made art school love, hungry, clawing sex paused by long mono-logues about Keith Haring and David Wojnarowicz.

She had a slight, waiflike body, fed on ramen noodle cups, cigarettes, and Diet Coke. Thrusting into her was like ravishing a Third World famine refugee. I took her to eat in oppressive low-lit over-priced steakhouses where you sat at a white tablecloth, drowning in dense mahogany, dull brass fixtures, and stifling chandeliers. They brought racks of lamb as big as butchered horses, big bowls of mint jelly, and small roast potatoes greasy with garlic butter. Her large, hungry urchin eyes devoured everything, but she only nibbled like a bird. I ate myself sick and washed it down with tall whiskeys and took her home and had her.

Sometimes I drank too much to be any fun and she kicked me out. Began to sleep at the office on an inflatable Boy Scout air mattress from a nearby sporting goods store. My employer was sympathetic. I could sleep suspended upside down from the ceiling like a bat, so long as I kept up my end of work and the money rolled in.

Greenwich Village points south became my roaming territory. At the invite of a poet acquaintance, I attended a reading where about a hundred bohos sat on the floor of a performance loft called the UpFront Muse, run by Tom Weiss. A succession of despera-does who were loath even to refer to themselves as "poets"—the poetry world, said one of them, is corrupt, the term *poet* become one of dishonor—read impassioned and I thought ingenious texts that sounded suspiciously like poetry, though they went beyond anything I'd ever heard or read in the *Norton Anthology of Modern Verse*: more raw, naked, personal, outraged, and streetwise than anything I'd encountered, including the Beats, who, by contrast, seemed almost self-consciously literary.

This new nonpoetic poetry was cement given voice, the revealed thoughts of alleys and gutters, the inner life of tumors.

"What do you think?" my friend asked.

"That's the greatest stuff I've ever heard from a contemporary," I said. And meant it. Was introduced, met everyone. These were just some of the beginnings of the Spoken Word scene in New York. R. Cephas Jones. Dave Hudson. B. Betterlife. David Huberman. Gail Schilke. Mike Tyler. One night, I joined a group of them to attend the opening of the Nuyorican Poets Café, the first slam night ever held in New York, and we all signed up for the open mike after. It went on until 4:00 a.m., poet after poet, and our poems burned the house down. That night met Bob Holman, Miguel Algarin. Returned Friday nights like it was religion and in time got to know Paul Beatty, Ron Kolm, Carol Wierzbicki, David Huberman, Jim Feast, Hal Sirowitz, Danny Shot, Kathy Acker, Eileen Myles, Pedro Pietri, Steve Cannon—amazing poets, editors, writers, novelists. Where had they all come from? Yet they kept pouring in from everywhere. Carl Watson and Tommy DiVinti from Baltimore, Bruce Isaacson and David West from San Francisco, Ken Dimaggio from Connecticut—poets from Boston, Chicago, LA, Ann Arbor, Detroit, London, even Johannesburg.

The Unbearables were a group of veteran downtown avant-gardists who crossed intelligent, urbane punk satire with serious poetry, fiction, and lit crit. Every so often they put out the call for an "assembly magazine" and the whole scene converged on the Pyramid Club or anywhere that had a pool table, each of us bearing fifty xeroxed copies of a poem, sketch, cartoon, or essay, and with Ron Kolm's huge industrial stapler we'd assemble them into magazines and have a reading.

Wednesday nights, Jennifer Blowdryer and Bruce Craven hauled a game show wheel into whichever performance space would have them and held "Wheel of Poets." You got a number as you came through the door and Blowdryer, renamed "Vanna" for the occasion, strutted about on high heels, tossing tiny rubber lobsters at your face. Craven spun the wheel as we chanted "Wheel of Poets," and if your number turned up, you jumped onstage, read a poem, and got a dime-store prize and a sexy hug from "Vanna."

At Max Fish, B. Betterlife, a lesbian Gertrude Stein look-alike with a gravel voice and a tender heart, hosted a reading so raucous that poets had to perform behind a chain link net to deflect beer bottles thrown by the art students. It was here that I saw David Huberman, dressed in a Wolfman mask, perform an astonishing rant as he backpedaled around the floor on his back screaming, "I'm afraid!"

But the focal point of it all was the Nuyorican Poets Café. On Friday nights, after you handed three bucks to Julio, the big Puerto Rican bouncer, you entered a brick-walled space hung with street art and saw at the end of the bar a black man in dark jazz sunglasses. This was Steve Cannon, the blind editor of *Tribes* magazine. About a hundred people led by Rome Neal salsaed to Latin music. "This is the shit," my poet friends laughed. We danced with beautiful women and drank ourselves into oblivion. The music quit and out slid Holman on one leg, hat in hand, vaudevillian, which in many ways he was, a W.C. Fields of slam, and said: "Welcome to the Nuyorican Poets Café! And this round of the New York City Poetry Slam Championship, where poets compete to be crowned Slam King of New York and win book publication by Nuyorican Poets Café Press! After the slam, we'll have open mike! And more dancing! And then more open mike! And more dancing!"

Audience judges were appointed. Holman went around to tables, handed out scorecards, asked us to score poems on a scale of zero to ten, zero being, he said, a poem that earned boos from the mouths of normally introspective and polite people, and ten a poem that caused the very stage to levitate.

It was a competition for money, prizes, glory, with poets throwing poems instead of punches, and it was more fun than anything I'd ever seen.

There were readings every night—I attended them all, night after night. I began to write in earnest, drunken stabs at nonpoetic poems, and noticed that I seemed to take well to this nameless new art form. We regulars encouraged each other, urged each other on and listened to each other carefully, to learn, acquire, steal, emulate, experiment. We were in the laboratory of language, trying to unlearn and so reclaim poetry; determined to rid ourselves, our very voices, of affectation, to write poems that could be read with the ears and heard with the eyes.

Different tribes arose: Nuyoricans, Unbearables, Big Cigar poets, Apathy poets, Wheel of Poets poets, the Tribes poets, The Upfront Muse poets, the ABC No Rio poets, and on the scene from San Francisco, the Babarians. There were similar uprisings in San Francisco, Baltimore, Chicago, an emergent avant-garde, and many of us were prepared to stake everything on the new development.

The characters were spectacular, especially some of the women, who called themselves kitty cats and dressed like felines, or were self-proclaimed fallen angels and wore wings, or white trash debutantes in dirty wedding gowns, or dangerous revolutionaries with toy plastic weapons, and aging Loisaida shamans who wandered around in pajamas and bathrobes. There were Dadaist musicians, a whole group of them, who appeared at gatherings with marching band instruments and exploded into a cacophonous call for street action, and whole parties emptied out to follow them into the streets, crazy parades at dawn through the East Village or Tribeca. We colonized clubs and bars all over town with our readings, as far north as the Paris Bar in Washington Heights, where Dave Hudson and B. Betterlife ran an open mike, and on Upper Broadway in the West End Bar, my former stamping grounds, where R. Cephas Jones and I led a group of jazz poets and musicians in a weekly open, then down to the Life Café, where the Unbearables, led by Ron Kolm and Jim Feast, held court, and farther south at Under Acme in the Bowery, where David Shapiro ran his open.

Some nights, though, all I wanted was to drink alone. Couldn't stand to think of Isadora, the broken bond, the impossibility of having the only real love that I had ever been given. To drown my grief, I'd go to Billy's Topless, get smashed. On those nights I belonged to nothing and no one, not poetry, not my daughter, and death was my road dog.

Awoke in gutters or curled up to keep warm on manhole covers and grates in cul-de-sacs, filthy, nauseous, hungover, astonished at my gargantuan appetite for the abyss, hands held despairingly to head and muttering "God almighty" over and over in a voice trembling with chilled amazement. And yet, no sooner had evening come than the morning's devastations were forgotten. Felt ready to entrust myself once more to the black snake of my unconscious, follow it anywhere.

My rapid, spectacular decline was no longer a secret. It was known at work that I had a serious drinking problem, and in the poetry scene I showed up to readings wasted. The legendary underground club the Knitting Factory featured me on a bill with some other rising names of the downtown scene, but I stumbled around onstage, incoherent, a drunken vomitous nightmare figure, and saw the pity in my poet friends' eyes. I realized even in my barely conscious state that I was blowing something that I would keenly regret, yet was helpless to do otherwise.

We all drank to excess, I reasoned, no point in singling myself out for special blame. Yet I had the sinking feeling that my star was waning fast even as my Spoken Word comrades started to ascend. The higher they rose, the lower I fell. They tried to bring me along, but everywhere I appeared I was an embarrassment, a stumbling drunk.

One night, I went home to stuff a cash wad into the measuring cup. The flat was dark. Esther and the kid asleep. I crept into the kitchen, not to wake the banshee; left money, turned to go. As I neared the front door, heard from behind a patter of tiny feet on hardwood floors, looked down, and there she was, my Isadora, all of a year and three-quarters, come out by herself, into the dark, so brave. She locked her little arms tight around my leg, a wordless plea for me to stay, as if to say: Daddy, please don't go.

Astonished, I leaned down gently and lifted her eye-level with my face. Her innocent blue eyes met my unfocused bloodshot gaze. Then her little arms hugged my neck, her sweet, soft blonde head tucked into my collar. She hugged me so tightly that guilty tears filled my eyes.

"Your daddy loves you, sweetheart. Really, I do." Never had I loved anyone as I loved her.

I kissed her forehead. She gazed at me, hopeful that I'd stay.

I put her back to bed. Left, returned to Manhattan, to Billy's Topless.

When I needed to drink, nothing, not even an angel, could bar my way.

46

NOW THERE WAS NO STOPPING.

In short order, was terminated from both jobs. My mistress, Eileen, tossed me out. I left home for good and moved into a flat in Washington Heights with three acid dealers; paid one hundred dollars a month in return for the right to crash there nights on a filthy sheetless mattress. In the morning I would awake in a fogbound purgatory where I lay for minutes or days staring at the familiar: a cockroach trying to stay afloat in a beer bottle on an unraveling cigarette. Lifting the bottle, gulped down the whole concoction, stumbled out to the day, passed a crack junkie—the neighborhood a major center of vicious drug gangs and crack houses—rummaging for food in a Dumpster outside a Burger King. Catching the disdain in my glance, he held up a half-eaten Whopper, said: "Why you lookin' at me like that, man? You think you better than me? They's some good food in here!"

What a loser, I thought. The next day, I got thrown out of the crash pad and played homeless hide-and-seek with a squad car downtown, outside a Sixth Avenue MacDonald's, waiting for the cruiser to pass so I could Dumpster-dive for my Happy Meal.

Sat down at restaurant tables from which others just rose, to finish their plates. Ate donuts from garbage cans, pizza crusts from sidewalks, half-rotten fruit found in doorways. I kept my cash for booze, which I drank in doorways, on bridges, on night docks overlooking the Hudson, and was kicked away from under tables on barroom floors and directed, drooling head hung low, out the door, face-first—staggered, fell, and passed out by storefront gates that rapped up at dawn, snapped me awake, with a proprietor's rough shouting, "Hey, pal! Wake up! Gotta open up! Mister! Get the hell up or I call the cops!"

I stumbled off in the pale-blue early waking city chill of morn, hungover, broke, sick to my guts. I had acquaintances so lonesome sometimes they let me stay over on cat-piss-reeking floors matted with filth and dust, in quarters that stank so bad you had to fight the urge to gag. It was out of the rain, a reprieve from the hard pavement, the all-night wind exposure, and a damp chill that burrowed deep into your bones, stayed there. Hugging a bottle, pretending interest in their oddball, hopeless prattle and talentless writing; invited to opine on their work, I lied, raved about how good it was. Anything to buy one more night that I wouldn't have to use the moon for a pillow.

The night was hard, its iron sometimes too fierce to withstand, its dark too menacing, and you just knew in your bones that were you to stay out in it tonight it would kill you—stab you as you lay blacked out or abduct and torture you in some basement or set you afire or kick you to death. At such times your nerves became so bad that the touch of a crawling fly on your skin made you cry out for your mother.

Despite this, I kept up my commitment to the Spoken Word

scene. Clung to it for life and meaning. Was all that stood between me and the abyss. The women and men who were each day founding the conditions for a new literature to exist didn't know at the time that they were not just fostering a revolutionary cultural direction but fashioning, reading by reading, event by event, book by book, a new reason for me to stay alive.

47

ONE NIGHT AT THE NUYORICAN POETS CAFÉ, MET an Australian woman named Bernadette, petite, with long red hair and sly blue sundowner eyes. She was an associate of the San Francisco poets, the Babarians, in for a few days to make the New York scene. Our attraction was immediate, strong. We were each in our own way gutter pirates, prowling life's open seas, targeting other people like so many merchant ships for the having, our roguish smiles nakedly exploitive, and we liked that about each other. Neither of us had real hopes for the future, so we were willing to stake everything on a good time had now.

I talked my friend Tom Weiss of the UpFront Muse performance space into letting us crash over at his place. Naively, he agreed. Bernadette and I took over his bedroom and were soon working our way through his pot stash and liquor hoard.

At first, annoyed but amused, he acceded, and then, as one night passed into several, made indignant speeches about our impertinence, which only made us want to hit his well-stocked larder that much more. We laughed, Bernadette and I, continuously drank, smoked pot, cigarettes, and made love. She had a small, pert, compact form that I wanted to hold firmly between my hands, penetrate, and plunder. We wrote poems to each other, read them aloud.

"You should come to San Francisco," she said. "Get the hell out of New York. You don't belong in the streets. Stay with me!"

Told me about the readings at Café Babar, Paradise Lounge, and the bookstore, City Lights, home of the Beats. Beat yet lived in the city streets, she said, a bohemian sprawl over North Beach, the Mission District, the Western Addition, the Haight-Ashbury.

When she left, Weiss, angry at the way I'd treated his generosity, wanted nothing more to do with me. I understood. I returned to street life. If I had anything like an address, it was Tompkins Square Park, a kind of outdoor commune for the damned, where I colonized a bench facing the Christodora, the Yuppie Condo high-rise.

Returning to my park bench from the Nuyorican Poets Café one night, I spotted a café regular entering the park, bearing a beer quart and a broken umbrella. Sauntered over in the charcoal gloom.

"I recognize you from the Nuyorican."

"Yeah? What? You want to keep me company? So, sit."

I sat.

"What brings you here?" he asked. "Can't sleep?"

"This be my current forwarding address."

"Oh yeah? Any mail come so far?"

"Yeah. Part of a newspaper. Used it as a pillow. It blew right up against my bench. Like a message."

"Well, you know what Kerouac said."

"What's that?

"Fame is like yesterday's newspaper blowing down Bleecker Street at dawn."

We both laughed.

"Here," he said, passing the bottle. "I know thirst when I see it. Thirst first."

I drew some, sighed, drank more. "Thanks. Goddamned needed that."

He nodded. "You're welcome. Got a name?"

I said it and saw him flip it through a mental index. No match turned up.

"Jim Brodey," he said.

I knew who that was. "You're in Anne Waldman's *Angel Hair* antho." He nodded, pleased.

"You were with the New York poets."

"I stand accused."

"You mean honored. You're a famous guy."

"To who?"

"Me. And other poets I know. I've read your stuff. Great work! You're not that regular at the Poets Café, though. I see you there just now and then."

"There, no. Here, often."

"I never saw you here before."

"Usually I'm on the other side of the Park. Near Life Café."

"So, how's a guy with your rep end up here?"

"How'd *you* end up here?"

"Me? I'm nobody. Just this, that, and the other."

"Yeah, me too." He held up the bottle. "This is my 'this.' " Then lifted his arm and let the unbuttoned sliding shirtsleeve reveal a poppy field of abscessed needle tracks. "That is my 'that.' My 'other' is I've got AIDS."

"With me, it's just this," I said, nodding at the bottle. "The

AIDS thing, I understand that's not so good."

"No, not so good." He pulled on the quart. "Lucky healthy you," he said. Held up the beer. "But this shit, bro, and the harder stuff, they will kill you over time just as dead."

"I feel like I'm dying inside."

Brodey drank, wiped his mouth, said: "In which part of you?"

"Every part," I said. And added: "My heart especially." Then I explained and Jim listened patiently to the whole litany of my complaints, the beatings from my mother, my early schoolyard soul-murders at the hands of molesters and my conversion to thuggish violence, my catastrophic failure to realize my gifts as a writer, my disillusioning experiences as a soldier, my disastrous inability to find love with a woman, especially my betrayal of true love with Anna, my ruined Ivy League career, my blackout bride and abandoned baby daughter. I spoke at length about Isadora.

When I was done, he said, simply: "That's not it."

"What d'ya mean?"

"I mean all that you just said, that's not why you're out here 'dying inside.'"

"No?" I laughed angrily. "Well, then, what the hell is it?"

"It's this," he said, hoisting the bottle. "This and nothing else but this. And this,"—surveying the park with his eyes—"here in hell is what 'this' gets you." Then added: "Gets us."

It began to rain. He snapped opened the umbrella. The bat-wing flaps hung broken-necked. We huddled for protection.

"Quick! Lift your feet!"

A soaked rat the size of a cat charged under, rain streaming from its coat.

"Yeah. That's very beautiful," said Brodey, shaking his head. "Fuggin' New York City."

Quietly we sat and drank, listening to the rain.

"It's weird to hear you say that," I said.

"What?"

"You know, about booze doing this. When I was at Columbia there was a reception for this visiting writer who came to give a talk to us grovelings. And I got, you know, totally sloshed."

"As usual," said Brodey.

"Right! I was sprawled out on this sofa with a dumb grin, cradling a bottle, and as he exited he passed me, looked, stopped, and said: 'I hear you're a pretty good writer.' And I said: 'Yeah? So?' You know: like a real wise guy. And he said, pointing at the wine, 'But that is gonna get in your way.' I forgot about that until just now. I mean, you're the second writer with rep to point to the booze."

"Sounds to me like someone's trying to tell you something. But will you listen?"

I shrugged.

"That's called: denial. And you know what they say about it?"

"Pass the beer."

He did. I took a long defiant pull, gasped, handed it back.

"They say that denial is not a river in Egypt."

"Looks to me," I said, "like I don't give a shit."

Brodey nodded that he understood. "You do. But you ignore dire warnings. I do too. But then something happens to make you think. Like you get AIDS. And what about that little girl of yours? Who're you kidding? You care about her."

I hung my head, broken-necked, like the umbrella. "Yeah. But I don't know what to do about that."

"Look. It's way too late for me, man. I got AIDS. But I figure, what's the point of saving yourself if you're gonna die anyway? It's too late for me. But it's not too late for you."

I didn't know much about AIDS at that time, no one did, and wondered as he spoke if it was catching, the infection crawling from his shirt to mine, huddled as we were in the rain, rubbing shoulders. And I was moved. Despite his fatal illness, despite that we sat with rats running under our feet, still something mattered to him, and it wasn't himself, not his fading fame or his ending life or the regrets that I saw eroding the light in his eyes: it was me.

"Save yourself," he said—so earnestly, with such intensity. I couldn't grasp why he would care. "It's too late for me. But not for you. You still can make it."

I felt something inside. Didn't know what. An Emotion. There was no self-pity in him. He cared about something more than his own plight. How could that be? I peered hard at the soaked paper bag, the brown bottle glass that would soon shatter on the pavement in shards, turning razor-sharp teeth to the moon.

"I'm telling you, man, you got a chance," he said. "To get out of these streets. Outta this park. You're not a true street person, you're a person in the streets who don't know how you got here. But there's still hope for you. You can do it."

"But I have nothing left inside me, man. Nothing."

"You got you. You got that little girl. Get into recovery."

I had never heard the word used in this way, as though it were some enterprise you embarked upon, some determined undertaking.

"Go to twelve-step meetings. Live one day at a time. Don't drink. Get help. Reach out. That sorta thing."

"I don't know what you're—what's twelve steps? Is that like 'How to Be a Millionaire in Six E-Z Lessons?' typa shit?"

He laughed. "No, man. No! Not like that. Look, I'm no great example. I keep going out. But maybe it will be different for you. So I'll tell you what I know."

And he did. In the rain, he told me everything he knew about recovery.

48

THE NEXT MORNING, I STUMBLED BACK TO TOM'S loft, drenched to the bone, with the inexplicable notion that I wanted to live, save myself, just because Jim Brodey, a poet I had heard of, thought that I deserved a chance. And I still don't quite get what happened next. Weiss let me back in. That alone was a miracle. Left me there with all his booze and stash, but I told him I didn't want it and somehow he believed me. For no reason that I will ever understand, I then phoned, out of the blue, a former classmate from Columbia University named Philip, who had last seen me with a published book, the departmental star in a London Fog, and now found myself telling him that I was a homeless drunk, near death and needing help.

Why had I not called sooner? he wanted to know, given his deep regard for me. "I'm going to put Jackie, my wife, on the phone. She wants to talk with you."

In no uncertain terms, Jackie told me to get in a cab and come to their Brooklyn Heights brownstone right away. She'd pay the fare.

I did as told, though it took a few cabs passing before one stopped. After sleeping in gutters, I didn't look so well.

They were out on their front steps, waiting. And from the shock in their eyes, I knew: I looked far worse than they'd imagined.

Jackie, pretty, blonde, in her early thirties, was very pregnant. Philip, a gifted screenwriter, tried to hide the pain in his eyes; smiled, shook my hand, and paid the cab as Jackie hugged me. I sort of cringed when she drew near, put her arms around me. Didn't want her or the baby in proximity, had just passed the night in the streets with a junkie's abscesses, drenched rats. But I let her. I was so tired.

Their mahogany-paneled home was tastefully furnished. In their kitchen, I sat down.

Jackie looked at Philip. "We'll be all right. I'd like a word alone with Alan."

"Of course," he said, grinning shyly. Told me: "I'm so happy to see you!"

"How goes the screenwriting?" I asked.

He mentioned the name of a director, one of the most famous in Hollywood, for whom he was writing under contract a new screenplay to a film I'd heard about.

"That's terrific, buddy! I'm glad one of us made it."

He smiled and left the room.

Jackie said: "He's so thrilled to see you. He admires you very much, you know."

"Undeserved admiration can be quite painful."

"It's not up to us to choose who appreciates us," she said.

"That's true."

She sat down, facing me. "Alan, I have something really important to say."

I leaned forward to better position myself to receive her confidence. My eyes grew unfocused. She began to recede, grew smaller.

My hands shook, my head filled with bat-winged demons. I glanced around the table, checking for knives or forks. A rising sense of panic lurked just beneath my ribs. A warning. She was coming close. I badly needed a drink to kill the echolalia of a screaming mother in my head. Her voice reverberated through the cavern walls of my dead soul.

"Yes, Jackie?"

"Alan, I'm an alcoholic."

I sat back in my chair to get a better view of her. Wondered why she was telling me this. Wondered if I could yet get out, walk out of here with a few bucks of their goodwill in my pocket, acquire some vodka, just a little to kill the shakes.

"I'm so sorry to hear that." My voice dropped, struck a soap-opera note of confidentiality. "Does Philip know?"

She laughed. "Of course he knows. I haven't had a drink in five years. We're both very proud of that."

She looked gravely at me, all business. "Have you ever considered that you might be an alcoholic yourself?"

"Sure." I nodded somberly. "I drink all the time."

"That's not what makes one an alcoholic," she said. "Plenty of folks drink all the time but are not drunks. An alcoholic drinks because he or she can't not drink. The alcoholic has to, even when they don't want to."

As she said this, I recalled what Jim Brodey had said, that so many times his brain had begged *NO!* as the needle slammed into his vein. Recalled times when my own mind had protested even as my hand tilted the bottle and poured the poison in—when another being seemed to possess me, drive me to drink, whether or not I wanted to.

"That's me exactly. The weak man."

"No. No, not weak, Alan! Have you ever considered what alcoholism really is? What you suffer from is not a moral failing but an actual disease. You have an illness, like diabetes or muscular dystrophy. You don't stop because you *can't* stop: it's impossible for an alcoholic to *stay* stopped for any amount of time. The world is divided into normal people and us drunks. And you're a drunk like me. You have a mental obsession combined with an allergy of the body. You're allergic to alcohol and obsessed with it at the same time. The combination is fatal and unstoppable. Once booze hits your system, the jig's up: you must drink. It's not the normal drinkers who end up in the park, it's not them who die in the gutter. It's us, with a condition that is recognized by the American Medical Association as incurable, and Alan, it's killing you."

I swallowed hard. "I never thought of anything like that."

She nodded. "Neither had I until I first came to recovery."

She told me drinking tales that made my hair quiver. Could not imagine that a pretty young woman could survive all that yet come out looking so well.

"There's a solution," she said. "I am proof."

"But Jackie, not for a hopeless nut like me. I know me like nobody's business. Trust me: don't waste your time. Nothing works on this blockhead." I tapped my skull with my forefinger. "It's like a wall. Good ideas just don't get through."

"But that's exactly the kind of case that recovery works best for. The more hopeless, the better. Since you have nothing to lose, you might be willing to gamble everything on getting free, which is exactly what's needed for this to work."

She repeated, in depth, things that Brodey had told me about 12-step meetings, where groups of drunks help each other stay sober one day at a time. How recovering drunks show up for you until you can show up for others. It all sounded very nice but it was flimsy stuff. The only thing that could stand between me and a

DRUNKEN ANGEL

drink would be handcuffing me to a bed and armed guards, 24/7. Besides, why would anyone invest more than a couple of hours' time in my type? A day, perhaps, a week. But longer? How long was needed to get this thing? A month? Year? A lifetime? Who could bear me for that long? I could barely stand myself.

"Why would anyone help me?"

"Because that's what keeps them sober."

I didn't quite grasp this. "And the twelve steps. What's that? Some religious thing?"

"No! Not religion. Spirituality. A commonsense, concrete way that gutter drunks like us connect to our spirits and to a Higher Power, whether you call it God or the Universe or whatever you like. It's what helps us to live comfortably in our own skin and stay sober."

"That sounds like religion," I said suspiciously. I was thinking "cult," actually. Next she was going to ask me to join her on the street corner to sell fund-raising bouquets for the Reverend Sun Myung Moon.

"Not religion: spirituality," she repeated.

"What's the difference?"

"Religion is for people who are afraid of going to hell. Spirituality is for people who have already been there. Alan, you and me, we've been in hell."

Tears started in my eyes. She took my hand, squeezed it. I flinched. Wondered what she was after.

And then I met the ugly truth of my desperation, that if selling street-corner flowers for the cult is what it took, I'd go. There was nothing left of my pride. Perhaps I'd never had any to begin with.

"Jackie, I don't know you as well as I know Philip. But if he trusts you, then, OK, I trust you. Maybe I just need some kind of help. I'll do what it takes. What do you want me to do? I can't believe

that anything will work on a hardhead like me." I pointed at my
moist eyes. "But you see this? You've got me. I'm out of options—I
can't go back to the streets. So, okay. Tell me, this recovery deal.
Where do I apply? When do I start? I'm done, Jackie. Believe me.
I'm finished."

Lightly she touched my shoulder, rose, and said very quietly and
gently that I should go upstairs and shower if I wanted, while she
washed and dried my clothes. And then I should nap while she made
me some food. And after dinner, we'd go to a meeting together.

I nodded tiredly and said: "O.K."

49

THE MEETING WAS IN A LARGE COMMUNITY-
center basement with dingy walls. There was a coffee urn, Styro-
foam cups, cookies, chairs in rows, a table and chair. I looked around
for drunks, couldn't see any, just successful-looking folks who stood
chatting and backslapping each other, some embracing intensely, a
convivial mood in the air. What kind of deal was this, I wondered.
Evidently, apart from Jackie, I seemed to be the only actual drunk
in the room. Perhaps this was some sort of anthropological group
devoted to the study of drunks, and I was their monkey specimen.
Some professor type to prod me with a stick, explain various points
about the way that drunks work. Well, if that's what it took to get
sober, I stood ready. I'd sell scented candles on street corners if they
asked me to. Now that I was resolved not to return to hell, I'd do
anything that would lift the obsession to drink.

She sat us somewhere in the middle of the crowd, who had
begun to seat themselves, and instead of calling me out to serve
as a lecture specimen, people shook my hand and welcomed me.

Three well-put-together specimens of mental health and professional attainment seated themselves up front and then, one after another, stood and told, with gentle humor and lots of laughs, the worst drinking stories I'd ever heard.

One, who now occupied a prominent place in the world of art museums, described her years as a jailbird, prostitute, and back-alley drug addict. And that's when things were going well for her. From there she descended into realms of nightmare that made my skid row seem like Sutton Place.

Another, a university professor, a wino, used to sleep blacked out under a highway overpass, unaware of his bodily functions.

The third, a top-level manager in a Fortune 500 company, had once made his home in the men's shelter and twice had been declared dead in the ER.

Newcomers were asked if they wished to introduce themselves. Nervously, I watched a few others. And then, as Jackie's eyes filled with emotion, my shaking hand rose. Jackie slipped her arm through mine, and I said: "My name is Alan. And I am an alcoholic."

PART TWO

BOOK SIX

50

I HAULED A BLACK TRASH BAG TO THE GREYHOUND
station. It contained the last five remaindered copies of *The New
Generation* from the Strand Bookstore along with a composition
notebook, Bic pens, and a sack of peanut butter sandwiches. Three
days. Three thousand miles. San Francisco.

In the pocket of my jeans I had sixty-seven bucks I borrowed
from Jackie and Philip and a pack of Marlboros.

Eight days sober. A recovery old-timer had told me: "Time takes
time. Don't be in any rush to get this thing. Let it filter in slow.
What's the hurry?"

I took it easy, one day at a time, and felt flooded to my marrow
with a new sense of hope. But still, I had to get out of Dodge, flee
New York: my blood stained every street in that town. Resolved
to stay sober no matter what, hungrily I absorbed advice from
those around me. One especially crusty old-timer had said: "On
that bus, do not drink, even if your ass falls off. Put it in a bag, stick
it in your pocket, bring it to the first meeting you hit in Frisco.

They'll glue it back on for ya."

I was like someone covered with fatal burns over 90 percent of his body who sees, without any rational explanation, portions of skin miraculously regenerate, and all just because he sat in some meetings, heard things, and began to follow a few simple suggestions:

A) Put the plug in the jug. Don't take that first drink. All your troubles begin with the first. Think it through. Ask yourself: what will be the consequence?

B) Don't drink, no matter what. Period.

C) Remember HALT: Hungry. Angry. Lonely. Tired. If you feel hungry, eat. (Carry a candy bar.) If you feel angry, calm down. Anger will get you drunk. Feel lonely? Isolated? Well, get the hell out of the house. Call someone. Go to a meeting. Connect. If you're tired, nap. Easy does it.

D) Just stay sober for today, twenty-four hours.

Simple guidelines for a complicated guy. When all else failed, they told me: pray.

"To what?" I'd asked.

"Don't matter," they'd said. "Whatever you like. Pray to the doorknob."

"But I'm no holy roller."

"This is not about religion," said one who had five years sober. "You ever heard of a religion where the words *God* and *fuck* get used by members in the same breath?" The five-year man pursed his lips thoughtfully and, leaning forward, said: "You been to hell?"

"That I have," I said, smiling sadly.

"Well, then, what the hell do you got to lose by giving heaven a try?"

★ ★ ★

"Thank you, fucking God," I said as I slid to a sit on the bus station floor.

In the busy station, desperate-looking travelers rushed to gates, driven by echoing loudspeakers. Bus terminals are not like airports or train depots, which tend to draw a moneyed clientele. Greyhound is the celestial ferry of the underclass, chariot of the poor. Those who ride the dog often don't look well. But even among these, I stood out as a sorry case. Only by the power of my newly awakened spirit and the tickled humor of my smile could I claim a place among them. For I was arisen not from the dead but from the undead, and if some might question whether I even existed at all, well, without a drink in my hand, I wasn't so sure myself.

And yet I felt a sense of newfound freedom. Had previously thought my life's purpose was to write great literature and champion causes. Now I understood: my first duty was to live. The knife was at my throat. Here was proof of life: I had tried so hard to die. And the blade was not in any other hand but mine, turned on me. So I must do anything not to drink. I had my work cut out.

I supposed that I now knew enough, had faith enough, to make it safely overland for three days aboard the bus, a fast-moving silver bullet on wheels, painted on both sides with the emblem of a dog running for its life.

I felt so relieved not to have a hangover. And though through sober eyes the world looked severely businesslike, frantic, joyless even, now and then inside I felt flashes of causeless happiness, cosmic winks, that brought smiles to my lips. In the meetings I had been promised that my shaking hands would soon be still. So here in the terminal there was nothing to do now but sit back with shaking hands and smoke a cigarette.

An old black woman in a wrinkled dress came along, dragging

a garbage bag identical to mine. Hers, filled to bursting, seemed to weigh a ton. Hauling it strained the sinews of her neck. She stopped about ten feet away, slid to a sit against my wall. Her feet were shod in Carolina work boots, untied laces trailing on the ground, and hair done up in little braids tied with colored rubber bands.

She searched the floor around her feet, and with a pleasure that I well knew from gutter days found a smoke and lit up, inhaled, exhaled, and spoke to herself. There is a kind of conversation with yourself that is sane and another sort that is with imaginaries—hers was the latter. When she noticed me looking her way, she gazed back with the disarming impudence of a child. Mad for sure, but sweetly so. Older too than I imagined. Must have been in her late seventies, early eighties, perhaps. What a world, I thought, to leave one like her homeless and hungry. What social order could allow this? What political system supports this? What economic theories justify this? Greed and indifference permit the old and infirm to die neglected. Being sober did not mean that I should ever make accommodation with a world that says: She is none of our affair.

And yet, here I was too, an Ivy League grad schooler with a published book, a writer, former museum program director, fund-raising wheeler-dealer, Israeli soldier—and had as little as she, maybe less. We shared the same dirty bus terminal floor.

The old woman was crazy, but so was I, with my long secret history of hearing voices, PTSD delusions, the stabbing phobia—all undocumented because I was good at hiding. But then, for twenty-two years, in full view of myself, I'd poured down my own throat a killing substance that drove me to ever-worsening depths of madness. I had, then, no cause to pity her. We were the same. Each hanging on by our fingernails. And realizing this, the strangest thing happened. I felt a sudden sense of warmth hatch

and spread through me and heard a small faint whisper of a voice-
less voice say: "Just smile." Which I did, straight back at her, and
in her face appeared the warmest, prettiest beaming little girl, and
there we sat on the terminal floor, two broken children, smiling
at each other.

51

I HAVE ALWAYS PREFERRED THE BACKS OF BUSES. Up front, the elderly, the migrant families, the single mother with kids, the young European backpackers, the theological student returning from seminary, but in back sat all us sinners. And here was quite a bunch of us: a pig farmer returning to Iowa from a whirlwind tour of New York's brothels that had left him penniless; an ex-con in a nylon stocking cap who had finished parole and planned to play out a new hand in the Promised Land of California; a still-pretty bottle blonde barfly type with boozy eyes.

Everyone began chatting as soon as we crossed into New Jersey and broke out bottles, joints, pipes, capsules, powders. I even saw one guy shift a rig from one pocket to another. I was seated next to a wino with cornflower-blue eyes and a trucker's cap announcing him to be a Proud Nam Vet. The vet had the wino's purplish bloat and inflamed potato nose.

"Corey," he said, offering a tough bony handshake, and that's all he said. He took out a pint of Mad Dog 20/20 and sat turned

to the aisle, sipping quick nips. I sat with eyes closed, reciting the
Serenity Prayer.

There wasn't an open seat down front or I would have moved
in a heartbeat, just to save my hide. A fifth of Wild Turkey was
circulating, and each time one of the back riders stepped from the
small bathroom a wave of pot smoke engulfed us all. This continued
unabated till we were halfway across Pennsylvania, when the driver,
an immense big-bellied man with nicotine-stained walrus mustache
and eyes bleached by a lifetime of hard travel, pulled us over, set the
brake, and slowly walked to the rear.

Leaning whiskers so close you could smell his Camels and coffee
breath, he said: "Now, you nice folks surely are aware that drugging
and drinking aboard a public interstate conveyance is punishable by
a fearsome fine and mandatory jail. It won't matter to the authorities
if you've never even crossed paths with a parking ticket. Highway
Patrol will take you off in cuffs and you will feel the full brunt of the
law. Is there anyone back here that don't understand them words?"

Everyone turned to stare coldly out the window, or at the ground,
fuming, eyes quicksilver with glaring insolence.

He came erect, surveyed the tops of our outraged heads with
amusement. "Do time in the joint just to get buzzed on rotgut on
a ninety-nine-buck one-way bus ride to nowhere? Makes no sense,
but what do I know? Well, no matter. When you get to where
you're going, pick a bar stool and stay on it till you can't tell your ass
from your elbow and hoist one for me. Okay? But no drinking or
drugging on my bus. We all understanding each other here?"

No one said anything.

Carefully, smiling at the passengers on both sides of the aisle,
he made his way back to his seat, started up the engine, and with a
great hydraulic clamor merged back into the high-speed traffic flow
and once more we were under way.

Almost immediately, the party resumed, and with even greater intensity. Wasn't until Chicago that I could change seats, advance into the drug-free zone. Until then, I sat with frozen smile, eyes glued to the scenery, nostrils filled with the reek of pot and the sour smell of cheap booze.

After Chicago, for a time, no one sat beside me, a welcome respite. But as we neared Iowa, Corey, the Nam vet, settled into the seat next to mine. My heart sank. It was night, most of the passengers asleep, even those in back, and Corey said: "It's crazy back there. Hope you don't mind. You got a friendly face."

"Don't mind at all," I lied, troubled. What did he want? Paranoia bells rang. Was it because we were both vets? Something in my demeanor that spelled "military vet"? Or "wino"? And if so, what did he want with me? My PTSD needed no interface with others' nightmares. I had plenty of my own.

"You got a minute to talk? Something private I'd wish to share with you."

Didn't say yes or no. Just looked at him. Then: "Why would you want to share your private stuff with me, a total stranger?"

"Because it's the only way I can. I'd consider it a favor."

I said nothing.

"I'll take that for a yes," Corey said. "Because it ain't a no." He removed his cap, ran his fingers through his gray-streaked brown hair. "I don't know where to begin," he said, groping for the right words. Everything inside me wanted to wall him out, scream, "Don't begin at all! Leave me the hell alone!" But my soul would not allow it. He was someone suffering for lack of human contact who needed to unload trouble, and it seemed incumbent on me as a recovering alcoholic, despite the inconvenience, to listen.

I said: "Well, why don't you begin at the beginning?"

He told me that before he got off the bus in Des Moines, where his old folks were waiting for him, he needed once and for all to clear his conscience of something that he had never told anyone.

"Why tell me?" I said. "Why not go to a priest?"

"I don't think a priest will get it."

"But I will?"

"You got a good face," he said. "I know faces. You've seen things. You're not like everyone. It's just a thing that I need to get rid of before I see my folks. I've been away for thirty years. In all that time, I haven't seen them face to face, not even once. Just post-cards and phone calls is all we've had."

"How does that feel?"

"Strange," he said. And the look in his eyes was familiar, I knew that look—had the same one each time I returned from duty in Gaza.

"What brings you back now?"

He looked at me in such a way that conveyed the full weight of his reply: "Going home."

"Home," I said. "I didn't know there was such a place left anymore."

"I hope so. Or I just blew my last stake for nothing on Des Moines, Iowa."

"Then there is home," I said. "There has to be."

A shadow appeared under the peaked brim of his Nam vet cap and cloaked his eyes in a bandit mask of murky memory light that seemed to engulf us, everyone aboard, in a single antechamber of recall. He told me how as a combat soldier on leave in Saigon he had shot a man in a drunken brawl in back of a gambling joint. Man pulled a knife. So he pulled his gun, one he'd lifted off a dead VC. And shot him point-blank in the head. He had killed boocoo Charlie in the bush, and it was like nothing to him. He wiped the gun clean of prints, left it next to the corpse, just walked away. The crime never followed, just the memory of it. Next, he was stateside, down South, in a bar. Some dumb disagreement became a fight, and when the other guy went out into the parking lot after him, with his gang, intending harm, he pulled a .45 and killed that man too. The others fled.

He looked at me to see how I was taking all this.

"Go on," I said, knowing that the story wasn't done, couldn't be. "There were others, right?"

He nodded. "I knew you'd see. In fact, there was one more. I won't say where. All I know is, he was armed and I was armed, but when the guns came out, he lost his nerve."

He hung his face, voice barely audible. "I had a choice."

"What choice?"

"I didn't have to. He just stood there. Couldn't follow through. I always said: you pull a gun, you use it. He couldn't. But I would not hesitate. Wasn't even angry. Just a matter of my code. You draw your gun, you fire. So, I dropped him. Almost like it was a lesson for him to learn. But that was the end of his education. It puzzled even me. You know what I'm saying?"

"Actually, I do."

"I thought you would."

We just sat there, heads leaned close.

"I never told anyone. It was all years ago. But that last time I knew was wrong. I couldn't get him out of my mind, his eyes. It hurt to think about. It isn't about the law. I don't give a crap for the law. The law don't know what happened to me in the Nam, shit-all! The law says over here you gotta act like a hairdresser but over there, in the jungle, you get to go Rambo. Double-standard shit is what it is. Schizo. Hell, in the Nam I was cutting off VC ears to prove my head count. I even scalped one or two, dried them in the sun, cured them, wore 'em around my neck. I left my uniform shoulder patches stuffed in the mouths of my dead enemy, like a calling card. I had no soul. Went there with one, returned without. The guy who killed those men was soulless, dead, in my way."

"So, how did you stop, if you couldn't before?"

I'd rather not talk about that either. Let's just say, I changed my life and I'm truly sorry about those men. They drew on me, pulled knives, came at me. I never once aggressed. I coulda been the dead man on every one of those occasions. I lived because I killed better than they did, but they were killers too."

"Except for that last one."

The pained look in his eyes showed to what degree he knew that, and suffered for it every waking moment of his life.

He swallowed hard and after a long reflective pause, said: "My parents are Christian folk. They believe in confession. But I can't go to no priest. Not in Des Moines. Not anywhere. I can't tell who might up and go to the authorities. I can put more trust in a stranger, like you. Be my priest, stranger. This was my confession."

"Done," I said. "I can't absolve you. No man can. Only God can do that, if there is one. Go to Him now. And be at peace. Good luck with your folks."

We shook hands. "I knew you'd be a good one," he said. "I know a soldier."

"I soldiered once," I said. "I'm just a bad drunk now but I'm trying to get better, man. I really am."

"You make it," he said. "You make it all the way." And Corey returned to his seat.

When the bus pulled into Des Moines, there were his parents, waiting. One on a walker, the other on a cane. They clasped Corey hard and close in their arms and his mother wept. His father swept away a tear.

I watched all this through the window.

52

IN IOWA I NAPPED. WHEN I AWOKE, AN ATTRACTIVE but bedraggled woman with a blackened eye, clutching a child in her lap and two other kids seated nearby, settled beside me.

"Hello," I said.

She scanned my face but didn't respond, her right eye ferociously bruised. I noticed scratches, abrasions, all fresh. The kids sat sucking thumbs and warily looking around, as children do in perilous times.

"How far you headed?" I asked.

She decided I was harmless. "Just to Reno," she said.

"Going to play the slots?"

"Oh, no. I've got a sister there."

"It must be a major production just to visit a sister out of state when you've got three young ones in tow."

Her face grew fierce, the wet shine preceding tears coating her eyes. "We're not visiting. We're moving."

"Oh, I see. To be close to Sis?"

"To get away from Des Moines."

"Oh."

After an uncomfortable pause, she added: "As far away as possible."

Couldn't think of what more to say or ask, and collapsed myself against the window, hugging the bus wall to give her more room, self-conscious, sensing her raw-nerved, painful state. After a time I said: "I guess I'll do a little reading," and took out a book about the 12 steps, covering the first chapter, about what powerlessness over alcohol is—an allergy of the body coupled to an obsession of the mind—and about the curious mental blank spot the alcoholic has, an inability to sufficiently recall the ravages of the previous night's horrors, a kind of lethal amnesia, as if nothing had occurred, and so the drunk goes at it all over again.

At some point I felt her eyes sneak-peek over my shoulder and pretended not to notice even as I eased a little closer, to help her read the page. The mental blank spot, said the book, always precedes the first drink. One feels a flush of unreal optimism about one's ability to process alcohol. Months, years, even decades of suffering and ruin are eclipsed once the alcoholic mind fixates on drink. One, taken just to wet the old whistle, becomes two, triggering the addiction that results in an unstoppable binge that can last anywhere from a day to twenty years.

"Do you have a drinking problem?" she asked softly.

Inwardly delighted, I looked up.

"I don't mean to pry," she whispered. "I just saw the book's title and couldn't help but sneak a look at what you're reading."

I smiled the nicest, most courtly smile that I could summon. "I don't mind your asking. I certainly do have a problem with drink, yes."

Her face grew somber. "I'm sorry to hear that. My brother has that problem too, I think. My uncle, Rickie, yes, him too, most likely. Well, what made you realize...you know...that you have the problem?"

"When I drink I break out in handcuffs, hospitals, shrinks, public parks, disappointed employers, angry wives, streets, Dumpsters. I keep waking up in gutters, rummaging in garbage cans for breakfast." I chuckled. "I got good at knowing which garbage cans had the best meals. Was a real connoisseur of trash food."

"Oh," she said. "Well, I've never had anything like that."

"Thank God for you."

"Yes, Thank God."

We enjoyed a comfortable pause.

Then: "I was a cocktail waitress."

"Oh." I smiled. "Well, I guess you've seen your share of drinkers like me."

"I certainly have. In fact, I got so that if a man drank I didn't want to date him."

"Do you drink?"

"Yes. But I can control it. I don't have the problem you seem to, I guess, where you can't stop?"

I nodded. "That's my problem in a nutshell. Once I start, I can't stop."

"Say," she said. "You couldn't spare a cigarette by any chance, could you?"

Gave her one, lit her up. She inhaled, and a sigh of sweet relief spread over her face, relaxing the lines into a smooth mask of narcotized bliss.

"Thank you."

"Are you just an occasional smoker?"

"I'm trying to quit. I never seem able to, though." She held up the cigarette, regarded it with wonder. "Actually, this is the reason

I gotta leave Des Moines."

"Oh?"

She told me that in the cocktail lounge one night she had met a man, a Peruvian rug salesman. Didn't drink or do drugs. In fact, had no bad habits. A religious thing. Polite, clean, well mannered, respectful, and very prosperous. Left her big tips and was always pleasant. He was very handsome and he loved America. " 'Oh, God bless America,' he used to say, and we'd both laugh. One night, he asked me in the sweetest, most chivalrous way if I would allow him to take me to a movie."

She inhaled and exhaled a plume of smoke. "*Allowed*. I liked that. I mean, American men never think, like, about *allowed*. They just grab and take, and what's a girl to do? If you say no they spread word around that you're a drag. And I thought that an evening out with a gent who asks permission would be good for me, like a visit to a foreign land or something—you know? I've never been out of Iowa except to visit the sister. My parents are dead. 'Sure,' I said. 'Pick me up at eight p.m. on my night off.'

"Come the night, I arranged for a babysitter, and was it ever worth it! We had the nicest date! After the movie we went someplace for ice cream sodas. I kept looking at his beautiful teeth. Perfect, white. And he smelled so good. He was something!"

"Sounds great," I said.

Her face darkened. "It was nice. It really was."

He took her out again. For three months they dated. He met the children, bought them toys. Paid for the babysitter when they went out. Said that he loved her, wanted them to marry. And one night, proposed that they live together, he'd pay for everything. She could quit her job as a cocktail waitress and just be a wife, mother, and good daughter-in-law. His old mother lived with him too. "I didn't like the bitch. But she was so old, I figured that she wouldn't be around forever."

She inhaled again, exhaled. "Well, I agreed. And it's funny. At home, with all that free time on my hands, I drank a little more than typical. But it was just for the readjustment. He was never home. Worked all the time. So I was there with his mom all day. And she began to go on about my smoking. Wanted me to stop."

She had finished her cigarette and asked if she could have another.

"Help yourself," I said; left out the pack to share.

"I love to smoke," she said, lighting up.

What happened was that she grew bored, restless, and began to think his nice big house was in fact a jail. Went out nights on her own nickel to the cocktail lounge, as a customer now. Missed the place. The action was fun. People she had once served now became friends. She went to other places, some of them rough trade but they were fun too. Put on little outfits that her boyfriend forbade her to wear when out with him or in the company of his mother. He wanted her to affect modesty. "Modesty!" she sneered. "Do I strike you as the modest type?"

I smiled. "You strike me as the nice person type."

She looked at me. "You're sweet."

Then he tried to put his foot down. Said no more going out. When she told him where to get off, he struck her, hard, across the face, while his mother stood by watching with approval. Outraged, she threatened to leave, but where could she take herself and three kids? All she knew were drunks. She had no choice but to stay put, for the kids' sake.

She determined to reform herself, meet the conditions of the situation. If enduring bouts of boredom would assure the children's welfare, then she would stop going out. They must come before herself.

But for the mother-in-law, it was not enough. She must stop smoking too. It was, she complained, not only a filthy habit but unseemly for a woman. Smoking was a vice of men. Only fallen women smoked, whores. She must quit smoking or leave.

She held up the cigarette for me to see, contemplated it. "This was my last refuge and friend. The last pleasure left to me. Take it away and what did I have?"

She looked blankly at me. I nodded that I understood.

She tried everything. Patches. Nicotine. Gum. Plastic cigarettes. This hypnotism tape. Nothing worked. And the old woman, that witch, was everywhere spying and reporting back to her son. And it's so hard to hide the smell. Lord knows, she tried perfumes and kept changing her deodorants—and the mouthwash, the strongest that money could buy. And in the belief that drinking the mouthwash would burn the smell right out of her system, she got drunk, and still it didn't hide the smell, but now she began to drink the mouthwash anyway, and then switched to harder stuff, bottles she smuggled into the house. At first, he was amused, then outraged. Told her that his mother had angina, couldn't be around smoke. That seeing her violate his mother's values was sending his own blood pressure through the roof. The former cocktail waitress was literally killing his mother.

She pleaded, tried to reason. This is America. Everyone drinks and smokes! But he flew into a fury, night after night, anger mounting into rages, and one night punched her so hard he knocked her wind right out, sent her flying across the room.

She lay there on the marble floor of his beautiful house with the old woman near, looking down on her in disgust, and the Peruvian with fists clenched shouting for her to get up and apologize to his dear wonderful mother, who was a woman of the old country and the old ways, such a woman as he should have, not some whore like you, and her children at the top of the stairs, watching, shocked, too afraid even to cry. And she came to her feet, made it to the front door, ran out, jumped into his SUV, drove like a bat out of hell to a local biker bar, told the bikers what her boyfriend had done. They swore up and down they'd crucify him. But what's the big hurry? Stay and have a drink. Here, have a cigarette. He gave you quite a shiner. Here, drink this. Big tattooed hand clasping her neck, tilting back her head as other bikers laughed, pouring in the drink, which ran down the sides of her mouth, and poured another in, and another, though she didn't need much help.

She left the bar with three of them, drunk out of her mind, riding on back, holding tight, shouting and laughing as they roared into the night, the Peruvian's SUV left behind with tires slashed and a pound of sugar funneled into the gas tank, to teach the sucker a lesson. And the next morning, awoke in a ditch with her skirt hiked over her head, panties stuffed into her mouth, face pounded and scratched, and made it to the highway, where a passerby drove her to the house. The Peruvian was gone, the old woman home with the children, screeching. She packed quick bags—the bags I saw; there wasn't much—threw together food and formula, got the kids into clothes, called a cab, and went to the Greyhound bus station. All this happened in the last twenty-four hours. Her sister had told her simply: "Come."

"Can you imagine all that trouble from just having a smoke now and then?"

I laughed sadly. "That's a terrible story. Can I be perfectly honest with you?"

"Sure."

I watched her face. It must have worn the same expression just before the Peruvian struck her.

"I want you to know that I think, first of all, that you're a hell of a brave lady, taking care of your children the best you humanly can. This is a hard world. It can't be easy, alone with three kids, and having to make some hard choices. I think you're really great."

Surprised tears started in her eyes. "Thank you," she said.

"And, well, about the smoking thing, I don't know. I smoke. Nasty habit. But it never got me to the streets. Drinking did that. And I heard some drinking in your story. I don't know. Wonder if that's a cause?"

She didn't look hurt. Taken aback, but not offended. "Well, maybe," she said. "It never—well, maybe it did occur to me, a little, but not as *the* problem. But I'm willing to think about that. Especially seeing as it comes from someone who knows about it a hell of a lot more than I do, and is very nice and helpful and well-intentioned."

I blushed. Told her about some of my experiences. And what getting into recovery had done for me already.

"How long's it been for you?"

"Eight days," I said proudly. "Going on nine."

She was impressed. Said: "I don't think I've ever gone eight hours without a little taste." She asked what she should do. I told her to look in the Reno *Yellow Pages* under "alcoholism." Recovery, I said, is all around us, if only we make an effort to find it and really want to change.

"I do," she said. "I'm done."

I nodded, and that's all there was to say.

In Reno, before she disembarked with the kids, a real operation, I handed her my recovery book. She clutched my hand tightly and gratefully and thanked me for helping. And could she have one last cigarette? I lit her up and sent her on her way.

It was my first effort to carry the message of recovery to another. And I don't know whether or not it took. But inside, I felt wonderful. And for the rest of the trip, I knew, I'd stay sober, right to California.

53

BERNADETTE LIVED IN THE MISSION DISTRICT. I called from the bus depot. She told me to come right over. I cabbed it, grinning out the window at the sunny San Francisco landscape, heart bursting with expectation. Arrived at a quaint white house on a pretty side street. Danced up the steps, garbage bag in hand, knocked. An angry, lanky, balding, goateed man in a black tee and blue jeans answered.

"You're Alan," he said with extreme displeasure.

"Yeah," I said, heart sinking.

"She's in there."

He stepped aside. I entered. She was in a bedroom, the door to which she slammed shut behind me and threw her arms around my neck.

"Who's the guy in the bad mood?" I asked, smiling uneasily.

"That's Brick. I rent a room from him. And now he thinks he owns me."

"He seemed very bummed that I'm here."

"Oh, to hell with him," she snarled. "It's his place and he's a damn control freak." And standing close to the door, she screamed out: "FREAK!"

"But you guys aren't together, right?"

Well, not exactly. Yes and no. He was a drug dealer. Had agreed to lie to the INS on her behalf. He was her only source of income. She dealt too, on the side, small-change stuff, mainly pot, also a little coke. It paid the rent. But never mind about him. FUCK HIM! How long would I stay? How much money did I have?

"Fifty-four dollars after the cab," I said.

We made love with desperate intensity. I was not to leave the room: Brick would be out there, lurking. Let her deal with him.

Come morning, she left to see friends who might help us move somewhere. She couldn't stand a day more with Brick.

But by midmorning, annoyed with my confinement, I left the room and found Brick seated at the wooden dining room table, cleaning a large-caliber silver-plated revolver.

"Mind if I sit?"

"Help yourself."

Watched him clean the weapon with slow deliberate strokes. "Forty-four Magnum?"

"Yes." He glared and went back to cleaning. "I hear," he said, "that you served in the Israeli Army."

"That's right."

He nodded. Ran a rag dipped in gun oil through the chambers. "You know," he said, "I'm the reason you're out here."

"How do you figure?"

"She's afraid of me. So, she's got you now to stand between us when she moves out. That's what she wants, right? To move? You're her muscle."

"I've got no truck with you. If she wants to move, what business is it of yours? Last I heard, this is a free country."

I saw his rage spurt up into his throat and how hard he struggled to swallow it back down, face visibly trembling. "So, she does want to move?"

"Seems so."

"That's where she went just now? To look for a place for the two of you?"

"Something like that."

He nodded. Thrust a brush down the long gun barrel, twisted in and out. "I hear you're a writer."

"Of sorts."

"What sort?"

"Poet."

"Poet. There's no money in that."

"Evidently not."

"Isn't that a kind of financial suicide? To be a poet?"

"Hey, Brick?"

He looked over.

"Do I strike you as the kind of person who gives a shit about money?"

He nodded, more to himself than me, as if assessing whether or not to take offense at my confident tone. Apparently, decided to let it go. If there was to be a showdown, he'd pick the time and place.

"So," he said. "You are in my house. Acting brave. How do you think this makes me feel?"

"I don't know," I said. "I didn't come here looking for trouble. You can choose to take that any way you like."

He laid down the gun and barrel brush. "You're here, screwing her in my house."

"It's her room," I said. "I'm not aware there's more to it than that."

He glared at me. "Oh, there's more. Much more."

"And what would that be?"

"That would be that before you showed up, I was screwing her."

"You mean, recently."

"Before that trip she made to New York, where she met you and suddenly between us all bets are off."

"People have a right to place their chips where they choose."

"Listen to me. She's a little cunt. A rat bitch. A real whore. You've let yourself in for hell. She's not worth dying for. I know her three years and it's been pain, nothing but pain. She's incapable of stringing together two truthful sentences in a row. If it's red, she says it's black. If it's wet, she says it's dry. She's a chronic liar."

He picked up a dry rag and began furiously scrubbing the gun barrel. It was almost sexual. Giving the gun a barrel job.

I stood up. "I'm going to see me some San Francisco," I said.

"You know," he whined, "I really don't like you being here in my house, banging my woman!"

I let the door slam on his reedy voice.

We found quarters in a Page Street dump near the Lower Haight Projects, in a seven-room ramshackle Victorian boardinghouse for drug addicts, secretaries, drifters, musicians, and the criminally insane. It was overrun with cockroaches and smelled like rancid old grease. To keep us afloat, Bernadette dealt drugs while searching for legit work. She wanted out of the game. We were both going to write poetry, make the local scene together. But until I could find my feet, she'd support us.

I went to 12-step meetings and poetry readings in the cafés and music clubs. Several hours each day sat in the Café International writing poems. Bernadette bought me a Walkman with headphones and a tape of Bob Dylan's *Blood on the Tracks*, which I listened to all day long as a way to combat the machine-gun thoughts in my brain ordering me to drink. When it got too much, when Dylan's voice couldn't drown out a craving so bad that the only way to stop it was to climb to the roof of the tallest building in San Francisco and swan-dive into the picture postcard, I shut my eyes, pleaded with God, whom I did not yet quite believe in, to please keep me sober. And each time, without fail, the urge left.

But still, I felt alone. Spoke to the other recovering drunks I encountered in the meetings, who shared with me their experiences, were encouraging, for which I was grateful. Yet something was missing. I couldn't imagine what.

"Help me, nonexistent God," I prayed. "Help me, damn you, in your goddamned exalted nonexistence!"

One day, in a meeting, a strange-looking man popped up before me like a little jack-in-the box and announced: "Ho, Little Brother! I'm your sponsor!"

"You are?" I said, warily inspecting the bizarre figure who stood before me, not altogether sure that I hadn't hallucinated him. Black, five foot four, if that, dressed in what I later learned was a West African shaman's cap, no shirt, a thick ugly scar dividing him belly to chest, a cowhide vest, old suit pants held by a limp-tongued belt, and heel-worn color-scraped blackish thrift-shop dress shoes with frayed laces. On a nearby chair lay something that could only belong to the weirdo: a medicine drum with eagle feather tied to it.

"I'm Carl Little Crow. Yesssss, Little Brother! And you, my new sponsee, are a newcomer to recovery. A new clean-and-sober baby."

Others had advised me that I was going to meet some rather

strange birds in the meetings, but this was too much.

"And what is your name, Little Brother?"

I wondered whether to say or not. Yielded reluctantly. "Alan."

His eyes widened in delight. "Yesssss, oh, yessssss! Alan! I don't know many Alans. Wasn't Robin Hood's minstrel friend called Alan-a-dale? You must be a minstrel!"

A smile crept over my lips. Clearly, he was harmless. Had a face that crossed Mount Rushmore with a chipmunk. A strange broad-nosed face with velvet black eyes and a curious dignity that I couldn't quite place, had never seen before—a kind of inherent royal defiance.

Whatever else he was, he was no phony. I felt that. Odd, yes; another's puppet, no. If I couldn't figure out what exactly he was, still, he was like no one else I'd ever met.

"Let me take you to coffee," he offered.

"Sure," I said, having all of eight cents to my name.

We went to *All You Knead* on Haight Street. A lot of the recovering drunks and addicts seemed to hang out there. Settling into a booth, we each ordered the $1.99 breakfast of scrambled eggs, home fries, toast, and all the coffee you could drink.

He asked where I was from, how much sober time I had. When I told him less than a month, he was overjoyed. "You're the most important person in the twelve-step meetings!"

"Why is that?"

"Because, Little Brother, you are closer to the last drink than many others. We have a tendency to forget. You'll remind us."

"How long have you been sober?"

"Eighteen years."

He bristled with a fierce happy energy that I'd never seen before in anyone in my entire experience.

I asked what was involved in sponsorship.

"Gently, slowly, Little Brother, one day at a time, we walk through sobriety together."

My heart sank. "Does that mean I have to see you every day?"

He laughed! Clapped his hands in glee. Happy as a child. "Noooo!!!! Oh, no, Little Brother! Nooooo! We just meet once in a while, to work the steps. If you get into trouble, call me. Have a question? I'll answer if I can. Feel frightened? Call me. Think you'll drink? Before you do, let's talk. And between our get-togethers, go to meetings, as many as you can, and don't drink, one day at a time, no matter what! Isn't that simple?"

It wasn't as if I had better options. And anyway, I was in California, land of the weird. Carl Little Crow fit right in with my sense of the Left Coast. I'd never met or seen anyone like him. A cross between Cochise and Ratso Rizzo.

"Sure," I said. "Okay. You're my sponsor." As if I were doing him a big favor.

Breakfast came. We dug in. I learned that he was not from here. A back-alley gutter drunk from Chicago, he had come west with a recovery poet buddy named Fritz, otherwise known as Red Man. Had I met Red Man yet?

"No."

"You will, Little Brother! You will!"

Asked me to tell him exactly what was going on in my life currently. I explained about losing my little girl, Isadora, how I ended up heartbroken, lost, in Tompkins Square Park, not caring anymore if I died, and how Jim Brodey the poet told me to save myself, and next I knew, Philip led me to Jackie, who 12-stepped me into my first meeting. I told about Bernadette and Brick, and where I now lived and what I was doing. Described the voices that spoke to me as I walked around on Haight Street, the glaring lantern-eyed toothless and tattooed devils that followed me, and what horrors I felt sure lay in store for me. I told him that right at that moment there were operatives of several intelligence agencies undertaking surveillance of my every move. They were outside the restaurant—in all likelihood our conversation was being recorded.

I asked him what he thought of all that.

"Wonderful!" he exclaimed, clapping his hands. "And yet, you're staying sober anyway. Why would you, if you're so sure that you will meet a terrible end?"

I didn't know how to answer that.

"Part of you suspects that it's not true, even though it seems so real. That part of you is the part that wants to live. The Great Spirit is watching over you. You are a sobriety warrior, offering your chest to the bullets like a brave on his pony charging the horseback soldiers, indifferent to death. And the bullets cannot touch you! You are immune! In fact, the soldiers are phantoms."

"It feels damned real when it's happening."

"But do you think it's real?

"Part of me does."

He nearly jumped out of his seat. In other booths, people looked around. "HO!" he cried. "Then do you think that you are crazy?"

"Yeah! I do!"

"Good! Wonderful! Because, Little Brother, you ARE crazy! And so what choice do you have but to enjoy it! Stop fighting how crazy you are! All your suffering comes from trying to pretend that you are sane."

I knew he was right. I began to laugh from deep down.

"So, tell me, Carl Little Crow. Let's say you're right. It's all delusions. Then what is real?"

"Sobriety is real. And the breath. The rest is mental, conjectural sleight of hand. God is in the breath. The Great Reality is deep within. And the way in is through the breath. You breathe involuntarily, despite yourself. It breathes you, without your permission. It doesn't need your cooperation. You are helpless not to breathe. If breath is cut off, you will do all you can to find air. Breath is the source of your life. Breath is the gateway to God."

Intellectually, I grasped what he meant, but viscerally had no real idea what he was talking about. Besides, was too worried about that strange, sinister-looking couple in an adjoining booth eyeballing me hungrily, no doubt thinking of the awful tortures they would subject me to once they had me in their clutches.

I told Carl about them. He turned, saw them, went over and chatted. When he returned he told me that they were not only good friends but also long-timers in recovery.

I looked pleadingly at him. All my defenses down. "Okay, so, you can see. I do need help, man. I think I'm insane. The fear is bad. It's like it fills the air, all around, in everything, a world of fear. I'm crazy. Really crazy." Tears filled my eyes. To think of me, in San Francisco, alone, confessing my madness to this Carl Little Crow, a self-described "Afro-Native American practitioner of shamanistic healing ways," whatever the hell that was. Less than a dime in my pocket, a thirty-seven-and-a-half-year-old man with a month sober. How had I gotten here?

But it's better than the park, the little voice inside reminded me, my Angel. *It's better than hangover, hunger, and hopelessness. Drinking got you here. But now, you have hope.*

"Do you think there's hope for me, Carl?"

His hands shot up, palms out, facing me. "HO! Little Brother! Do you see these hands?"

"Yes."

"Are they steady?"

"Yes."

"Look at my eyes."

"So?"

"Are they clear?"

"Yes."

"Look into my heart."

"How?"

"Close your eyes."

I did.

"What do you see?"

"Chaos."

But then something else appeared. A sort of calm, gentle, rhythmic breathing. "Is that me or you?" I said, a bit spooked.

"There's no difference," he said. "We are all one heart, one mind, one breath, brothers and sisters, members of the same family, the Society of the Last Chance."

I opened my eyes and felt calmer.

"Little Brother. Come, walk with me."

We strolled down Haight Street, past all the shops. Carl fit right in with the other weirdos out in the midmorning sun on the sidewalk, strumming guitars or reading tarot or just panhandling. As we walked, Carl glanced down at my shoes. "Slow your feet, Little Brother. Slow down. When we drink we are running from consciousness, from feelings, from the sight of the world. But now, we take it in. We savor it. We walk slow, observing our breath, letting our thoughts think themselves, without trying to interfere or control them. Slow your feet and breathe the perfume of clean-and-sober air."

As he slowed, so did I, and as we walked he beat a slow tattoo on the medicine drum, as if announcing our clean-and-sober passage to passersby, who smiled, thinking us holy fools, a piece of local color, and the street folk grinned and nodded. Some called out to Carl, knew him. We passed a liquor store, and it was as though we moved under the murderous gaze of a gigantic panting tiger hungry for our flesh—and yet, nothing happened. We paused before a tree, one of those rotting on Haight Street, with shriveled sooty leaves and an emaciated trunk scarred with slogans, names, dates, crudely etched with pocket knives. Around Carl's feet, small black birds with rainbow glints of bluish light in their coat feathers hopped by his ankles, as he leaned an ear close to the tree trunk and said to me: "Shhhhhh! It's trying to tell us something."

"Carl, what are you doing?"

"Listening, Little Brother."

"To what?"

"To the tree."

"Oh, yeah? And what's Mister Tree saying?"

"It says to tell you, Little Brother: 'Don't drink!' "

54

CARL WOULD COME TO MY ROOM WHEN
Bernadette was gone and sit on the floor cross-legged, listening to
whatever I had to say. When he left, there'd be a ten-dollar bill on
the table. He came by once with sage and "cleansed" the room of
"bad spirits"—lit the sage and waved the thick smudge stick over
each corner of the room with solemn incantations as I stood by with
arms crossed and a condescending smile.

He had me sit out with him on the little back porch watching
clouds pass as my brain screamed with boredom and dread, racing
at light speed, wondering whether he was insane, or I, or both of
us, and what on earth did it mean in the big scheme of things that I
was seated on rusty metal folding chairs with a bizarro named Little
Crow who had me occupied with watching clouds float over San
Francisco?

All this wasn't in the existential game book of my strategy for
life. He came by once with a half-gallon of Peach Melba ice cream,
asked if I had two large spoons, which I produced. Carl jumped up

and down like a kid at a birthday party as I pried off the lid and dug out my first spoonful. "Yesssssss!" he crooned gleefully. "Thank you, Great Spirit! Little Brother and I having a clean-and-sober ice cream party on Wednesday afternoon, and there's nothing else we have to do right now! AYE!-AYE! HO!-HO! HEE!-HEE! HEE!-HEE!"

We ate ourselves into a sugar coma, conversation fading to a battery-dying tape-recorder drawl, and when he said goodbye, I collapsed into bed and slept until the next day. That was how I got in yet another twenty-four hours clean and sober.

He liked to walk around San Francisco with me, hitting 12-step meetings where he shared with the fiery cant of an Elmer Gantry crossed with a Dakota war chief. We'd go to visit specific trees in Golden Gate Park that he claimed friendship with, and he stood unashamedly talking aloud to them as though visiting regal monarchs. The granddaddy of them all was an immense and nameless bark monument which he called, simply, "Grandfather," and from the moment we saw it at a distance his feet slowed and he began to beat his medicine drum in slow parade step, me trailing behind, mortified, pretending not to know him and watching as tourists and parkgoers, especially children, paused to observe him with smiles ranging from admiring to ridiculing. Then, at a certain remove, he stopped, laid down his drum, and raising hands, palms out, shouted at the tree: "HO! Grandfather! How are you today?" And listened respectfully as I stood there, looking around, not hearing anything.

"HO, Grandfather!" Carl Little Crow called again. "Here is little Brother, my friend. He is a warrior initiate in matters of the spirit. He is learning. We are walking together on the path as we cast off the great shadow of alcoholism from our hearts. Come, Little Brother! Say hello to Grandfather!"

He waved me forward as a group of Japanese tourists with cameras hung around their necks gathered and began to snap shots. I made a shrugging approach to the tree, tinged with skepticism and insolence.

"Little Brother," whispered Little Crow. "Give Grandfather a loving hug! Go ahead! He's so excited to meet you! He likes hugs!"

"Look, uh, Carl," I said. "You know, I'm really glad you're helping me, but, uh, you know, is this really necessary?"

"Yessssssss, Little Brother! Go on! He's waiting!"

Horrified, I stepped up to the tree, glanced over my shoulder as the tourists hoisted their cameras and Carl beat a slow tom-tom on the drum. Got my arms around the trunk as best I could and hugged Grandfather.

And the damndest thing happened. I felt as though something warm and alive from the tree passed into me. The bark felt flesh-like, kindly, and I smelled its wood odor and leaves with the warm sun on my hair as a breeze stroked my cheek, and it felt good, nurturing. Something inside me longed for a grandfather, which I'd never really had, and I forgot all about the tourists, who lost interest, dispersed. I remained with eyes closed, cheek pressed to the tree as Little Crow beat the drum softly in my thoughts, like the pulse of the world, and when I let go the bark turned hard, the breeze fell, a cloud passed before the sun, and my hand grew cold. I stood in shadow, experienced a pang of separation, as though I had let go of the hand of my real grandfather, who in actuality had died when I was very young, and the other before I was ever born.

55

ONE DAY, I AWOKE CLUTCHING AT MY THROAT. A
wolf burrowed bared teeth into my Adam's apple, big paws pinning
down my chest, trying to sink long incisors into my jugular. I
thrashed, hands at my windpipe, shouting for help.

"What's wrong?" Bernadette leaned over my face, kissing me.
"Dearie! You're having a nightmare."

"I'm awake!" I gasped. "I just can't seem to swallow!"

Sat up with a start, peered around the room, windpipe lax,
esophagus paralyzed. "Can't swallow," I gasped, pointing at my
throat with a look of anguish.

Bernadette grinned uneasily. "Huh? Of course you can."

"No," I muttered, "help me!"

"Honey, just relax. Try to breathe!"

What in God's name was she talking about? How do you relax
when choking to death? Ran to the bathroom, slammed the door
shut, fell to my knees, laid my cheek on the toilet seat lid, and
prayed there, helpless as a child.

"Please, God. I'm choking. Help me." And with that, heaved a great sigh and gulped down spittle, air. My lungs began to work.

It happened again in a movie theater. Bernadette had given me enough scratch to go see three films at the Strand Theatre. I bought a big sack of dollar burgers from Carl's Jr., smuggled them in, settled down, and began happily watching the second film, *Death Wish*. In the climactic scene where Charles Bronson is cornered by police, my ability to swallow went kaput, just like that. Hand at throat, heart pounding, I looked around in wild-eyed terror for someone to help among the hoboes, derelicts, addicts, mentally ill, homeless, prostitutes, criminals, and young hipster film buffs, but no one looked as if they could care less or would even know how to assist. I stood up, hands at throat, tried to change posture, but the dark flashing images, the loud cheap speakers, remote and alienating, just increased my panic. I wanted to scream "Help! I've forgotten how to swallow! I'm dying!" but couldn't speak.

I left the theater and hurried down Market Street, rushing past hustlers flashing stolen jewelry, evil-looking street buccaneers with gold teeth and derisive eyes, and it came to me that these were an advanced guard of infiltrating satanic henchmen out to get me. I shifted into evasion mode, weaving and bobbing through a kaleidoscope of threats from which there was no rest, reversing course, then pivoting to the opposite direction, attempting to elude and surprise my pursuers with illogical and spontaneous zigs and zags, like some cosmic broken-field kickoff return performed in a field of flaming asteroids. Then, head ducked, I marched up Market Street to Church, a friendly little street unlikely to host killers. But still my pursuers were closing fast, and, panic-stricken, I couldn't decide whether to duck into Aardvark Bookstore or pretend to go for a leisurely bite in Azteca Taqueria.

Hunger won out. Burrito it was. Ducked in there, ordered a

Chicken Super Burrito. And the moment I did so recognized my fatal error. At the counter, the big-bellied man in bean-stained apron fixed me with his pockmarked face and listless gaze. What was he looking at? I noted an open office door and a video monitor of some kind. Quickly scanned the ceiling: security camera. They had me on tape! Wouldn't even need to send operatives now: knew exactly what I looked like, my every mannerism, where to find me, even— would calculate that it must be someplace approximate to here.

GET OUT NOW! screamed my panicking brain. But if I did, I'd tip my hand, force them prematurely to attempt my abduction and slaughter. The counter worker's lips moved, forming words. Terror froze me. What was he saying? I leaned close.

"Refried or whole beans?" he asked.

An obvious trick. The wrong answer would surely seal my fate. Refried or whole? How to answer? It was agonizing. I realized: there wasn't any right answer. Either way, I was doomed. The trap lay in stalling while trying to decide. *GET OUT,* screamed my brain, and with a pounding heart and exploding head I turned and bolted out, ran down the sidewalk. Glancing back, I tripped and went sprawling headfirst across the pavement, where I lay, wind knocked out, gasping for breath. "Where are you, Carl Little Crow?" I cried out, tears welling in my eyes. I felt so abandoned and ashamed. "Help me, please!"

Suddenly, I heard the voice of Carl Little Crow advising me to pray to whatever God was mine, and found myself calling upon YHWH, ancient God of the Jews, right there on Church Street in San Francisco. I felt a flow of warm solace, and a hand lifted me to my feet. I hurried to get to a 12-step meeting, knew there was one starting soon in the Haight and that there, waiting for me, would be cookies, coffee, my alcoholic brothers and sisters who would understand the nightmare that I had just gone through.

56

WHEN I WAS TWO MONTHS SOBER, IRAQ INVADED
Kuwait and, in turn, America invaded Iraq. Iraq responded by
shooting missiles into Israel's largest city, Tel Aviv, where my
daughter, Isadora, and her mother were holed up in a hotel room
lined with plastic against chemical attack, my daughter's screaming
face strapped into a gas mask.

I called Esther, who held the telephone up to the window so that
I would hear the air raid sirens and Iraqi Scuds. Then she held it
close to Isadora so that I could hear her crying protests as she struggled to wrestle the gas mask off. Three-year-olds and gas masks
don't make a good fit.

"That's your daugh-ter!" Esther raged scornfully. "The one that
you abandoned. She's in a gas mask, under missile attack, while you
muck around playing the poet in San Francisco!" And slammed
down the phone.

Frantic, I called Carl, who said: "Little Brother, you must now
pray to the Great Father, your God, Yahweh, and I will pray to the

Great Spirit of the Dakotas. Pray for a miracle! But don't drink, Little Brother. You're powerless over Bush, Saddam Hussein, and Scud missiles. Killing yourself with alcohol will not help Isadora. And no matter what that woman, your ex-wife, said, forget it. You're an alcoholic with a life-threatening disease, getting sober, taking care of yourself, learning how to live without a drink one day at a time. You will see, Little Brother: someday that will help your daughter more than anything else you can do."

But frantic, I called the Israeli consulate to see if Israeli Army veterans were needed. I'll go right now, I offered. My daughter...I broke down, wept, nerves shot. The Israeli at the other end listened with kind patience and said: "Do not worry, Mr. Kaufman. Your daughter will be fine."

"I hope so," I sniffled. "I do hope so!"

But when I hung up, the thought of anything happening to Isadora was unbearable. Knew that she was a remarkable child destined to become a remarkable woman—that she must live! That she, no less than I, was the reason my mother had struggled to survive the Holocaust, and was not only the future, but the truest incarnation and redemption of my mother's lost and vanquished youth—a youth destroyed by five years of hunger, hiding, death-fear, during the interminable Nazi occupation of Europe and systematic slaughter of the Jews. Isadora was the little daughter my mother had lost at term, who turned her from a melancholic but essentially sweet and good-natured young woman into a mentally ill pill addict given to explosive violence, as if venting on me not only her own thwarted aspirations but frustration at the trap of her marriage to an illiterate and largely indifferent gambling addict. The bruises and welts that covered my arms, neck, and back throughout my youth told the true story of her life—an Aramaic narrative of wounds that others did not want to read or believe. Isadora was a sweet, sane, beautiful child—a hopeful light born out of darkness, a living candle, and I would gladly lay down my newly sober body and life to save her if I could.

But I couldn't. Not only was I not wanted or needed in Israel, but without a drink to steady me I was too mentally ill even to apply for welfare assistance. A few times I'd gone down to the welfare office at 1440 Harrison, where lines of homeless kept melting through the doors without anyone seeming to emerge, and I developed a paranoid conviction that the poor were being euthanized in there. Here I was, too crazy even to apply for the sort of assistance that the mentally ill are eligible for. And to my name I had, at the time of Iraq's missile attack on Israel, exactly $3.24 and a pack of cigarettes.

Depressed, I lay on my bed, closed my eyes, and prayed for death to simply come finish me off. Was so helpless. Useless. Please, God, I prayed: help Isadora. And the remotest whisper of the voice of my Angel said: *When your mother was a child, there was no safe haven on earth for a Jew, and she was hunted like an animal with no one to care for her or defend her. Millions of her fellow Jews were gassed, burned, shot, and the world said nothing, did nothing. Then there was the state of Israel. And then your mother had you. You became Israeli, served as a soldier in Israel's defense, and fathered Isadora, who is now Israeli too. And though Saddam and his army want to chemically gas the Jews of Israel, Isadora is in her own country now, surrounded and defended by a Jewish army, and against gas she has a mask to wear in a plastic-sealed room—which is by no means a good thing, but compared to what your mother had a great improvement—and Isadora will be fine.*

So, reassured, I went mercifully to sleep. Later, in accounts of this episode in Israel's history, it became known as a kind of modern miracle that so few Jews were killed by Saddam's rockets. They were intercepted by both the Israeli Air Force and American patriot missiles; and any that somehow landed successfully failed, for the most part, to take Jewish life.

It was a smaller, lesser sidebar miracle, but one nonetheless, that in distant San Francisco an alcoholic Israeli-American Jew, terrified for his daughter's life, yet did not take a drink and reposed, instead, in the arms of his 12-step program and in a God that he still only vaguely sensed the presence and meaning of.

57

CARL LITTLE CROW CALLED ME ONE DAY GASPING
for breath, barely able to speak. "Little Brother," he gasped, "I'm
having a heart attack. Must go to the hospital. I don't want an
ambulance. Need your help to get there. Sorry for the trouble."

"I'll be right there, Carl!"

I called Suzy, a friend from the 12-step meetings, who rushed
over with her car, picked me up, and drove us at top speed to his
apartment. Carl was stretched on the floor clad only in white briefs,
unable to move, barely conscious. The apartment unfurnished, dirty.
Food-encrusted plates and butt-heaped ashtrays lay about. There was
no television, no books, no pictures on the hand-smudged walls.
Clothes were piled on the floor. I stood there stunned. "Carl," I
whispered. "Oh, my God!"

He was my chief link to recovery, my lifeline, the first human
being in the entire world for whom I'd felt unequivocal trust.

"We need to call an ambulance," said Suzy.

"No," Carl whispered.

"No? But you need to get to a hospital now!"

"You take me," he whispered.

"Alan, you'll have to help me dress him."

We did, first his pants, then shirt—the first time I'd ever seen him in one—then the shoes. We found his wallet and keys and I carried him in my arms out the door and downstairs to Suzy's car, where we laid him out as best we could in the backseat and drove at breakneck speed to San Francisco General Hospital. Suzy apologized and said she was expected back home. I remained at Carl's side, unable to let go, as he lay on the gurney. A doctor said he would be taken to emergency surgery. Terrified, wondering what would become of my sobriety without him, I held on to his hospital gown, refusing to release him, even when they began to wheel him to surgery. Carl whispered hoarsely, "Little Brother, you must let go. I can't help you now. These nice people will care for me. Go, Little Brother. Don't drink! Go to a meeting! I love you."

"I love you, Carl," I said, tears filling my eyes.

Shocked, I stumbled from the hospital, wandered through Mission streets where bars called out to me and liquor stores beckoned. Gutter drunks and junkies leered with amused smiles, as though the demons possessing them—the kind that had once inhabited me—knew by what a fragile thread my recovery now hung.

I was too numb to understand where I was going, and yet somehow my feet took me to a 12-step meeting on Valencia Street. I sat at the large table in the center of the room, head buried in my arms. "Carl, what will I do now? Oh, God, please, don't let Carl die. He's the only one who understands me. The kindest, best person in the world, my sobriety brother. Please, O Lord, I need him to stay sober or I will die."

I was praying, face hidden, when there came loud applause and I felt hands slapping my shoulders and back.

When I lifted my head, someone growled: "Congratulations!"

"Uh—what for?"

"You've just been elected to run our meeting for a term of six months!"

"But I can't! I'm brand-new! I've only got two months sober."

"Well, that's two months more than anyone else in this room got! Congratulations!"

During one of my first meetings as the new secretary, a gutter drunk came in bearing a forty-ounce beer bottle and sat in back, drinking and making a racket. A muscle-bound biker and amateur boxer named Monk stood up, accompanied by two sober brawler types, and approached the wet drunk, snatched the bottle from his fist, dragged him screaming and protesting onto the sidewalk, and poured the bottle into the gutter. The trio then proceeded to beat the living hell out of him, shouting that if he ever dared bring booze into a meeting again they'd break him in two.

Appalled, I ran out and pushed them off the drunk, who ran for his life, hurling insults over his shoulder as he went.

When we were all back in our seats, I gravely surveyed the room and, bringing to bear the accumulated gravitas and wisdom of my full two months of sobriety, said: "That sort of behavior is unacceptable. Twelve-step recovery is supposed to be about us loving one another, helping each other. I want to pass a motion here and now that no such scene ever again occurs in this meeting. All in favor raise your hand."

"But wait!" said a fellow named Jack. "First there's gotta be discussion. We're democratic."

"All right, then. Who has got something to say?" Skeptically, I looked around.

"I do!" spoke up an eighty-nine-year-old woman with snow-white hair named Irene. "I think that Monk and the boys did great. It was real loving. We're recovering drunks, hanging on for our lives. Bringing booze into our meeting is like pointing a gun right in our face and pulling the trigger. This is supposed to be a safe place for us to come."

The room exploded in thunderous applause.

"Now, wait a minute—"

"I got another motion!" said Irene. "I say let's make Monk our official bouncer and give him our okay to bust any alkie's ass but good who tries to put us all at risk by bringing booze into this here meeting! All in favor?"

Every hand in the room shot up with cries of "AYE!"

"All opposed?"

Not a one.

"Motion passes," Irene declared. "Monk, honey, congrats! C'mere and give Ireney a big kiss."

Monk lumbered over and planted a wet one on Irene's cheek. "That's my boy," she said, smiling coquettishly, patting his face with her dainty hand.

By then the meeting had ended. We all said the Serenity Prayer and I sat at my desk, watching, dejected, as the room emptied out. Someone came up to me and said, grinning: "Every meeting makes its own rules. There are no el presidentes in twelve-step recovery. We're all just a bunch of drunks helping each other stay sober one day at a time."

"But a bouncer?"

"Whatever works," he said with a smile.

BOOK SEVEN

58

AT FOUR MONTHS SOBER IT WAS NICE TO LIVE OFF Haight Street, apartment-managing seven boardinghouse rooms in a flophouse Victorian. I got the job just after Carl's release from the hospital. He was too weak to sponsor me, but I still called him in emergencies, which were frequent. When Bernadette decided that I was too insane to cohabit with—which I was—and bailed, leaving me penniless, foodless, cigaretteless, and furnitureless with the rent and telephone bills due, I called Carl.

Still quite weak, he spoke barely in a whisper. "Yes, Little Brother? What's going on with you?"

"I thought you said that if I stayed sober and worked my program, my Higher Power would take care of all the rest, especially for the first year. Well, Bernadette has split, I'm flat broke, rent's due, telephone about to be cut off. I got no food and I'm sleeping on a bare mattress on the floor. Is this what I got clean and sober for? To go homeless? I mean, how in hell is some hocus-pocus Higher Power going to get my goddamned rent paid? Can you tell me that?"

"Little Brother, what did I tell you to do when problems occur?"

My mind raced. Couldn't think of what it could be. "I don't remember!" I snapped. And then I did. "Oh, yeah. You said when it gets hard, go to a meeting and things will get better."

"That's right."

"But how will going to a meeting help with this?"

"Little Brother, all we ask in recovery is that you keep an open mind and try what we suggest. So, here's my suggestion: go to a meeting and see whether or not things get better."

"But I don't—"

"Just try, Little Brother. Okay? Let me know what happens."

I hung up, cursing Carl under my breath. Damned brainwashed 12-step zombie! But I rose from the mattress, begrudgingly slipped on my heel-worn Durango boots, and headed out the door, down Page Street, to a 12-step meeting in a community center by Golden Gate Park.

About halfway through the meeting, I found myself grinning. Three-quarters through, and I was laughing to split my sides. By meeting's end, I was positively ecstatic. For one hour I hadn't thought about my trouble, except to talk about it in the meeting and get lots of hugs and well-wishing, plus a few offers of piecework for a little pickup cash, which I declined.

"No need," I said, smiling. "My Higher Power's got it!" And really believed that as I tripped down Page Street, smiling from ear to ear like a holy happy fool. So what if I go homeless tomorrow, I conjectured. So long as I'm clean and sober today, there's a ball game. You never know: things just might improve.

I found a barely smoked three-quarter-length cigarette on the pavement, and gratefully lifting it to the sky said aloud: "Thank you, God!" and put it in my pocket for later. At home, stretched out on the mattress, lit up my found butt and just whiled the time away, blowing smoke rings and not worrying about much.

There was a knock on the door. "C'mon in!" I called cheerfully.

It was Mark, the apartment manager. "Mind if I have a word, Alan?"

"Not at all," I said, smiling, knowing he was here to throw me out. I'd make it easy on him. "Come on in, bub. Sorry there's no place to sit. She took it all."

He nodded.

"What can I do you for, Mark?"

"Well," said Mark, "you see, I'm getting married."

"Oh!" I exclaimed. "Why, that's damned wonderful! Congratulations!"

"Hey, thanks." He smiled. "And I, well, this job, apartment manager, I can't keep it now. And, well, I know that you're kind of strapped. And I just wondered if, maybe, well, Alan, would you consider taking over as manager here? I know this is short notice. It's free rent plus a monthly stipend to cover incidentals, food and such." To which he added: "I mean, you're the sanest guy in this place."

Which goes far to show just what sort of place it was.

I lay there, nonplussed, blew a smoke ring, and said: "Yeah, sure. Why not?"

"Oh, thank you! Thank you! That gets me off the hook. I gotta leave right away. You'll take over tomorrow. Is that okay? Here's the keys. I've left instructions on the kitchen table."

"I got your back, bro. Have a great honeymoon!"

When he left, I called Carl, half out of my mind. "You won't believe what just happened! It's a fugging miracle!" I shouted.

"But Little Brother. Why so surprised? Your Higher Power is always watching out for you."

★ ★ ★

I had the back room to myself, with a little porch overlooking a patchwork of bedraggled and abandoned backyards with big rusting chunks of junk metal recumbent in the sun. Soot-covered hole-punctured deteriorated bedsheets that had been left out for years hung uncollected on rotting clotheslines, and across the way was a row of houses fronting on the Webster Street Projects. Every so often as I sat out there with eyes shut, dragging on a cigarette, the warm sun on my face, I heard piercing shrieks: someone being tortured by the drug gang that ruled over this hood.

These were "bitch snitches" or two-timing street soldiers who had gone somehow awry. Recall one who, though horribly hurt, seemed somehow, more than others, to retain a semblance of control through his ordeal. His pleas formed a kind of melodic refrain: "DON'T...DO...THAT!" endlessly repeated, before his ampli-fying howls became flat-out animal screams.

Otherwise, it was pleasant back there. Orange-breasted robins scavenged about in the trash and an occasional red-crested wood-pecker beat out mysterious Morse on the old rotting cruciform tele-phone poles that ran along the alleys.

In my room was a mattress covered by a sheet and a neatly folded blanket and pillow. On a small wooden table lay a marbled compo-sition notebook and two blue-ink Bic pens—the same writing tools that I had first used as a schoolboy. In them I wrote three poems per week to read at Café Babar on Thursday nights and on Sunday nights at Paradise Lounge—the major open mikes in town.

On the windowsill were sunglasses, a few recovery books, and a schedule for 12-step meetings. On the floor, a small hippie shoulder bag I'd fished from the Tuesday morning trash collection, my main wardrobe source. I still wore the same pale-blue collarless India shirt and blue jeans, and my indestructible Durangos still had nails stabbing my heels as I walked, drawing blood—a sensation I actually relished, as some sort of penitent self-chastisement.

I was a heavy smoker and could afford to buy my own, but old habits die hard and I still mainly picked up my tobacco quota off the streets, where butts were plentiful. As I walked down Haight Street, nails stabbing my heels and Dylan on the earphones, my eyes scanned the sidewalk for butts, which I would pounce on and keep stashed in a plastic ziplock in my shoulder bag.

I didn't even own a jacket, though I badly needed one for the chameleon San Francisco weather. Not only could it change instantly from cold to tropical, but this is one of the few cities in the world, I ventured, that has multiple seasons simultaneously: if it's springlike in the Lower Haight, it can be wintry in the Sunset but tropically warm in the Mission, even as it's autumnal downtown. Couldn't begin to guess what season might prevail up on windy Twin Peaks, where a gigantic satanic-looking communications tower glared down with one red blinking Cyclopean eye burning jewellike in the center of its forehead.

I kept a lightweight fishing knife tucked in my boot, just in case, and my fear du jour revolved from day to day, like the colors in a child's prismatic kaleidoscope. On a given day, as I kicked down Haight Street en route to a meeting, a tattooed and toothless old street wino might glance at me with maniacal glee that triggered me to think he was a plant, a ploy, intentionally signaling the presence of innumerable agents in the vicinity—a revelation meant to throw me off my game, spark a panicked response that would precipitate wrong decisions.

In 12-step meetings I found reprieve from this sense of constant threat, could sit for an hour or so and relax, blend into the room of anonymous faces whose names, for the most part, I didn't know.

Between the long stretches of panic were lucid intervals when I realized that I was completely insane. This, in turn, both terrified and depressed me: a development I was quick to report to my new sponsor, Eugene.

"I think I may be completely off my rocker. I don't know what to do! Oh, God! What if I really am insane? And don't even know it!"

"Well," said Eugene, "let me put your mind at ease on that particular point once and for all. You are completely insane. In fact, I've never met anyone loonier. So you might as well stop fighting it. Just give up, since you're powerless over it."

This is the same sponsor who said, when we began working together on the 12 steps: "Just one thing. I want you to know that it's not in my power to get you sober, or for that matter in the power of anyone in a twelve-step program."

"Well, what can keep me sober, then?"

He looked at me hard. "Only God can keep you sober."

I gaped back at him, outraged. "God! You gotta be kidding! I can't bring myself to really believe in that crap! If that's what it takes, then I'm fucked!"

"That's right," he said. "That's what I've been trying to tell you. You're fucked."

I often lunched in the soup kitchens, too mentally disheveled to contemplate enrolling in the General Assistance welfare program—a step that Eugene strongly advised me to take, as a way to augment my small income.

"It wouldn't hurt you to eat regular meals," he said. "What do you eat? One or two meals a day?"

I shrugged. "Yeah. Like that."

"Not enough. You're a big guy. What are you? Six two? Two ten?"

"That's right."

"You need food. Protein. Vegetables. Fruit. What did you eat this morning for breakfast?"

Was ashamed to say. Breakfast usually consisted of whatever kinds of cookies were offered up at my regular 12-step meetings, plus endless cups of coffee spiked with big helpings of white granulated sugar. But that morning someone had brought to the meeting two cartons of green-frosted Teenage Mutant Ninja Custard Pies. Knowing that rigorous honesty at all times was a mandatory precondition of remaining sober, I said, embarrassed: "Well, this morning someone brought a couple of boxes of Teenage Mutant Ninja Custard Pies and I had me a couple."

I couldn't look him in the eyes as I said this.

"Uh-huh," he said, voice flatlined in that tone I'd come to recognize when he was struggling especially hard to remain neutral and nonjudgmental in the face of some of my just plain outright imbecilities. "Uh-huh. And how many of these Ninja pies did you have?"

I winced. "Three." And before he could respond, corrected: "Four."

"Uh-huh. And how much sugar you figure might be in one of these Turtle Pies?"

I pursed my lips thoughtfully. "You mean on average?"

"Yes. Your best guesstimate."

"Well, a lot."

"Uh-huh. And you also like to put a lot of sugar in your coffee, right?"

Grimly, I nodded.

"Well, no wonder you're nuts. You're crazy enough without all that. But the way you eat sugar, you're ramping it up into full-blown psychosis."

"Oh," I said.

The rate and even the severity of my delusions decreased with improved diet, but not enough yet to permit me to sign up for General Assistance and food stamps. For now, that must wait. I felt too frail. Ate on the wing and lived off the cuff, smoking sidewalk butts and crisscrossing San Francisco on foot, notebook along, going from one recovery meeting to the next, sitting on park benches and building stoops, or on the steps of friendly-looking Victorians, writing poems to read at the open mikes—which Eugene had more or less ordered me to do.

Carl Little Crow had been the first to say that he thought, given my history, that I had no choice but to become a poet or else return to drinking. To this Eugene added an additional proviso. "There's no question that you want to be a writer, but you've betrayed your gift by not really making a serious try. You can never do that again. Or, as your Carl indicated, you're sure to drink."

"But I'm such a loser," I said. "I've got no books to my name except for that out-of-print anthology. I'm thirty-seven years old and feel like it's too late for me."

"You're right," he said. "For the man you were, it's too late. But it's not too late for the man you are becoming, as far as God is concerned. If you stay sober and write with discipline, someday you'll have a shelf or two of books printed with your name."

"You think?" I said hopefully.

"Yes," he said firmly. "I do."

My heart soared. "Okay," I said excitedly. "What do I do?"

"Go to meetings and write," he said.

"Write what?"

"Poems."

"But I really want to be a prose writer."

"Well, that's fine. But right now you've got the attention span of a flea. Write poems. They're short and you can probably do it fast. Bring me three a week."

The next week, I showed him three poems. He barely glanced at them. "That's fine. Put them in a folder and next week bring me three more."

"But aren't you going to read them?" I asked, offended at such scant attention paid.

"What for?" said the Philistine. "I hate poetry. Write three more. Bring them next week."

Months later, I had several poems that I felt quite proud of and that were well received at the open mikes. Jack Hirschman, a well-known poet then in his late fifties, came up to me after I'd read two of them one Sunday afternoon in North Beach, leaned his big walrus mustache close to my face, and said, "You write one hell of a poem. I haven't seen you before. Who are you?"

I told him that I was newly arrived from New York. Recognizing something in his accent, asked: "Are you by any chance from the Bronx?"

"Why, yes, I am, originally. For sure." We exchanged Bronx credentials and it turned out that we had both attended DeWitt Clinton High School, though twenty years apart.

"Look," he said. "You ever publish a book, let me know."

"Would you write an intro for it?"

"If they're as good as those two poems you read today, it will be my pleasure."

At this same reading, David Lerner, co-ringleader of the group of underground poets who congregated at Café Babar and called themselves the Babarians, stood next to me, his immense shaggy buffalo body quivering with nervous intellect as he puffed existentially from a cigarette held in a clenched fist—and said in his humorous, deep-throated, velvety voice: "Zeitgeist Press might consider doing a book of those. Are there more?"

"I've got twelve that I respect."

"All that good?"

I nodded.

"The two you read need editing."

"Why?"

"Show me one."

I showed him a poem titled "On Reading Whitman's 'Song of Myself' at One O'clock in the Morning." Lerner patted the pocket of his loud tropical shirt, fumbled out a pencil stub, and, peering at the poem with a look of frenzied concentration, snorting and huffing like a giant beast, went through it in about three minutes, drawing neat lines through words as he went and making professional proofreading symbols. He handed it back. I read it over, twice. It was perfect.

"That's amazing!" I said. "I didn't think it could be improved."

"Everything can be improved. I just cut repetitious statements, changed polysyllabic words to monosyllabic ones where possible, and inserted stanza breaks to give the eye some rest. Simple stuff. And you see what I did here? You use the word *democratic* twice in the same stanza. That's called an 'echo.' Unless you have good reason to repeat words for effect, like Hemingway or Gertrude Stein, don't."

"Those are rules of poetics?"

"We don't do 'poetics' at Café Babar," he sneered. "Those are rules that journalists like Jimmy Breslin and Hunter Thompson might use on tabloid prose. So, why not on poetry?"

59

AMERICAN CRUISER CAME OUT UNDER THE
Zeitgeist imprint, as a slender volume with an introduction by
Jack Hirschman. Two hundred were printed, and I sold them at
three bucks apiece in the cafés around San Francisco. The additional income from books and my interface with pretty women at
café tables emboldened me to approach my sponsor one day and
announce: "I'm ready for a relationship."

He looked at me. "With what?"

"A woman!"

"You mean an actual animate one? No, I don't think that's such
a good idea. You're not ready."

"But I'm lonely," I said. "You say that my loneliness is alcoholism
and that the only real relief is to help other drunks, which I try to
do, and sure, it helps, but I have a simple human need to get laid."

"Do you want to get laid or have a relationship? They're not the
same."

I thought. "Well, to be truthful, yeah, I want a relationship. You know. Be with the same woman over days and weeks. Something steady. Love."

His squinty eyes got all flinty. "You haven't yet learned what real love is. Your idea of it is sick. You know what they say about love in early sobriety. It's like putting Miracle-Gro on your character defects. You'll be in bad pain in no time. And that'll get you drunk. I suggest that you wait until you've got at least a year sober."

"I'm desperate."

He studied me. "So, what I'm hearing is that you want to be in a relationship with something that's not your own mind."

A sweet little light of profound relief blossomed in my chest. "That's right." I smiled.

"Well, that's different. Hell, why, that even falls under the category of sane. You're having a healthy urge to be in communion with something other than your own mind. Congratulations!"

Shyly, I said: "Thanks."

"It's just a question of what is small enough, primitive enough, that you could safely have a relationship with it, because you are a selfish, delusional, paranoid, clean-and-sober horse thief who doesn't care about anything or anyone but himself."

"That's it exactly," I said.

"Well, I'd start you out with some tiny organism like an amoeba or protozoan and say start with that. They're kind of self-sustaining and self-replicating, so they wouldn't need you, which is perfect for where you are. But without the right equipment, the high-powered microscopes and expensive petri dishes and whatnot necessary to commune with a pet amoeba, I guess it won't work."

"No, I don't suppose it would."

"What about a cactus plant? They're tough. You could piss on it once a year and that would be enough to keep it going. That's a task about equal to your skill set in matters of responsibility."

I grimaced. "I'm not really the plant type."

"They say that people talk to them, that plants can hear. And the plants don't talk back. That'd be perfect for you, wouldn't it? Isn't your problem with women that they have personalities of their own that occasionally force them to have needs and even talk back?"

"Don't make fun of me."

"I'm not. I'm dead serious. Isn't that part of your problem? The women have minds and needs. They talk back. You can't control them. When it's too much, you drink yourself into a blackout to kill the pain of the sheer impossibility for you of coexisting in the same space with a woman with a mind of her own."

I didn't need to think hard about that to admit that he was right.

"Then I suggest that if you want to stay sober, you set aside women for now and try for something simple. How about a bird? A parrot?" He thought. "No. They might talk back and you'll get bent out of shape and drink."

He looked up. "I've got it! A goldfish! They're easy. You just change out the water now and then. And feed them a pinch of food each day. They don't talk back. In fact, they don't talk at all. Since you're still hearing voices and having paranoid delusions of persecution, you might think the fish is talking to you, but at some point you'll realize that you're just nuts, and you'll be okay."

One day, after a meeting, I stepped outside with Willie Deuce, an addict whose crack implosion not only cost him whatever cachet he'd had in the world of bikers, his backseat momma, his colors, and any last trace of self-respect he'd ever had, but now the teeth were rotted from his head and he lived in a cockroach-infested Tenderloin room with a TV and an ashtray. He passed me a cigarette and we stood gazing out at the Golden Gate Park tree line across Stanyan Street. It was one of those hot blue San Francisco early-autumn days that are like an Indian summer's Indian summer but that at any moment might turn cold as the fog grayed over everything.

"What now?" he said. Looked old, faded, his face torn up. Couldn't seem to get more than a week or two sober before hitting the pipe, getting into even worse predicaments, and crawling back into recovery beaten to a pulp, flat broke, discredited, on hands and knees. This last time, he'd been diagnosed with hep C and his liver was giving out. Now he had about four days back, his denim still bore fresh-looking blood and puke stains. The bottoms of his eyes were green bags of disease.

"You eat yet today?" I asked.

He shook his head no, dragged so hard on a smoke his collapsed cheekbones drysucked his face into a granny look.

"Well, how about we go get some grub?"

"You got dough? Or you thinking Fort Hamilton?"

"No. But I know this," I said. "I ain't eatin' one more salad of fresh-mown lawn grass and tomato rings at the Fort Hamilton Church Free Lunch."

"Getting particular, huh?"

"Tell you what. There's an open mike in North Beach that runs every Wednesday afternoon. Starts at three and runs to five. What say me and you hoof it across town, I'll read, sell some books, and we'll blow what we make on big plates of beef lo mein down in old Chinatown?"

"Bet."

It was a couple of miles, but we had nothing else to do and just sauntered along, slowly, to conserve our strength. He hadn't eaten in over sixteen hours, I in about ten, and those hadn't been spectacular feedings. So we both felt light-headed and paused frequently to rest, sitting hunched on the sidewalk, shoulder to shoulder, passing a cigarette back and forth. At least the weather held.

"I feel like a butterfly nailed to a wall," he said, adjusting sunglasses with a tap from a grubby fingernail.

"Why do you say that? Don't you like being sober?"

"Do you?" he asked skeptically.

"It's better than the gutter, man."

Willie Deuces looked incredulous. "What do you call this?" he said, pointing to the pavement holding up our tired hungry asses.

"I call this grooving on Haight Street in the weekday sun, with nothing to do but go read poems and maybe stuff our faces with Chinese chow."

"Man, you're on Pink Cloud Number Nine," he said.

"Just practicing gratitude. It works, you know. Everything starts to look better. The world gets its shine back."

"Who's your sponsor?"

"Eugene."

"He's a good one. Hard-ass, I hear."

"He keeps it real."

"You look a lot better than when you walked in. You were pretty torn up. And nuts. I can see whatever you're doing is working."

"I go to a meeting every day, man. Sometimes two, three, or four. Meet my sponsor every week. Pray to this thing I don't even believe in completely yet, though I'm starting to. There is something. I don't know what it is. But it's not me or you and it's there when I need it. Some kind of Higher Power."

"At least you're staying with it. I can't seem to get a month clean. Keep going out at one week, two weeks. Three weeks. Three days! Three hours!" He shook his head. "I'm sick and tired of being sick and tired. I don't know why I can't seem to get this thing."

We stood to our feet and shuffled along some more down the hot sidewalk, keeping one eye on the sky, checking for shifts in the wind, hints of gray, but it stayed blue and we ogled and grinned at the pretty San Francisco girls in their hippie dresses and Bettie Page haircuts and sweet tattoos of she-devils and swallows.

"So what makes you feel like a butterfly nailed to a wall?"

"I don't really want to be in sobriety, okay? I'm not even court ordered. I don't much like sober life."

"So what makes you keep trying to get this?"

He didn't answer right off. Face withdrew into sadness. Then said: "I once spat up a piece of my lung when I was hitting the pipe. And I got so desperate when I ran out of crack that I figured the piece I'd spat up must have crack residue on it, so I put it in the pipe and smoked it. I guess when you smoke your own lung it's time to quit. What do you think?"

I grinned. "I'm trying to think of a name for that. How about Addictive Respiratory Autocannibalism."

"I want to fly free, man. But my wing's nailed to the wall. All I can do is flap around and look better and better, but when do I get to fly?"

I didn't try to answer, though I knew just what he meant. But to me, this sobriety thing was limitless. To me, the blue sky above our heads was a miracle. Passing clean-and-sober time together was a miracle. That I didn't have a ball-peen hammer of a hangover smashing my brain was a miracle. That my body did not groan and scream with pain was a miracle. That I did not crave alcohol was sheer science fiction. That I could just walk around breathing and being and talking and doing without a black sucking abyss on my insides demanding more booze was more happiness than I had ever known. There was no dense wall of impenetrable glass dividing me from Willie Deuce and every other human being on planet Earth. His presence resonated in me, fed a part of me that craved companionship. I didn't know his real name or anything about him, but it didn't matter. There was no separation. We were recovering alcoholics kicking it on Haight Street, alive when we should have been dead, disporting in a kind of living afterlife, since whatever we once had been was to all intents and purposes gone. We were both new in the city—he came from Southern Cal—and for me the city still held wonders, a sense of magic. You felt it not just on Haight Street but in the Mission, North Beach, even the Tenderloin, where what had gone down in the Fifties and Sixties revolutions, the ghosts of old bands and countercultural legends—Jefferson Airplane, Big Brother and the Holding Company, Richard Brautigan, Charlie Parker, the Dead, Miles Davis, Bob Dylan, Sonny Barger and the Hells Angels, Hunter Thompson, Kesey's Merry Pranksters, Allen Ginsberg, Jack Kerouac, Diane Di Prima—arose like specters from the sidewalks, beckoning to new unknowns with an electrifying thrill that charged the clear blue air with a sense of purpose and possibility.

My virgin nerve endings, which had lain dormant for years blacked out on vodka, tingled now with a sense of joyous freedom. And what was freedom? First, freedom from addiction. No longer a slave to my thoughts or impulses, or to chemical dependency, I could dance beneath the open sky with one hand waving free! That was huge. I grasped that recovery from alcohol and all substances must serve as the baseline for freedom's pursuit. But once that was solidly in place, the possibilities were limitless. Political freedom. Sexual freedom. Personal freedom. Artistic freedom. Spiritual freedom. Were they all one and the same? Did one find freedom in all these ways through the diligent pursuit of a single freedom? I didn't know.

Was desperate to find out. And that little voice of the whispering Angel said: *When you have become what you wish for through your own experience, then you will truly be free.*

But what should I wish to be? On this, the Angel was mute.

At the North Beach open mike I read the title poem, "American Cruiser," from my book and received a rousing ovation from the twenty or so people present, mostly other poets come to read their own work. Among them was a black woman in a wheelchair who was not a poet.

She waved me over. "How much for that book?" she asked.

"Three dollars, ma'am."

"Give me one, please. No, give me two. I want to give one to my son."

She removed a small bead-covered purse, unsnapped it, and counted out six singles, all she had.

Heart wrenched, I held out the two books and said: "Ma'am, it would be my pleasure and honor to sell you two for the price of one."

"Nonsense!" she snapped, wagging the bills at me. "Take your money. Give me my books. That's a beautiful poem you wrote, and real poets like you gotta eat, just like the rest of us. You don't look to me like you're getting properly fed. Big tall good-looking fellow like you should eat well. Who's taking care of you, son? I can see your momma's not around for a thousand miles. Is that right?"

"Right now, I'm in God's hands, ma'am." And to my own amazement, realized that I truly meant it.

She began a reply but the words caught in her throat and her eyes grew moist. Though I took the money, her hand remained aloft, inviting me to hold it, which I did. She said: "Not too many people would give that answer these days, son. You're a very beautiful man. A very beautiful man! And you are God's poet. It's God puts words like that in a beautiful man's mind. Will you sign my books, please? Make mine out to Lucille and his out to Bobby."

I did as asked, thanked her, and went around to other tables hawking my wares. To my utter amazement, the books sold. Willie Deuce rejoiced at the prospect of lo mein.

"Dude! You made about twenty-five bucks in there!" he panted as we cut across Columbus Avenue, past City Lights Books, and down Kerouac Alley to Sam Ho's Noodle Shop, a little dive with steamy old dumbwaiters and crawlspace tables, but the food was cheap and plentiful and we each ordered big plates of egg rolls, bowls of wonton soup, and heaping portions of beef lo mein.

We didn't speak until the food came, realized there was nothing to say, and fell to it, slurping down the noodles, spooning in the wontons, ravenous, crunching down on egg rolls; washed it all down with big drafts of hot tea. It was a great feast and we made it last. Not a speck of food left. Finished off with fortune cookies that we recited to each other.

Willie Deuce read his: "To have good friends you must be a good friend."

I read mine: "You have only one life. Live it clean and sober."

He looked at me. "You made that shit up."

I smiled and said, "Let's go have a cigarette."

Bellies full, we walked over to a good spot in the sun, a wall off Columbus Avenue, and, sliding to a sit, contentedly lit up cigarettes. Willie Deuce put his hand out and shook mine. "I know you don't want to hear me say thank you and how much I appreciate you taking me along like this, buying me this good meal—"

Before he could finish the thought, I peeled off ten bucks, stuffed it into his shirt pocket, and said: "And are you also eternally grateful for the tenner I just gave you and you will never be able to repay me?"

Willie Deuce laughed. "Don't get all hard-assed on me, now. We both know you're a good man. No point avoiding that fact, bud."

"Okay." I grinned. "I'm a good guy. Just take care of yourself, okay, Willie Deuce? Don't drink today. Agreed?"

He stood up, smiled. Walked off.

I never saw him again.

60

IN A TENDERLOIN SPECIALTY PET SHOP I BOUGHT a pretty little goldfish that I named "Debra." Only later did I realize that Debra is the name of my brother, Howard's, wife. What possible psychological implications this might have I dared not even to consider.

At first, she was just a nice surprise when I got home to my room—to find her gliding in her small round bowl, alive, a life other than mine. The pleasure that I took in her surprised me. Fed her a pinch of food, watched her nibble on a flake, her mobile color form antidote to the drab rooming house.

And then, one day, I came home hurting inside. Though I'd gone to a meeting, and written some poems, the whole reality of my life, being nearly thirty-eight, had crashed in on me. I was living flat broke and still newly sober, managing a run-down flophouse in a sketchy neighborhood, a member of a poetry avant-garde that had little chance of breaking through, let alone of earning money—and to make things worse, at the meeting, a fellow named Charles who had the same length of sober time as me, six months, showed up dressed to the nines, hair styled, with a knockout girlfriend on his arm and leading a leashed Saint Bernard.

He announced to the group that he could no longer attend our meeting because he'd just landed a great new high-paying union-ized job as a master carpenter, and in addition he'd just acquired a cherry vintage black Chevelle SS. He owed it all to recovery, he said, and he looked forward to more great things that his Higher Power had in store for him. Hoped he'd be able to drop in on meet-ings now and then just to stay in touch.

At his mention of a Higher Power, my insides lurched. Still couldn't claim to have found one or even to have given it much thought. Eugene, my sponsor, had told me not to worry about it. "Anytime you find another alcoholic standing in front of you," he had said, "looking you in the eye and talking about sobriety, consider that God is there, speaking through him or her to you. Or anytime you're sitting in a meeting, consider that God is there. For now, think of God as an acronym for 'Group of Drunks.' "

Those were instructions I could follow. Needed to be baby-fed sobriety a teaspoonful at a time. Too much too fast spooked me. When I told Eugene that, he said: "Sure. That's right. That's why we say fear is just an acronym for 'Fuck Everything and Run.' "

Always quick to catch him out, quickly I shot back: "But you once said fear stands for 'False Evidence Appearing Real.' Which is it?"

"Both. You'll see."

And he was right.

But now, there was Charles. My age, same time sober. But he was dressed in fine threads, driving a sweet car, hooked up with a high-heeled blonde bombshell, and master of a gigantic and lovable Saint Bernard, a terrific breed, especially when one considered their

ALAN KAUFMAN   309

traditional use as brandy-bearing rescuers bounding over avalanche snows to deliver a keg full of schnapps right to you. What drunk would not love such a creature?

One day, I confessed my envy of Charles's good fortune to Eugene, who said: "I'm skeptical of whatever it is that you think he's got. What you've got is far more important."

"What I've got? I've got nothing! A crazy nonjob as custodian of a dumping ground for psychos, malcontents, and petty hoods. A little book of poems that maybe fifty people have read. And a goldfish in a bowl. I'm penniless, heading into middle age, and still eating in soup kitchens. And my ex-wife won't even let me talk to my daughter. What I've got? I'm pathetic!"

"How many meetings did you get to today?"

"Three. I was feeling so poor over Charles's good luck."

"Uh-huh. Well, while you were feeling sorry for yourself did you do anything to pitch in and help at the meeting in any way?"

"Yeah. I stepped up to make coffee for one of the groups when their regular coffeemaker didn't show."

"And you wrote today?"

"Yeah. A new poem."

"You ate?"

"It tasted like mud. But it was food."

"This guy with the Saint Bernard, he's been in recovery the same amount of time as you, but look at what conclusions he's reached. That he can handle a relationship, care for a Saint Bernard, hold down a full-time job, keep up a high-maintenance car, and he'll do that by dropping in now and then on meetings when he has time. Let's see how well that works. How's that goldfish of yours, by the way? Debra?"

"Swimming."

"Well, that's wonderful! I would have thought she'd be dead by now. What's it been? A whole two weeks that you've fed her and changed the water in her bowl?"

"Something like that."

"So have you figured out why you gave her your brother's wife's name?" He was grinning now from ear to ear.

A black cloud of gloom overtook me. I leaned forward, hands clasped anxiously. "What do you think? Any significance to my choice of that name?"

"Not unless your brother's married to a goldfish. Then I'd say we might need to have a professional look at you. But you're nuts anyway, so what does it matter? You're doing better than I ever expected. I already told you, you're the worst alcoholic I've ever met, and I've seen some bad ones. When I first met you I wouldn't have given five cents for your staying dry a single day. But you're doing great. The hell with Charles. I'll tell you what. You just decide that from here on in, since your life is already a great big loss, you're going to be a pathetic recovery loser who does loser shit like go to lots of meetings and helping other drunks and writing poetry. Let Charles get the bimbos and Saint Bernards. You're the loser who puts recovery and spiritual life before everything. We'll see who comes out on top."

When I entered my small room, Debra would circle the bowl, small, orange, and streamlined, backlit by a soft lamp. I leaned close, said: "Hi, Deb!" She looked incredibly pretty to me, beautiful even. Had doe eyes and a pert little nose and naturally large wide lips without any silicone. Filling a water glass, I used a small net to transfer her out of her bowl while I cleaned it and changed the water. I returned Deb to her fishbowl and sat with my face close to the convex glass. She came over.

"Look what I got you. A friend!"

I removed from my pocket a tiny rubber deep-sea diver that I'd found in a toy store, and dropped it in. She darted away. It sank right to the bottom and lay there, looking dead. She swam away to avoid it.

"What's the matter, Deb? Don't you like the dead deep-sea diver? That's what I feel like. That's what I find when I go down deep: a diver half dead. I'm so tired."

I placed Debra's bowl on a chair where I could watch her circling from my cot. She always seemed to pause on the side facing me, as if she wanted to see me as much as I wanted to see her. And in this way, it seemed, we kept each other company.

"Can it be?" I asked her. "Do you have feelings? Are you as lonely as I am? All alone here in this crazy little room and you all alone in your crazy little bowl. Did last night's gunshots from the projects scare you? They woke me. The gangbangers go on the roof and shoot off their guns. They get high and aim at the stars. Can you imagine being in so much pain that you shoot at stars with a gun? I'm in pain, Debra. What have I got to show for my life? What have I done? Did you know that I have a daughter, Debra? Her name is Isadora. She's in Israel. I have no money to see her. I worry about her. I miss her. Every day, I miss her. It's a constant ache in my gut, hurts all the time. How was your day? What'd you do? I saw the food flake gone. Which reminds me, it's your dinner time."

Swung my legs off the cot, rose, found her food, removed a big flake, and dropped it in. As it floated to the bottom she swam to it, took a big bite, and cut a lazy graceful happy diagonal, nibbling the flake, tiny trapped air pockets bubbling to the water's surface.

"You really are a sweet little fish, aren't you? Huh! I'm surprised how much I like you."

But as I continued to watch her, and talk, open up more about myself, how I felt, something occurred that worried me. Immediately, I called my sponsor.

"I just want to ask you something. It's weird, but you said that no matter how weird I shouldn't hesitate to share it with you if I feel truly disturbed."

"Yeah, that's right."

"Well, I find myself truly disturbed."

"By what?"

I hesitated. But knew that rigorous honesty was absolutely crucial to my sobriety. So.

"I'm having sexual feelings for the fish."

After a pause, my sponsor said: "Okay. So, what's the problem?"

"Isn't that sorta sick?"

"No. Feeling sexual is sane."

"But for a goldfish? One named after my brother's wife?"

"My guess is, it's more complicated than that."

"How so?"

"Probably you're projecting feelings onto Deb. I mean, Debra the fish, not your brother's wife. Feelings, all feelings, have some sort of sexual component. You haven't felt anything in years, so it might be a little confusing to you. Some of your wires got crossed. Anyway, why worry about it? You're not going to screw the fish, right? Even if you wanted to, you couldn't. So, enjoy the feelings. It'll all work out in the end. You'll see. My guess is, you're bonding with Deb. And there might be some sensual component to the feeling that makes you uncomfortable. You probably have mixed or confused feelings about sensuality. But also, you're taking an emotional risk by bonding with her. Because it means the possibility of loss."

"You mean she might run off with someone else."

"Just let the bonding with her continue."

"Check out Freud of the Fishes." I laughed.

He didn't. "You mustn't let yourself get Hungry, Angry, Lonely, Tired. HALT. Take care of those. Everything will work out. Did you eat?"

"Not really."

"Eat something. Are you tired?"

"A little, yeah."

"Angry?"

"No. Not at the moment."

"Lonely?"

"A little."

"Tell it to Deb. She'll listen."

She did. Not just that night but every night, I poured out my soul to Debra. And came to believe in time that the little goldfish not only heard but understood everything I told her. Knew about my fearsome delusions of being stalked by death squads, my feeling of failure as a writer, my anger to find myself in my mid-thirties so utterly defeated, my sense of betrayal and mourning for alcohol, my constant low-grade grief for Isadora, whom I feared I would never see again. And as the months passed, each time I came home I called out: "Hi, Deb! I'm home!" and she swam to whatever side of the bowl I was on and hovered there, as though to greet me. In time I came to identify my feeling for her as love.

"Can you love a fish?" I asked my sponsor. "Because I love Deb. No ifs or buts about it. She's such a great little sweetheart of a fish and there isn't anything I wouldn't do for her."

By this time I had obtained for her a big bowl that I lined with colored gravel, marbles, and pretty plants to oxygenate the water, where she could hide among the soft, furry leaves, make it a home. And I loved watching her safely nestled and resting, content. Some days, I came rushing through the door, couldn't wait to see her.

Set the clock next to her bowl on a chair and watched it ticking off clean-and-sober time. Deb, first member of my new sobriety family, happily circled her watery living room. To this happy scene I hoped someday to add my daughter, a girlfriend, a dog, male friends, numerous acquaintances, and literary colleagues, fellow writers who believed in my work and wished me well.

Returning from a meeting one afternoon on the 71–Haight bus, I watched a scrawny man in rags with a Civil War–length beard jump aboard through the exit door without paying. He walked up and down the aisle, thrusting a carpenter's tool bag into people's faces, shaking it to make the metal parts clink, and asked in a loud, slurred, hectic voice: "You wanna buy? I'm selling cheap."

He thrust the bag at me. Our eyes met. I knew this man. His eyes shrank back.

"Charles?" I said, shocked.

"Alan," he said. "Alan, Alan, Alan. How you been, man? You wanna buy these?" He held the bag out. "I'm broke. Need money bad."

"I don't want those. But tell me: what happened?"

"Alan, Alan, man. I went out, man. Somebody offered me a beer at work. Screwed up! The next day, a joint. By the end of the week I was smoking crack. Went on a run and when I came back, everything was gone."

"What happened to the dog?"

"It warn't mine. Belonged to that chick you saw me with. She dumped me, man. Bitch!"

"And the car?"

"Hers."

"And the job's gone?"

"Gone, man, Alan, all gone."

"You better come to a meeting. Let's get you back to recovery right now. C'mon, I'll take you."

He recoiled. "Can't do that. Not yet. Got important business first. These tools is just to hold me over till my big check comes in. Any day now."

"Uh-huh. Well, you know where to find me."

"Yeah, man! Later!"

One day, I came home running through the door, tired and happy from a long fruitful afternoon during which I had attended two meetings, composed new poems, and hung out with sober friends at *All You Knead*, talking about lit, politics, spirituality, sobriety, and then went kicking down Haight Street through one of those ineffable orange-pink San Francisco sunsets that look like a Sixties rock album cover—so grateful to be sober, to have Deb to come home to. By now felt sure that she couldn't wait each day to see me.

"Deb!" I laughed as I entered the kitchen, threw on the lights, set down my backpack.

Deb lay afloat on her side in a terrible stillness. I ran to her, scooped her out. She was barely alive. Some horrible illness sickened her sweet eye. She peered at me with a sidelong look of resignation, fins expanding and deflating, mouth puffing out slow asphyxiated breaths.

I don't know why I thought running fresh tap water over her as she floated in a cup would make it better. I was nearly hysterical, a child desperate to believe in good fairies. I stood at the sink, splashing water over Deb and praying aloud: "Hang in there, Deb! Don't die, Deb! Please breathe, baby, breathe! I know you can do it!"

But she couldn't. She couldn't make it.

Gently, coldly, softly, the light in her eye went out.

And then Deb was no more.

DRUNKEN ANGEL

I don't know how long I sat struck numb in a chair, or who came
or went as Deb lay in a little matchbox on the dinette table. For a
period of time that could have been minutes or hours—couldn't
tell—I poked and prodded her, bringing my ear close, my eye up
to hers, holding her up, turning her this way, that. It didn't seem
possible that she was dead. Couldn't bear the thought that her
reddish-gold skin would rot, her doe eyes shrivel, her flesh disintegrate. Brought my mouth close, breathed on her, to warm her, or
maybe, like God, bring her inanimate matter to life. I'm not God.
It didn't work. Nothing would.

And when I knew this in my bones, it was dusk. I brought her
to my room, placed her on the chair, lay down, stared at her lifeless
form for two days: lay there, sometimes slept. When I woke, read
from the stack of library books at my bedside—Brassaï's *Picasso and
Company.* Hilberg's *The Destruction of European Jewry.* Hemingway's
For Whom the Bell Tolls—books to pass the time while my heart
lay down like a tired animal in the cave of its grief. I did not once
think of God or pray or blame Him for this. In my bones, knew:
this death was not malevolent, an angry thing, but the gateway to
silence so profound that it is beyond all blame, all remembrance, an
elegiac stillness that narrates itself in a void.

Two days later, I rose and moved around my room with a great
sense of purpose. I assembled a bigger box, ribbon, paints, a paper
and pen, and plastic wrap. First, I painted the matchbox into a beautiful coffin, and then put pen to page and wrote a secret note to Deb
in which I said that I would always love her and thanked her for all
the love she showed for me, the happiness she brought to my life. I
sealed the note in plastic wrap and laid it in the coffin, inserted over
it a tissue-paper bed, and on this bed of words and soft white I laid
Deb. Tied the coffin closed with ribbon. Put it in my pocket, left

the house. I rode the 22–Fillmore bus to the Marina and walked out to the water.

When I had found what I thought was an ideal spot, one with a view of Angel Island, I clasped the coffin between both hands, closed my eyes, and said: "God, who watches over me, over all things, I give to you the body of my friend Deb, a goldfish who showed me that I am capable of love and that even when that which you love dies, still love remains in the heart, the heart that cannot bear not to love. Thank you, God, for sending Deb, your little golden messenger, to me."

And with that, I put her in the water. I returned her to the sea.

BOOK EIGHT

61

AT A YEAR SOBER, I BEGAN TO FEEL AS THOUGH A big foot was crushing my chest. Couldn't properly breathe, had no drive. Days on end, stretched on my cot, smoking cigarette after cigarette, piling ashtrays with butts, the room dense with smoke.

Thought I must be depressed. In the meetings, heard some speak of the onset of vicious blues. Asked them what they thought. Go on meds, they said, or jog or stop to smell the flowers. Yet another told me to get in touch with my Inner Child, listen to John Bradshaw tapes. I even invited my good old Columbia University bud the poet John Lane, now moved to Berkeley with his wife Kevi, to sit witness as I watched a Bradshaw video and bawled "cleansing tears" of Inner Childishness. Appalled, not knowing what to say or do, he sat there as I sobbed and gagged about God knows what.

When I reported back to the Bradshaw enthusiast that nothing had changed, she suggested I fondle cheap Walgreens baby toys to satisfy my Inner Child. "Buy yourself a rattler and shake it," this person said, smiling with New Age luminescence. I did. Sat there at the dinette table, shaking a Walgreens baby rattle and smoking endless Marlboros, face haggard, energy level still minus zero, until my displeased Inner Child smashed the rattle underfoot and ground a Durango boot heel into the pieces. Concluded that I don't got an Inner Child: it's an Inner Hit Man.

The depression continued. Asked for more suggestions. Fly a kite. Walk barefoot in grass. Go to Ocean Beach and shout "FUCK YOU!" at the waves. Finally, one old-timer said: "Why don't you ask your sponsor what he thinks"—the last thing I would have thought to do, since his answer is always the last thing I want to hear and usually what no one else on earth would have the guts to tell me to my face.

Eugene didn't hesitate; looked at the cigarette burning down in my hand and said: "It looks to me like the Marlboro man's gotten between you and your Higher Power."

"What, this?" I said, holding up the last vice in the world that still made me feel alive.

"Uh-huh," said the smug know-it-all son of a bitch.

"Well, what do you suggest I do?"

"Quit."

"Completely?"

"You know what recovery says about things done in half measures, how it avails nothing."

My heart sank. He couldn't be serious.

Of course he was.

What does he know? I told myself. Prayed for an answer, and smoked. Lost more energy. It got so bad I couldn't be bothered to answer the door if someone knocked. Pretended not to be at home. One day, Eugene came by, knocked. When I didn't answer he gently pushed open the door with fingertips and stood there as dense smoke and rancid air washed over his self-satisfied face. Wore that smile he'd get when confronting the obvious. Looked down at the overflowing ashtrays, my grayish lifeless face, and immobilized, corpselike form stretched on the cot, incapacitated, and said: "So, how's goes it? Are we happy, joyous, and free today?"

"Screw you," I said.

He just laughed and said: "Well, try to get to a meeting, okay? And don't drink, no matter what."

He left, chuckling to himself.

Knew I was in trouble when I tried, later, severely depressed, to get to a meeting but couldn't rise from the cot, not due to any particular "issues" but because I had smoked myself comatose. Cigarettes, my second-oldest friend and consolation after alcohol, had turned on me, just as booze once had.

Couldn't breathe, couldn't move. Was in a state of living death, which is the condition that addictions always seem to reduce me to en route to actual death. I called Eugene.

"All right," I hissed. "I give up. Cigarettes have kicked my ass. What now?"

"Get help."

He informed me that just as there are 12-step programs for people to stay off booze or drugs, there are programs to stay off cigarettes.

The first one I attended was held in a small hospital conference room adjoining the cafeteria. I arrived early. A woman in a hospital gown, nose clipped to a portable oxygen tank, shuffled in, and, seating herself, informed me her name was Carol and inquired if this was my first meeting. Sullenly, I nodded that it was. Hers too. She was ten years sober and had thought that that would be enough. "No one in the meetings for alcoholics ever talked about cigarettes." She had smoked to her heart's content, even when it sapped her energy, even when she could no longer feel the presence of a Higher Power in her life; things began to fall apart and nothing felt good anymore.

By then, she knew that she was running her life on self-will alone. "I didn't drink," she said. "Figured that was good enough. It wasn't." Now she had emphysema, was back in the hospital being tested for lung cancer. "I'm scared," she said.

Now so was I. And then a well-known North Beach Beat poet walked in. Why was it that well-known poets always seemed to appear at important junctures in my recovery? Couldn't believe he was there. He recognized me, a little embarrassed, spoke in a hoarse whisper.

"You got a problem with the coffin nails too, huh?"

I nodded.

"They're killing me," he whispered.

Needed no more convincing that I was on the right path. Don't recall what was said at that meeting, but remember the sound of anxious fingers drumming angrily on tabletops, the pneumatic shaking of nervous legs, the surface clawing and excavating fingernails, and jaws chewing gum so hard you heard teeth grind.

For six months I attended those meetings once a week. As with alcohol, it required all my focus to kick cigarettes. I took it a minute, sometimes a second at a time. My throat clenched hungrily for a whiff of smoke. Muscles crawled under my skin like bugs, rummaging through my veins for one last trace of nicotine. One night I lay in bed sucking on my thumb. Didn't care. My brain ceased to function. Would never write again. So be it. How sad, I thought, that a literary career that was an abortion to start with should end at the point of a stubbed-out cigarette.

Told this to Eugene, who always paused before responding and did so now. Then: "Well, let me ask you this. Your desire to be a writer, where did that come from?"

"What do you mean?" I bristled, annoyed, my fuse a millimeter long.

"Well," he said. "Take me, for example. I have no desire to write. I never write if I don't have to. I find it difficult, unrewarding. But writing seems to make you feel alive and gives you a purpose. You seem to be good at it, too. You've been published. You're the only published writer I've ever met. I've met a lot of wannabes but never one that somebody else thought good enough to publish. So, you must be the real thing. I can't say if you're a great writer or a good writer or a fair writer. But I'd say you're a writer. Well, it seems that God put that in you, both the desire to be a writer and the ability to do it. He didn't put it in me or anyone else I know. So, I guess God made you a writer."

"That's what Carl Little Crow told me too."

"Uh-huh. Well, I can see why. So, let me ask you this. Why would God make you a writer and then create a circumstance that makes it impossible for you to write?"

"How do you mean?"

"Maybe God is removing cigarettes from your life to make you write better and open doors for you that have stayed shut until now."

"But I've always smoked and written. The two go hand in hand."

"Well, you always feel that you should have gone farther as a writer. Maybe the smokes are what held you back, like the booze. We don't know what God intends. We only try to find out to the best of our ability and act in accordance. Looks to me like He's removing tobacco addiction from your life."

I just couldn't imagine such a thing. To my mind, it made no sense, but in my heart lurked a suspicion that he might after all be right.

"I got an idea," he said.

"What?" I said forlornly.

"Writers often write from their own experience, huh? Why don't you write about what it's like to stop smoking?"

"Okay," I said, always more or less ready to try a sponsor's suggestion, even if with a brooding sense of futility.

"Remember," he said. "God didn't get you sober to fuck you over."

"Nice rhyme," I said wryly.

Sat down at my twenty-dollar thrift-shop Smith Corona and in one sitting banged out a ranting freestyle performance poem titled "Last Emphysema Gasp of the Marlboro Man," which that Thursday night at Café Babar I read with vehement fury. As I read, a camera flashed again and again. The audience howled with laughter at my expiation of the cigarette demon and applauded and banged their feet appreciatively against the grandstand-style seats.

After the reading, a man and the woman who'd snapped my picture came up, introduced themselves as a reporter-photographer team on assignment from SF Weekly to do a feature on the newly emergent Spoken Word scene. They had some great shots of me reading. Would I grant an interview? The reporter's name was Cary Tennis. Not long after, he published a second feature story with me again as the focus, in the San Francisco Bay Guardian, replete with a huge photo of me atop the cigarette machine at Babar, performing "Emphysema Man."

One day, as I passed a room in the boardinghouse that I managed, one of the tenants stepped out, an Austrian named Norbert Gstrein. I vaguely remembered renting the room to him but rarely saw him, though each time I'd pass his door would hear the tap-tap of a manual typewriter.

He said that he had read about me in *SF Weekly*, saw my photo. "I have no idea you are famous poet!"

"Well," I stammered shyly, "Hardly famous."

"But this is good newspaper, no?"

"It's all right."

"The whole city reads it."

"I guess."

"So, you are a famous in San Francisco poet!"

I smiled.

"I too am a writer," he announced.

Crap in a basket, I thought. Not another one.

"That's great," I said half-heartedly.

"No, really," he said, reading the disdain in my eyes. "Come. I show you!"

He did. Novels under his name published in stately editions from Germany's best-known publisher. I held the books with great respect, wished that I could read German, to sample them. Regardless, I knew: here was the real item. Just the feel of the books, their look, told me they were serious literary works. He had submitted his claim to the ages. I respected that.

"I would wish to hear this poetry you do. I think they would like it very much in Germany."

"I've got no money for bus fare, let alone airfare to Germany.

"They don't pay you, these clubs you read in?"

"Not a dime."

"So, you do all this for love only?"

"Not for love. Out of psychological and spiritual necessity. Otherwise, I'd go nuts. You can take my word on that."

"Yes, yes, of course, of course," he said. "This I well understand.

But at least I am paid. It's a scandal that you don't get something. But the paper: they paid you for this interview, yes?"

"Nope."

He muttered something indignant-sounding in German.

"Well, I would like to come and hear you. I am very well connected to the German cultural institutes. They could bring you over."

"Again, I have no money to travel."

"Oh, no. They would pay for everything. And for your readings! A lot!"

"Be my guest."

He came to the DNA Lounge, a rock club, where he saw me perform among several poets on the bill. After, he came up: "This is wonderful! Spectacular! You are the best of these. I will arrange for you to fly over. I am returning to Germany soon. You will hear from them."

Before he left, we spent more time together. He was writing a novel about a woman whom he'd come with to San Francisco and who abandoned him for someone else. Crushed, he wandered the city alone, exploiting his internal anguish for material and transposing it to prose. I had never seen anyone put heartache into art with as much discipline as Norbert. He had a wonderful sense of humor, but the pain in his eyes was ineradicable. He had suffered too many setbacks in love, almost as many as I had, and he thought it astonishing that one could ever fall in love, knowing it would turn against you with the viciousness of a knife-wielding assassin and carve out your guts. Who made such a world, his eyes seemed to ask. I guess his books were his effort at an answer.

Novel completed, he left the country. I didn't expect ever to see him again and gave no more thought to performing abroad.

★ ★ ★

In the meantime, new levels of anger manifested, surprising, potentially lethal. Sans cigarettes, I became an ambulatory hand grenade. If someone dared raise a voice I jumped exploding down their eyeballs. I was dating Lana, a shy kindergarten teacher with a Bambi temperament. I raged at her about any jealous thought that blipped across my brain. She cried. Eugene dared suggest that in my crazed state I might not be the best partner, recommended that I think of her needs before my own, maybe remove myself before I caused her any more emotional and psychological harm, which, in turn, would jeopardize my sobriety.

In response, I did what any self-respecting alcoholic in early sobriety does. I fired him and asked her to move in.

62

SPONSORLESS, LIVING WITH LANA, EVERYTHING seemed to be going so well until that three-day spell hiding underneath my bed from a squadron of satanic kidnap killers posing as a choir of black Baptist singers who just happened to be exiting from a church down the street from where I lived.

Persuaded there were new conspiracies afoot, I concluded that having a sponsor might not be such a bad idea after all. Asked Old Ray to sponsor me—a sagacious thirty-two-year veteran of recovery whose shares in the meetings always were right on the spiritual and psychological money.

He said sure.

Old Ray had no training in psychology, hadn't made it through high school. A former underworld figure out of Kansas City who had come west as a young man, he rode in early forerunner motorcycle clubs that prefigured the Hells Angels and ended up serving a long prison stretch, during which he got sober, read Tolstoy's *War and Peace*, Hemingway's *A Moveable Feast*, and the complete works of Sigmund Freud, and then proceeded to read everything else that he could lay hands on.

I never once saw him without a paperback jammed into the pocket of his windbreaker. He was one of the best read people I'd ever met. To get by, he bartended and on the side managed a strip joint.

Short, pugnacious-looking, with a cloud of white hair and hard blue eyes that twinkled with a hint of mirth, he was not the sort to let you run a game on him, and he could easily deflect my bouts of willfulness. Also an outsider of sorts, he didn't toe anyone else's line. I could tell that he grasped the signature difference between artistic eccentricity and destructive egotism. In response to my complaint that I felt sure I was insane, one of the first things he told me was: "You're a poet. That's your job."

It made me feel better instantly.

Soon after, we sat down and he spelled out in no uncertain terms how he envisioned my recovery program might look. "The way I see it is, you're doubly cursed. Most alcoholics just have to deal with alcoholism, which is tough enough. But you're also a writer. That's a kind of disease too. You can't just get away with working the steps. You have to do more. You need to write just in order to stay sane, never mind about having a career. Career or not, if you don't write, you'll drink for sure."

"Every sponsor has told me that," I said.

"Well, they're right. I've watched you over the last fifteen months," he said. "I think I've gotten to know you a little. You're complicated. So let's keep recovery for you as simple as can be. From here on your program consists of two parts: recovery and your writing. A day of writing without recovery, the steps, meetings, practicing your principles, being of service to other alcoholics, won't work. And a day with steps but no writing also won't do it.

So your day must consist of both writing and recovery. And a day that has both, no matter how it turns out, will always be, for you, a good day, a day well lived, in which you can feel fully alive because you've discharged your intended purpose on this earth."

He leaned forward, looked me in the eye. "Do you realize how lucky you are to know what you're here on this planet for? Do you have any idea how many people, normies or in recovery, wander around clueless to why they're here? Be grateful and make good on the gift. You're a writer: write! And don't mess it up."

On a day when it was pouring outside, with emergency flood conditions announced on the radio, I was depressed, lethargic. I had written that day but not gone to a meeting. I called Old Ray.

He sent me out into the near hurricane, had me run in the downpour as dressed, in boots, jeans, shirt, no coat, face turned to the black sky, pelted full on by bathtubs' worth of splashing deluge—had me run and walk and breathe in the heart of the maelstrom. When I returned home, I scrubbed myself down and put on some warm clean clothes, made love with Lana, and felt as happy, as whole, as a young kid.

Other times, he had me "hang out" with my Higher Power as I walked around the city on my ceaseless rounds of meetings and to cafés where I sat to write poems or met with other poets. He had me pray to my God, talk with Him in my head as I walked, asking to be nearer, to be inspired, asking Him to show Himself to me. And once, on Geary Boulevard near Octavia Street, while following these suggestions, I had the riveting impression that my Higher Power had somehow internally materialized in such a way that I could clearly see Him as an old Chinese sage with a long white goatee, somber, peaceful, who had journeyed to me from thousands of years ago—an ancient poet who spoke to me now of the need for self-discipline and simplicity, patience and spiritual power.

"Be still now," said the old sage. "Slow your feet, watch your breath, as Carl Little Crow showed you. Slow down, and you slow down time. A minute is an eternity. You will see."

Did exactly as instructed; must have looked strange there on Geary as traffic shot past, breathing slowly, eyes crossed with focus, body moving in a stop-motion manner, which later I discovered is an actual ancient Zen walking meditation practice known as *kinhin*. As I slowly moved inches over minutes, I never felt so calm or connected to God.

Old Ray had me plan a schedule that included a certain number of writing hours per day and at least one daily 12-step meeting; in his experience, recovery only lasts for twenty-four hours, after which one must re-up, begin anew. I could not bank, he said, on yesterday's actions to keep me sober today. He also asked that at any given time I work individually with no fewer than three recovering drunks, help them do the steps, assist where needed. I should also, he advised, have recovery commitments. Make the coffee in a meeting. Visit rehabs and homeless shelters. And be sure that whenever anyone needed help, I would make myself available to assist in every way I could, without fail.

I did all that, and the anger waned. Also the fear. Began to feel stabilized, and discovered a sense of profound interest in my own internal states. My torso no longer felt like a torture chamber, my emotions like a constant anguish that I must externalize and project onto the minds and motives of strangers. The pain very simply was gone. And when I felt the paranoia coming on, Old Ray would say: "You've got PTSD. You're a military veteran. This is normal. Don't fight it. Just remember: you're safe. Be gentle with yourself."

I would need, Old Ray said, to learn how to meditate. "Go to the experts," he suggested. I visited the San Francisco Zen Center, where shaven-headed men and women in black robes sat in a plain

wooden room called a *zendo*, on round black *zafu* cushions, facing
beige screens. They sat perfectly still for thirty minutes at a time.
I could sit for five, at which point I resembled Linda Blair in *The
Exorcist*, head twisting 360 degrees, moving, twitching, scratching,
sneezing, laughing, crying, and suppressing an urge to projectile-
vomit supernatural green bile into their Buddhist faces.

My knees hurt as I sat and my brain flew away on interplan-
etary missions to the darkest recesses of the alcoholic universe, but
I attained a sense of calm repose, a tone of well-being. The whole
world became a meditation through which I moved with a mystical
sense of union. This I realized must be the Fourth Dimension I'd
heard about in meetings, where one did not believe in God as some
idea but rather experienced Him directly as action in the living
world.

One day, from Munich, Germany, a letter came with an invitation
to perform my poetry at an international writers' conference. I was
to call Mona Winters collect, discuss details.

I called. Charges were accepted. A good sign. A German-
accented woman answering to the name of Mona said that the
prominent Austrian writer Norbert Gstrein had referred my name
to the prestigious Literarisches Colloquium Berlin, which in turn
had requested her to extend an official invitation to come read my
work in an upcoming festival of international writers in Munich. I
could also bring along any other American poet of my choice—but
one who belonged to my "Spoken Word movement."

"That's very nice," I said. "So who pays for this?"

"The festival."

"I mean, how do I get to Munich?"

"We'll fly you and the other poet round-trip on Lufthansa or
any airline that you prefer."

"Yeah? And where do I stay in Munich?"

"At a first-class hotel, paid by us."

"Food, too?"

"Yes. Of course."

"Okay. And when I get to Munich, how do I get from the airport to the hotel?"

"We will send a limo to pick you up. Of course!"

"I got one more question."

"Yes?"

"How do I get from my house to the airport?"

After a pause, she said: "You are so poor?"

"Lady. I'm picking my wardrobe out of the sidewalk garbage collection."

"I do not know what that means," she said. "But I assure you that you will not just be reimbursed for your fare to the airport but every stage of your trip will be paid in full. There will also be out-of-pocket expenses. And, of course, you'll be compensated for your reading."

"How much?"

"A thousand US dollars. Cash."

After a pause of slow-blinking disbelief, I said: "Same goes for the poet I invite?"

"He gets less but almost as good."

I called Bob Holman of the Nuyorican Poets Café in New York, who said: "I'm there."

Then I called Old Ray and said: "A miracle has just occurred."

63

GOD DID NOT GET YOU SOBER JUST TO FUCK YOU over. But did God want the son of a Holocaust survivor to fly to Germany to read his poems? This thought plunged me into doubt and then despair. How could I go? Accept anything from a nation that gassed and murdered my people, hunted my own mother? A country whose nightmarish shadow had loomed over the entirety of my life?

A few days later met with Old Ray in our usual coffee shop, a nondescript place whose anonymity was comforting.

Old Ray searched my eyes. "Congratulations," he said.

"I'm not going," I said, and could tell that somehow he already knew that.

"I see," he said. "Why are you not going?"

I told him. He considered. "Okay," he said. "Well, let me ask you this. Would you say that it's God's will for you not to go, or Alan's will?"

"God's."

"I see. But if you don't go that would be in accordance with how you have been thinking about such things your whole life, wouldn't it?"

"I suppose so, yes."

"In other words, old thinking. Your usual take."

"I don't see where you're going with this."

"Well, isn't it your old way of looking at life that got you drunk in the first place? So, by not going, you're just reinforcing what you've always felt and thought and admitting no other possibility, no other view. Just more of the same. Going would be different though, wouldn't it? That would mean a journey to the heart of your nightmare to see firsthand what has always been for you secondhand history. If you went, you can make your own history; see up close the concentration camps, the destroyed synagogues, the desecrated cemeteries, and so forth. Make a pilgrimage. You could also go to twelve-step meetings in Germany and stay sober in the middle of what you have most feared. This would all be the unknown for you. That is where we want to go, not into the known—which got us drunk to begin with—but into the great unknown, to experience new life firsthand, fresh adventures, your own new experiences witnessed by your own clear clean-and-sober eyes. You must go, it seems to me. God has chosen you to bring back news. What's happening there in Germany? What about the Jews there now? Isn't neo-Nazism on the rise? There's no better candidate to go than you. God wants you to be His hands and feet. So go do God's will, as it is revealed to you along each step of the way. And at the end of it, see what it all adds up to, what it means. That's my suggestion."

At Munich airport a black sedan met me, whisked me off to the center of town, where a black-tie reception was in full swing at the city hall. Dressed in a frayed weather-beaten San Francisco Giants cap that a Haight Street bum had given me, a striped boho shirt, cutoff denim jacket, raggedy jeans, and a pair of brown work boots with steel-reinforced toes that I'd fished out of Tuesday's trash, I sauntered in Reporters and photographers circled me as though Madonna had just entered the hall. The Burgermeister of Munich came forward, hand extended. "You are the hottest new poet of San Francisco. We have heard all about you!"

Cameras rolled, shutters clicked.

"Well..." I smiled. "I don't know about the hottest..."

But no one wanted self-effacement. The moment I hit Germany, I was the "hottest" and that was that. As far as they were concerned, they had scored a big coup. I stopped trying to dissuade them of my importance and settled into the strange new feeling of being, just for now, a literary star.

In the lobby of my first-class hotel Mona Winters handed me an envelope containing a thick wad of deutschmarks "for incidentals." From my room I called Old Ray. He had suggested I do so when I got there.

"Ray," I said.

"You're in Munich, I presume?"

I told him about my reception.

"Yes, well. It's not your job to decide whether people should think you're important or not, hey? Huh? What others think of us is none of our business. Maybe you're more important than you give yourself credit for. This could be God's way of showing you something you should know but don't."

"Yeah, but Ray, that's part of what I'm worried about. I know that there's God in San Francisco. But is there God in Germany? My God?"

"Well, let's see."

"How?"

"Go to a meeting."

"How do I do that?"

"You've got that contact number you said someone gave you for twelve-step meetings in Munich?"

"Yeah."

"Call it."

One hour later, as I waited in front of the hotel, a Brit named Dick pulled up in a Saab, rolled down the window: "Are you Alan, then?"

"That's me!"

"Well, get in. We'll just make it to the meeting." And as the sun set Dick drove off, asking a million questions about recovery in San Francisco, on a drive that seemed to take hours. Then we were in a forest, the darkest and most ominous I'd ever seen.

I said, apprehensively: "What's this place called?"

"Black Forest," he said.

Didn't like the sound of that. Few cars, bigger trees, dense woods, expected wild wolves and big razor-tusked boars and immense dagger-clawed black bears bounding from the brush across our path—but in deeper Dick went, and then deeper still, turned off onto a side road and I thought: Well, here we go. I'm now officially fucked. We'll be met by machine gun-toting Sieg Heilers, and that will be that.

Ahead loomed a military base. I prepared for the worst. The sentries, though, were American. "Here for the meeting," Dick told the sentries, who waved him through to a Quonset hut. Inside, circled chairs filled with an assortment of civilians and military personnel. Dick announced: "Everyone! This is Alan from San Francisco. Shall we ask him to be our guest speaker?"

"I should say so!" exclaimed another Brit, a woman with bright red hair and intense blue eyes. "It'll be a nice change from listening to your boring stories every week." Everyone laughed and Dick nodded in appreciation.

And so I sat at the head of the group and told the story of how, just a year and a half earlier, I had lain on a bench in Tompkins Square Park, dying, and now here I was, an invited poet at an international literary festival, on an all-expenses-paid professional junket, telling my story to a group of clean-and-sober alcoholics. When I finished, met with a round of warm and appreciative applause, there was no doubt in my mind that my Higher Power had traveled with me from San Francisco to Germany.

Mona Winters informed me that news of my coming had spread throughout the network of German and Austrian literary institutes known as *Literaturhäuser* and I had received an additional four invitations to perform in Frankfurt, Hamburg, Salzburg, and Berlin. Holman could join me for three of those, she said, but in Berlin only I had been requested. In return for this, my ticket would be extended at their expense, I would stay in hotels and private apartments as a guest, and would receive travel expenses to each city, out-of-pocket expenses, and fees ranging from $500 to $1,000 per reading. Would this be, she wanted to know, all right?

Certainly.

Holman arrived the next day. That evening we performed for the festival. My reading was telecast live nationwide to 60 million viewers on Germany's equivalent of *Sixty Minutes*. As I read "Last Emphysema Gasp of the Marlboro Man," I glanced down at one point to the foot of the stage, where a mob of camera lenses was aimed at me. A month before, I had performed the same poem to an audience of ten, most of them half asleep, at a Sunday afternoon reading in San Francisco.

★ ★ ★

I had another pact to keep, one I'd made with Old Ray, to visit sites of the Holocaust wherever I went. In Munich took a suburban commuter train to Dachau, where I found drunken German soldiers clutching beer bottles as they weaved arm in arm, singing, through the concentration camp, a tourist site replete with gift shop and a soccer field right behind the gas chamber complex, where a soccer match was in progress, fanatical fans cheering good plays near the crematoria. I had brought a prayer book and yarmulke and stood over a mass grave, said Kaddish, the Jewish prayer for the dead.

The next day visited a Munich synagogue walled in by security barriers and barbed wire. An Israeli sentry in a small watchtower with bulletproof windows kept vigilant watch. He asked questions and checked my papers before allowing me into a modest-sized synagogue with a tiny congregation of bent old men and one or two youngsters with sallow, inbred-looking faces such as I had seen in photos from the Warsaw ghetto. They were a man short for a minyan, the quorum of ten required to hold a proper prayer service, and so greeted my arrival with considerable fanfare.

I was called up to the Torah to read—an honor. After, they crowded around me. They were, compared to me, so small, tiny even, many with numbers on their arms. They insisted that I remain for lunch, which I couldn't refuse. We sat to a long table in the synagogue attic, their wives and daughters bearing trays of kosher food. More prayers were said, and then my plate piled with one delicacy after another, all homemade, and no sooner had I eaten than more was heaped on. They all watched happily as I ate, seemed to enjoy my pleasure in the food even more than eating it themselves, and asked me numerous questions.

Then the head rabbi, a large, bearish man with a gentle bearded face, broke his silence to ask: "So what brings you all the way from San Francisco to our little synagogue?"

They all waited for my answer.

"I'm a poet and a Jew. So I'm making sure to visit Jewish points of interest. And you are one."

"I see," said the Rabbi, smiling. "So, we are a point of interest. What, if I may ask, do you find interesting about us?"

"How few of you there are. Not enough to make a minyan. And many of you have numbers on your arms."

A few of them nodded to confirm my observations. The rabbi said, "This is something we talk about all the time. What will happen to our congregation, so many of us are old, just a few young people come." He shook his head. "I'm not sure that we'll survive another generation."

"Your English is fantastic," I interjected.

He smiled, grateful for the compliment.

"We'll survive!" exclaimed one of the young men, his English also excellent. "You'll see. We'll get married, have lots of children. The shul will go on."

But no one else seemed to agree.

The rabbi said: "Imagine. All the way you came from San Francisco, just so you can make the tenth man at our minyan. God must have a special love for you, to entrust you with such a mission."

I couldn't help but think of what Old Ray had said about new experiences emerging from new choices, new ways of looking.

"My mother," I said, "was in the Holocaust. A French Jew. She was twelve years old when the Germans marched into Paris. She escaped from a round-up of Jews deported to Drancy and then Auschwitz. She fled to Italy, where she was arrested and put in Borgo concentration camp. But somehow she escaped from there too and into the mountains around Torino, where Italian Communist partisans found her and took her in. She saw terrible battles fought. She saw terrible things. When the war ended, she came back to Paris, where she learned that half her family had died in the camps. And her own name was on the list of the murdered. Her escape had gone unnoticed. The Nazis had marked her for dead. She was seventeen years old."

At this, the table grew quiet. All stopped eating to look at me, listen to the Rabbi, who was preparing to speak.

"Then you cannot know how much this means to us. We are the last Jews of Munich, the remnant of the thousands who perished under Hitler. We remain to show Germany that to snuff us out is not so easy. And now, here you are, from the French branch of the same murdered family. Alan, welcome. You are among your own here. And we are grateful that you are here."

In Hamburg Holman and I stormed the city with a new level of ferocious impudence. The fact that the Beatles had premiered here drove us in part. We were messengers of a new avant-garde. Now, we thought, half seriously, our turn had come. We toured the Reeperbahn, the red-light district where the Beatles had debuted and rocked the Hamburg nights.

We were booked to perform in a former palace, now converted into the Hamburg Literary Institute, or Literaturhaus Hamburg. At long tables sat the assembled dignitaries, attired in evening wear. We were expected to perform on a stage while the guests supped on haute cuisine. Holman and I exchanged a look that said we were nobody's dinner act. While Holman rocked the mike dressed in a punk cheetah-patterned lounge jacket, I jumped onto a row of tables and proceeded to rant a loud poem that equated gluttony with fascism while storming up and down, sending dinner plates and cutlery every which way. Our hosts were exhilarated and appalled. A review of our performance appeared the next day in Hamburg's biggest German-language daily beneath the headline "Wild Tigers Attack the Stage."

I continued on to Berlin alone while Holman returned to America. On the train to Berlin, no one spoke except a passenger who noted the camera around my neck.

"American?" he asked, smiling. A young, sallow-faced man with a trim blond mustache.

"Yes."

"You want to see something very funny? Quite amusing?"

"What?"

"Stand up, point your camera at the passengers as if to take a picture, and see what happens."

"Your English is excellent," I said, trying to change the subject.

"Yes. I studied your English in school. We all do. English is the new lingua franca, huh? Go ahead: do it, as they say in Nike. See what happens! You will see something. It is very amusing."

Curious, I stood up, pointed my camera at the passengers.

Every head, as if on cue, ducked, noses tucked into coat collars, eyes averted, some passengers pretending to tie shoelaces. Not a single passenger remained upright or looked ahead.

My fellow passenger grinned, delighted. "You see what is this? Reflexes of the old GDR! Ha! Ha! Ha! Is so funny, yes? They still think there are Stasi going around like the old days, photographing and informing to the authorities. Everyone in GDR spied on his friends. Everyone was Stasi."

"And you? You were Stasi?"

"Everyone," he said.

"And now?"

"Now is no one to report to. The Stasi is over. Everyone feels lost." He laughed himself sick over this.

Just then, a flood of uniformed men in greatcoats and military boots appeared, an entire battalion, it seemed, laughing and shouting, arms around each other's shoulders. In my car, a stampede of passengers rushed to get out, into the next car. My fellow passenger stayed, but his face, on seeing the soldiers, grew hard, ugly with hate.

The seats filled up with troops. They were, I gathered from the insignia on their caps, Russian tank soldiers.

My newly unamused fellow passenger said: "The occupiers. They're unemployed now. Since the collapse of the Soviet Union the whole Russian occupation force is on unemployment benefits paid to them by us, the occupied! Germany pays them their salaries because there are no jobs for them in Russia or here and we don't want these rogues to turn their guns on us. They have nothing to do but get drunk and make fools of themselves. Look at them. Idiots!"

He stood up. "Excuse me, my American friend. But this is more than I can bear," he said, and exited into the next car.

The Russians filled every seat, including his. The train pulled out. I was the one civilian left among them. Soon, the Soviets broke out bottles of vodka. Everywhere, bottles circling my head, passing under my nose, swung in big-knuckled fists, contents splashing on me. The tank soldiers sang and shouted, laughed and shoved, falling over each other.

"Americanski!" someone howled. Next I knew, there were vodka bottles shoved in my face, soldiers urging me to drink, drink! Vodka breath all around me. Vodka-soaked whiskers brushed my face and hands. The car reeked of it. The laughter was soaked in it. The songs sung were vodka songs. The Russian blood of my father's father did a mazurka in my veins. Vodka! My ancestral beverage! Purim! Dostoyevsky! Taras Bulba! Tevye the milkman! It all pressed in on me, urging me to drink. I closed my eyes. Prayed: Oh, God, help me now. And God's voice came back loud and clear: *Why don't you just leave this car and go to the next one?*

That hadn't occurred to me. Stood up and elbowed my way into the next car and the next—a strange nightmarish pastiche of silent sallow oppressed-looking East Germans and drunken brawling Russians—until the vodka-soaked tank brigade was far behind. At last found a quiet spot, a kind of dining car with hard little seats to discourage lingering, and sat, closed my eyes, imagined my favorite 12-step meeting in San Francisco. And there they all were, my beloved clean-and-sober friends. Eugene, Old Ray and Carl Little Crow and Suzy and Kevin and Si and Red Man, everyone I knew and loved in recovery, seated around the table in my mind.

My name is Alan, I said. I'm an alcoholic. And held a meeting in my head: said the Serenity Prayer, then the 12 steps, and, appointing myself as guest speaker, shared about the experience I'd just had with Russian soldiers and endless vodka. I don't know how long I sat like that—it was a long meeting, so peaceful—and when I opened my eyes I felt safe and good, my Higher Power with me in this most improbable of places, as was my recovery network, their spirits and examples. Each face kept me company right until I reached Berlin. And they are always with me, to this day, the meeting that I carry in my soul.

BOOK NINE

64

MY LONGING FOR MY DAUGHTER WAS A CONSTANT ache. Year after year, I didn't know what to do. An impossible situation. Despite my repeated calls, Esther refused to allow me to speak with Isadora and often just used my calls as an opportunity to scream at me and then hang up. It had been seven long years since I had last seen my daughter. In the interim, my mother had died, and despite my efforts to reconcile with them I was hopelessly estranged from my father and brother, who wanted nothing to do with me. Slowly I was struggling to get on my feet, making headway as a writer. But it wasn't enough. The way that Isadora had slept in my arms as an infant, the complete trust and understanding that we seemed to feel with each other at the most gut level—I needed to see my little girl.

I knew that somehow she needed to see me. Yet to think of it filled me with dread. The thought of facing Esther again made me angry, sick inside. I hated her. She had stolen my daughter from me and, no doubt, filled Isadora's head with poison about me. She was a lunatic.

I told this to Old Ray. He looked at me. "Resentment, justified or not, will kill you," he said. "It seems to me that you need to take some personal inventory about it. Do a fourth step. We'll have a look."

I wrote out a full inventory about Esther, outlining not only my resentments against her and how I perceived that her actions had affected me, but also my part in things, where I had been in the wrong. This was harder to do. Harder to see. But it was clear. I certainly had my fair share of responsibility for the wreckage of this situation. I had married the woman, a stranger, while on a binge. Had never really stopped drinking during our entire time together. And when things went from bad to worse, I resorted to alcohol—the very action that had fueled the problem in the first place—because my solution to any crisis was to black out, destroy myself and my life entirely. In the process I had deprived Isadora of a father and had abandoned her to a crazy mother—one nearly as psychotic as the one I had had.

It was also clear that, as I was then construed, with the tools for life then in my possession, I could not have done otherwise. Did what I had always done, acted as I'd always had when things got hard—whether as an athlete, a writer, a student, a lover, an employee, or as a father: I quit.

Seated across from Old Ray, in our usual café spot, I went through all this, detail by painful detail, fully expecting that Old Ray—as he had so many times before when I brought up on fourth steps that, love apart, purely on a person-to-person human level, I owed that little girl an amends, to somehow be in her life—would say: "Yes. But not yet."

This time, he said: "You're right. Go home, do steps six and seven. And on your eighth step, list of amends owed to people you've harmed, just put two names: Isadora and Esther. You owe that little girl. It's time to make amends."

I stared at him, astonished. "You do? Now, when I haven't a dime to my name and I owe all this money on unpaid back taxes and student loans and I'm unclear how to pay this month's phone bill—now, of all times, you say: 'It's time.' Esther won't even put her on the phone to me."

"Alan," said Old Ray, voice quieting into that calm inflectionless tone it acquires whenever he stands face to face with my anxieties. "Are you in charge, or is God? Either God is, or God isn't. Which is it?"

"God is…" I said reluctantly. "But."

"And if God is in charge of amends and this amends is owed, then you'll need His help to make it, won't you?"

"Yes, but…"

"So, all you need to do is the footwork and leave the outcome to your Higher Power. Yes? No? Huh? Which?"

"Yes," I said sullenly. "So, what am I supposed to do?"

"How much does a ticket to Israel cost?"

"A lot. Round trip? Plus hotel? And out-of-pocket expenses, food, cabs to and from the airport, and what about gifts? I'd want to get her things. I'm her daddy…" I looked down. "Her daddy," I said hopelessly. I looked Ray in the eyes. "I haven't seen that kind of money in years."

His eyes did not soften. "Make a budget for how much you'd need. Call me when you're done."

I looked at him, dejected, a little resentful.

Old Ray leaned forward. "Do the footwork. Turn over the results. Isn't that what we say in recovery? Do the footwork? Turn over the results?"

"Yes, but…"

He smiled. "So, do it."

★ ★ ★

With heavyhearted reluctance, spiritually winded, went to see a travel agent who specialized in flights to Israel, hotel bookings, etc. She quoted prices to me so beyond my means that I had to fight to keep a straight face when I heard them. Wanted to blurt out: "It's all my sponsor's fault. There's not a hope in hell that I can afford the prices you've quoted, or even a flight for a quarter of those sums. I don't have nickel one to my name."

But straight-faced, played out the farce to the end, thanked her, returned home with the useless, unobtainable figures in hand.

That night, at home, I received a fax from the Berlin Jewish Cultural Festival requesting me to perform alongside Allen Ginsberg and asking if I could think of some other California writers to invite; they hoped to assemble a program on California alternative Jewish culture. In return for my reading, as well as the work of recommending other writers, they would pay me a few thousand dollars in addition to the round-trip flight and my stay in a first-class hotel in Charlottenburg, where Ginsberg would also room.

I stared at the fax trembling in my hand, then listed names on a napkin: Kathy Acker, Jerome Rothenberg, Rabbi Michael Lerner. Called Old Ray. Could barely get the words out: "You won't believe this…"

He suggested that when I fax back my acceptance I request that the festival add a Tel Aviv stop on the return leg of my air ticket. I did, and included the names of proposed invitees. They faxed back that adding Tel Aviv was no problem, thanked me, and named the travel agent in Union Square where I could pick up my ticket. I had just received, in a matter of moments, more than enough to visit Isadora.

★ ★ ★

There are no accidents in God's universe. The invitation, coming when it did, was no coincidence. It was a miracle.

But there was yet the matter of Esther, who would hang up each time I called, after shrieking my ear off. She had even once refused to let my parents see Isadora after they had flown all the way to Israel expressly for that purpose. What would prevent her from doing the same to me?

I called. She answered. I calmly explained about the festival, said I'd stop in Israel for a week to visit Isadora en route home. Wasn't even so surprised when, this time, she agreed. By now, nothing could surprise me. Was doing my Higher Power's bidding. All I had to do was stay sober, show up.

I flew to the festival with Kathy Acker, who was a friend. Compact, pretty, pierced and tattooed, with short-cropped bottle-blonde hair, a studded motorcycle jacket painted with roses and skulls, and an assertive voice that brooked no nonsense, she was also one of the sweetest people I'd ever met, but only if she liked you. She liked me and we laughed a lot, reminiscing about the old days at the Nuyorican Poets Café, where we had first met on a second-floor balcony and blown pot smoke into each other's mouths and puppy-kissed. These days, she was exploring the still relatively new social medium of online anonymous sex chat rooms and finding that it showed a whole new side to herself, including the strange realization that though the sex games were pure fantasy, her partners anonymous, still, she had feelings for them and they for "her," despite neither party having a clue to the other's identity. What, then, is identity, she wondered. What is love?

Our hotel was in Charlottenburg, one of the poshest districts of Berlin. The festival organizers explained that I would perform solo, but I was also invited, along with Allen Ginsberg, to perform poetry with the Klezmatics on backup. After my set, where I read "Marlboro Man," "Relationshit," and other rants, Allen Ginsberg took the stage. Though in frail health, he performed with the power of a dharma lion.

When it was over, a beautiful Nordic couple with white-blond hair and green-blue eyes came up. The man introduced himself as Carl-Johan Vallgren, a Swedish novelist. He said my performance was a revelation, would like to translate my poems into Swedish, write a profile about me for *Bonniers Litterära Magasin*, Sweden's most important periodical of literature. Could we meet the next day? I handed him a sheaf of poems and said: "I'll see you tomorrow."

That afternoon, Ginsberg, Jerry Rothenberg, and I gave a press conference. Of course, Ginsberg was the main act, the center of attention, as was right. He was the guest of the Berlin Turkish community, which had sponsored his fee to the tune of thousands. In return, Ginsberg would speak out on behalf of the Turkish immigrants who were being incinerated in their homes by mobs of firebombing neo-Nazi skinheads. The government response had amounted to a shrug.

The German press, as well as reporters from France and Italy, listened respectfully to Ginsberg's opening remarks. He deplored Bonn's apathy, called on Kohl to stop the killings of Turks at once. Then he appealed to the film stars of Germany to raise their voices.

"Why film stars?" asked one of the reporters.

"Because if American film stars had raised their voices against Nazism, they would have prevented the Holocaust!"

This I could not countenance.

"Excuse me, Allen," I spoke up.

"Everyone," said Ginsberg, "this is Alan Kaufman from San

Francisco, one of the new breed of Spoken Word poets, making a new scene in America. Yes, Alan?"

"With all due respect, Allen—there's no poet I more admire than you—you can't seriously believe that Gary Cooper and Shirley Temple could have stopped Adolf Hitler and Heinrich Himmler!"

"I believe exactly that," he snapped, face darkening with anger. "The collective force of popular culture could have prevented World War Two."

Numerous reporters groaned and rolled their eyes or sat with pained, bewildered smiles. Beside me, a beautiful Italian photographer leaned close and squeezed my wrist. "What nonsense! I completely agree with you!"

After much back-and-forth between Ginsberg and the astonished reporters, Ginsberg turned to me and said: "Alan. I apologize for losing my temper. You angered me but that doesn't justify my behavior."

"No problem, Allen."

You had to like Ginsberg, no matter how offbeat his perspectives sometimes were. In publicly apologizing to a relative unknown, he showed real class, I thought.

At the festival Kathy Acker spoke to me about her ambivalence toward the whole matter of Jewish identity, the prohibition against tattoos, Orthodox treatment of women, her sense of estrangement from Judaism's institutions. Kathy did not seem to like Berlin that much. It was a harsh winter of searing cold, the city buried under snow and ice. She left the festival site as often as possible. My impression was she couldn't wait to return to San Francisco, where she drove a motorcycle and occupied one of the punkiest Goth apartments I'd ever seen, draped in velvet nineteenth-century Baudelairean decor and hung with original shotgun art by William Burroughs and David Wojnarowicz.

The next day, I breakfasted with Allen Ginsberg and Michael Lerner. I have never been fond of small talk in such encounters, where everyone butters their toast with a sense of momentous occasion. Perhaps this time great things were said, but I don't recall. Was too busy wolfing down my eggs as Lerner spoke at length about his magazine, *Tikkun*, to which he invited both Ginsberg and me to contribute. I do recall that at one point Ginsberg exchanged a fatigued look with me. When I left, Lerner was still talking.

That afternoon, Carl-Johan Vallgren took me for a walk around Berlin. At the site of a former train station that had served as the central round-up point for the deportation of Berlin Jews to the death camps during the Holocaust, we stood in silence. And I listened. Vallgren had mentioned the large number of Jewish children who had gone to their deaths from here. I heard a child crying. A mother pulling a very upset little girl. For an instant could imagine the cries of children as they were pushed or sometimes thrown into overcrowded cattle cars for journeys of two and three days, standing the whole time, unfed, parched with thirst, hurtling toward gas and, as often, incineration while yet alive.

I thought of my mother, who had succeeded in escaping this fate, and of my daughter, Isadora, in Israel.

I looked at Carl. "I hear them."

"Who do you hear, Alan?" he asked respectfully.

"The dead, Carl. I hear the dead. I've been listening for them my whole life. And sometimes, I hear them everywhere. And I hear them now in this place."

"I think I understand," he said.

65

THE PLANE'S WINGS DIPPED, AND THERE WAS ISRAEL.
As always when I see Israel, I felt overtaken by the sad, warm drows-
iness of the place, the inexorable link between her harsh brown
unforgiving soil and my soul. The knot within, which Jews abroad
live unaware of, relaxed. I was home, safe, back among my own.

At the airport passport control, used my Israeli passport to enter.
Took a taxi into Tel Aviv and from there a bus to Jerusalem, my
old hometown, where I booked myself into a cheap hotel. Called
Esther immediately, let her know that I'd arrived. She was cool but
cordial. We arranged to meet the next day in Ashdod, where they
made their home. She refused to give me an address, asked instead
to meet at a café near the town's main post office.

The next morning, wandering too early along Ben Yehuda street
in the center of town, hardly able to grasp that I was actually here,
I bought a miniature Casio piano keyboard for Isadora. Don't know
why. What do you get for a nine-year-old girl? Hadn't thought to
ask before leaving, and, on my own, my aching brain scrambled the

task into an anxious muddle. Could hardly believe that I was really about to see my daughter. It had been so long.

What would I say? How to speak to her? Would she forgive me? How would I state my amends? When would the right moment come? Oh, please, YHWH, I prayed, God of my people, help me to make amends to this innocent who has harmed no one but has been hurt by my drinking. Please, I ask that you allow me to be the kind of father that I should have been before.

66

ASHDOD WAS A POOR IMMIGRANT SEACOAST TOWN, with a more upscale district along the shore. With wide, dusty streets of rows on rows of ugly housing blocks, it was known both for its blue-collar uncouthness and its burgeoning criminal class—a whole stratum of the population engaged in illegal activity, as is common in slums, where hope and money are scarce.

The rendezvous point was a typical cheap kiosk café with a few outdoor tables—a place that sold coffee, tea, ice cream, cigarettes, and lottery tickets. Bought tea and took a seat at an umbrella-shaded table, out of the burning sun.

And then I saw them—Isadora holding the hand of Esther, who was rushing along in a kind of frantic charge. Spotting me, she stopped and stared with wet eyes. I came to my feet, searched my heart for rancor. Despite all that we had gone through, I felt none. But kept close internal watch nonetheless for some resentment that might lurk somewhere, hidden, and lash out, ruin everything. Whether or not she could forgive me, I must completely forgive her and remain in a state of forgiveness.

But I couldn't bear to look at Isadora, who was the only reason I had come. If not for her, I would simply have sent Esther an amends letter and left it at that. Isadora was the reason I was here.

Isadora did not approach and also did not look my way. And then she looked.

The last time I had seen her, she was a toddler, less than two years old. Now she was nine, a developed little girl with a full head of dirty-blonde ringlets and the most angelic face, with big blue eyes and a lovely mouth and a perfect little nose. And there was something of the tomboy about her. But I couldn't tell what she felt on seeing me. Her true face, the one beneath her face, kept itself secret. I wanted to put my arms around her so tightly and warmly and tell her I love her and promise never to disappear on her ever again. But stood there, restrained, trying to relax. And slowly, reluctantly, Esther and Isadora came up to me and we all stood there transfixed by the sheer awkwardness of the moment.

Esther giggled. Then said, in a voice husky with drama: "Hel-lo."

"Hi." I smiled.

"Izzy," she said. "This is your father. Say hello to him."

Isadora regarded me. Still couldn't tell what she was thinking. Though she stood in full sight, something, a kind of ambivalence, yet veiled her from me. I realized that it was the presence of Esther.

"Hello, Daddy," she said, trying to seem controlled, the voice flattened, just a touch, as if reading from a script, her face struggling not to show a feeling.

But I fought back tears to hear her call me "Daddy" and it must have showed. Didn't deserve such a precious gift, though I had yearned to hear those words every day since the time I left, never to return.

"Hello, sweetheart, my daughter," I said. Her face changed.

There she was. As if we hadn't been apart for a single day: my Izzy! But Esther must have seen it: the illusion of her control slip for a single instant. She tensed. And Izzy vanished again from her own body. And the walls were up once more.

We sat and I ordered them whatever they wanted. Esther talked about some career difficulty she had and I did my best to be attentive, but internally my focus was all on Isadora, her every gesture, expression, body posture. In me an unfilled space made sacred for her was desperate for her content, and each time she just breathed, another item was added as I sat there, registering each flicker of her golden eyelids, shift in skin tone, the fall of her hair, trying to discern subtle hints of mood, noting how she gradually relaxed, particularly when the ice cream came, and how she simply stood up, leaned against my leg, placed her hand on my shoulder, and, ignoring Esther, stood there, listening, leaning into me, as if it were the most natural thing in the world, which it was.

I died of happiness. Had to restrain myself from shouting joyfully. Against my body, hers, which in part had come of me, emanated an essential distillation of familiarity unavailable anywhere on earth except from her in relation to me. She was my little girl and I was her daddy. Breath of my breath. Love of my love.

Esther didn't like it. "Izzy," she snapped, "Stop bothering your fa-ther. It's hot!"

I put my arm around Izzy, as if to hold her in place. "No," I said. "She's fine."

But Izzy slipped away and stood off to the side, apart from the table, and began to play some mental game with herself and hop around. I was fine now. Knew that she was thinking about me, a thousand thoughts, and about other things probably, her friends, and whom she would tell about me first and what she would say and how to describe me. Intuited all this immediately, relaxed. It was going to be fine.

Let Esther talk as long as she liked; I heard none of it. Finally, when she had spent herself—talk was her way of staying calm—she said: "What now?"

I suggested that we take some photographs. Sensed how important it was that Isadora experience a moment, if ever so briefly, of normal family life, like posing together for photographs, to break the ice of her estrangement not only from me but from any sense whatsoever of sane family closeness.

"Izzy," I said. "For a proper photo, you should sit on Daddy's shoulders."

Her face lit up. "Okay, Daddy."

I offered her a hand up, and effortlessly, like a little monkey, she swung onto my back and carefully placed one leg after the other over my shoulders as I held her firmly. Laughing, she blindfolded my eyes with her hands and I pretended to stumble around confused and teeter on the brink while she held fast, squealing and laughing.

Esther shot some photos of us, and then Izzy came down and Esther asked someone to shoot all three of us, as I took note of how my emotions protested against appearing in a picture with her, an idea as repugnant to me as ever—I evidently had not forgiven her enough even to pretend to allow a relationship, and perhaps she sensed this, perhaps in this I failed to maintain my spiritual stance. For though I intended to speak with her in private, to make amends face to face about the wrongs I had done, I also wanted her to be very clear that my only reason to be here was Isadora. I did not quite grasp that she, in turn, wanted me to understand that she controlled Isadora's every breath and step—that nothing I could do would take her away. As if that had been my intention, then or ever.

"Would you like to come see where we live?" said Esther.

It was more than I dared to hope for.

"I'd be honored," I said.

"You won't feel so honored when you see the dump we live in."

She was right. It was awful. The building sat, old and ugly, in a neighborhood overrun with feral cats where laundry flapped on outdoor clotheslines amid knee-high weeds.

A large balcony thrust from the flat like a pouting lip. This was heaped with a compacted avalanche of discarded clothes, photos, hairbrushes, newspapers, and anthologies containing my poems, mangled into rain-twisted mulch. Clothes, books, shoes, dinner plates were strewn everywhere throughout the flat. It looked as if some biblical flood had hit, then abated, and everything it destroyed was left as is.

I wanted to buy something for Isadora. The Casio piano had flopped, I could tell, as well it should have: there was nothing of me in it. Would Esther permit me to go off alone with my daughter to shop in the local mall? I asked nervously, remembering the pitched battles that Esther had waged in the past when I tried to take Isadora out in the stroller for a walk through Brooklyn's shady Park Slope streets. Feared sparking more of her paranoia. But something in my manner reassured her. Amazingly, she agreed. The sober man had calmed the skittish fox. Hand in hand with my daughter I left the flat, unescorted, unmonitored, just she and I.

Air and light returned to the planet's surface. I walked along, smiling, as Isadora skipped ahead and turned frequently to see if I was still really there and not some mirage that might dematerialize back into the sad surroundings. I'm still here, sweetheart! my smile signaled. Not going anywhere. Just with you. I love you!

In the mall, everything was closed. We found a single store open, from which we came away with a small fishing rod. Isadora had told me of her great fondness for beaches and water, but this gift, too, was all wrong. She led me to her favorite haunt, a huge ugly manufacturing plant with chemical-green pools that Isadora traversed by means of plank bridges, and then to the shore, to shoals and tide pools where she squatted, pointing out the various sea-life amusements, starfish and anemones and shells—and then we walked hand in hand down the beach. It seemed like the right time to bring up the amends that I had come to make, even though I was already living it just by being here. Still, some words, I felt, were in order.

"Izzy, do you know what an alcoholic is?"

"No," she said, quickly shaking her head without meeting my eyes.

"It's someone who gets very, very sick, and also crazy, when they drink beer or wine or brandy or whiskey. Anything with alcohol in it. So, they call such a person an alcoholic."

She now stared at me with interest.

"It makes them so sick that they could die, but they can't stop drinking it."

"Are you an alcoholic?" she asked.

Sharp kid!

"Yes, yes, I am. And that's the reason why you haven't seen me all these years. I've been very, very sick and trying very hard to get well."

"Are you better?"

"Yes, I think I am."

"So, are you going to stay now with me and Mommy?"

"Your mother and I are only friends now. We're not married anymore. I'm your father, and for as long as you let me, I promise to be in your life."

"Then why do you have to go? Why can't you stay?"

"Well, I've got a home and a girlfriend and all my friends and a career in San Francisco. My whole life is there now, except for you."

"Why don't you live in Israel?"

"I love Israel, Izzy. But I'm a writer in English. To do what I do, I really need to be there, where English is spoken and written."

"But you could if you wanted."

"The best would be if I could live some of the time here and some there. But I'm afraid I don't have that kind of money."

"Why don't you get the money?"

I closed my eyes, said a little prayer to know what to say, how to answer. And the answer was to be who I really am, as truthful as I could be. Never to lie to her, even if I didn't come out looking the way I'd like her to see me.

"I can't seem to, Izzy. I try, but I have a long way to go. I'm a writer and I don't make much money at it and I'm still learning. I'm doing the best I know how. But I need a lot more time.

She thought about it. And then she said, "But Mummy said you were a soldier in the IDF? Were you?"

"Yes," I said. "Yes, I was."

She looked extremely proud of me and said: "You're Alan Kaufman! You can do anything!" and with her little hand slapped the small of my back encouragingly.

There is no greater encouragement in life than your own daughter's belief in you.

"Thank you, sweetheart. We'll see. I'll try. I swear, I will."

"Promise!"

"I promise!"

She was so happy that she danced spinning over the sand with arms outflung against the sunset, a bronze-fired silhouette, and I felt that I had made the verbal amends that I had come for, and that now, in earnest, the living part of the amends could really commence, for a relationship had been established between her and me. Never again would I disappear from her life. From here on, we would be in whatever kind of communication life and circumstances would allow, and through it all she would know: she has a father who loves her.

67

I TRAVELED BACK TO JERUSALEM THAT NIGHT, promising to return first thing the next day. Izzy looked so stricken when I departed. I made sure to call when I got back, to let her know that I was thinking of her. Esther put her on the phone and we talked for a long time.

That night, I went to a 12-step meeting, my first in Israel, where often they are held in unused bomb shelters that serve when full-scale war erupts but then revert back to community centers in less threatening times. This one, though, was held in a rehab clinic. All kinds of people showed up to the meeting, including a religious Jew and an Israeli Arab. Wherever one stood in the complex spectrum of life, one left it at the meeting door. Alcoholism and drug addiction are the great equalizers, reducing all to the same common denominator: a dying human whose body and mind no longer make life viable and who, regardless of social station, religion, or politics, must reach out to others in recovery for survival and must find a Higher Power through pursuit of a spiritual life grounded in love, unity, and service.

When I told of my purpose in coming to Israel, to make amends to my daughter, they all nodded approvingly and spoke of the great example that I was setting for them.

The religious Jew said· "You have the willingness to go halfway around the world to set things straight. That is willingness to go to any length to stay sober. But also, it shows a certain truth about life. The more sober you get, the more clearly you feel, the more you want to see your Isadora. Love keeps pushing to the surface. And moving you to do what is right. That is what I called God."

The Israeli Arab spoke of his estrangement from his family, whom he had dishonored and abandoned. My story gave him hope that if he stayed sober he may yet sit to table with them.

"May Allah make it so," said the religious Jew.

At meeting's end, we all joined hands and heads lowered, said the Serenity Prayer.

The next morning, I arrived in Ashdod and hurried to Isadora. A short, slender, swarthy man in house slippers let me in. Esther introduced him as Yaacov, a Bosnian refugee working in construction. We shook hands.

"He's my lover," she said in the kitchen as Yaacov descended to the outdoor trash receptacles with a bag of garbage.

"Good for you," I said. "How do he and Izzy get along?"

"They love each other."

"Great!" I said.

He seemed nice enough, nondescript, plainspoken, pleasant smile. Isadora appeared a little awkward around him, not as loving as Esther claimed, but I saw no special significance in this. I wanted to be alone with my daughter, but Esther insisted that we all remain together, and so we did. There was no chance of one-on-one communication with Isadora. We went out to the seaside and walked around eating ices, taking in the festive, bustling oceanfront scene. That evening, they insisted that I sleep over rather than return on the late bus to Jerusalem. Isadora couldn't bear the thought of my going. Of course I agreed.

I was to sleep on the kitchen floor, where I curled on a blanket amid caked cat food, hairballs, and dust. I would have slept on a bed of hot coals to be near her. Later in the evening, Esther decided to sleep with Isadora and I should come off the floor to share the large living-room sofa bed with Yaacov. I complied.

Yaacov and I made some stilted small talk before he dozed. I lay awake, thinking of Izzy, wondering how she was, grieving a little to find her in such squalor. What a mess. An alcoholic father, a mentally unbalanced mother, and on both sides penniless bohemians.

She appeared, whispering on bare feet out of the dark to the foot of the bed, and crawled in and cuddled up against me. I encircled her with my arm, heart pounding, held her. My little daughter. My Isadora. This I could give her, the sense of me, my speechless, wordless love. My warmth. The love of my bones and blood. My adult solidity and protection. This I could give, regardless of my empty bank account. It did not add up in dollars and cents. Just breathe, I told myself, and let her breathe beside you. That's enough.

It was more than I could have hoped for. I prayed: God, watch over this child. Give me strength to be her father, to stay sober, and give her strength to live despite all.

Just then, Yaacov stirred. Izzy's body froze. She went completely cold. He said: "Izzy?" and she slipped away, disappeared.

The next day, she insisted, to my extreme joy, that I take her to school. Off we went, hand in hand, she with her little backpack, pointing out things special to her in the run-down landscape: a playground where she and her friends liked to go, certain cats she had named, places where friends lived. At the school she released my hand and said: "Come in with me. To meet my teacher."

"I will, sweetheart. I'm just going to stand out here for a moment, okay? And I'll be right in."

She trundled down the path, her little backpack on her shoulders. I paused to watch her, overcome with sorrow, grief, to realize all the days of her life that I had missed, the special occasions, the first day at school, school plays, performances, sports events, bake sales. How many days of seeing her in her little backpack had I missed? They haunted me, embodied ghosts of lost, wasted years—a black hole. I hung my head and wept to think of it. And waited for the fierce sun of Israel to dry my tears before entering.

The teacher stood to receive me. "How is your Hebrew?" she asked in English.

"My speaking level is good."

"Welcome," she said in Hebrew.

Isadora turned to the owl-eyed curious class and said boldly, standing beside me: "This is my father, Alan, from San Francisco. He was an IDF soldier."

In Israel, every father is a soldier, serves in the army. It is a sign of normalcy, and my having served normalized her in their eyes, was one less way in which she would have to feel different.

"He is a writer."

They stared at me.

I smiled and waved and said: "I'm Izzy's father. I love her very much. It's nice to meet you."

They applauded, and the teacher smiled and nodded that this would be a good time to leave.

★ ★ ★

That week, I helped Izzy with her homework every night. We spent every possible moment together. I passed hours with her and her friends—a little friend club of which I became a full-fledged temporary member.

Yaacov and I spoke little and stayed out of each other's way. But at one point I said: "I'm very glad that Esther has you and that Izzy can depend on you when I'm not here. Let's both be good fathers to that wonderful little girl."

He only smiled. I found it hard to get a sense of him, but I was only a guest here, felt fortunate even to be allowed to see Isadora. I chalked up my inability to read Yaacov to language barriers, cultural differences. Or there may have been a problem lurking, some jealousy he felt at my suddenly showing up. Perhaps my appearance had raised tensions between him and Esther, or set him against me, which in turn might confuse Izzy, her love divided between him and me: a very tough dilemma for a child who had already lost, for a time, her dad. In truth, I just didn't know. I had to remind myself that just a while ago I had been little short of Satan to my ex. And then the moment I dreaded, that Isadora feared, arrived: I must leave.

She seemed fine for a little while, but as the hour approached she began to ask, at first calmly and then ever more emphatically, why I must go.

Then it was time. Esther and Yaacov left the room so that Isadora and I could say our goodbyes.

"Why must you go, Daddy?"

"Sweetheart, I love you. But I don't live here. I live in San Francisco. All my work is there, my friends, my recovery groups, my partner, Lana, my apartment. I have nothing here to make a beginning with—no money, no possibility of employment. You are here and you are important to my life and I will be back, I swear that I will. I will always be in your life for as long as you let me. I will never disappear on you ever again. We can talk by phone, we can write. I'm your daddy, Isadora, and I'll always love you."

Words. Empty words. Sometimes I hate words. Sometimes they fail human experience. Sometimes words are a way to avoid the truth. But in the mouth of an innocent child, words have the clarity and pinpoint precision of a laser beam.

She collapsed onto the bed and began to sob inconsolably, sobs that shook her little body, that seemed to begin in a place buried so deep away, a grief so dark and great that no one could find it and from which violent tremors shuddered to the surface and convulsed her in an agony of loss.

I closed my eyes, prayed to my Higher Power to know what to do, and the answer came: *Let her have her feelings, let her say what she needs to say and remain by her side until you have to go.*

I laid my hand on her gently and said: "I love you."

And she cried out: "Why do you have to go? Why? Why are you always going?"

The truth of it cut me to the soul.

Why are you always going?

All my life, I had been going, fleeing, leaving. Home, friends, jobs. Cities, countries, armies. Marriages, families—everything, everyone, everywhere, always. For a time I was there and then, gone.

Why was I always going?

Even as a writer, what had defeated me, in part, was my inability to complete anything. I didn't finish what I began. Left things half done, grew bored or frightened, or frustrated, and lit out for other, another, elsewhere, different: anything but this, anyone but you, anywhere but here.

Why are you always going?

I didn't know. For once in my life was answerless.

But as she wept I remembered her little feet on the hardwood floors of our Park Slope apartment, the way she clung to my leg, cheek pressed to my shin, as I waited to head back to the bar at Billy's Topless, wordlessly begging me not to go—and how I looked into her eyes and felt so much love yet was helpless not to leave, had to go have my alcohol. Not even her love could stand between me and booze. Booze had been my lord and master, the tyrant that posed as a liberator, destroyed what it seemed to liberate.

And I saw, understood, here before me as she cried, the full consequences of my drinking career: how the innocent suffer, how unforgivable it is, how utterly irresponsible.

I hung my head in shame. Esther looked in, said: "You'll miss your bus."

Slowly, I stood. Isadora clasped my hand. We held on to each other so fiercely, with so much longing.

"Come with me to the bus," I said. "Sweetheart, let's go together."

She sat up, eyes puffed with tears, clinging to my hand, and we left with Esther and Yaacov following behind. At the bus, I knelt before her and said: "Give me a hug so big it will hug us both all the way home."

She encircled my neck and buried her crying face into my shoulder and held on and squeezed, squeezed with all her love, all her longing, all her hope, all her heart, all her wanting to have a daddy.

Then it was time to board. She couldn't believe it, wouldn't release me. Esther pried away Isadora's arms.

"This is not goodbye," I said. "I'm your father. I'll always be your father. That never ends."

And turned and walked to the bus and boarded with her cries in my ears.

Yaacov held her back. I took a seat, pushed open the window. Izzy reached out with both arms, imploring. I stretched out my arm. Our fingers touched. The bus began to move. And then she was gone.

68

WHEN I RETURNED TO SAN FRANCISCO, I COULDN'T bear the thought of giving another poetry reading or ever writing another poem again. Sat in cafés bleakly staring out of windows. All of it—Isadora, Germany, Israel—triggered a sadness that lodged in my chest, wouldn't budge, and petrified my spirit in stone.

I told Old Ray about Isadora. What should I do? More would be revealed, he said. But for now, aspects of life long repressed with drinking had come to the fore and I should stay open, see what my Higher Power had in store. In the meantime, why not look further into Judaism, even for a possible synagogue to attend?

Tore the list of shuls from an old Yellow Pages and went on a quest, from one to the next, to see which, if any, resonated.

None did.

Conservative, Reform. Orthodox. A barrier stood between me and the congregants, the very settings. I disliked having to pay an annual fee for full membership in a shul. Shouldn't worship be free? Reform temple services seemed too Christian, Conservative temples too middle class, Orthodox too rigid.

Anshei Ha'sefer at 23rd and Taraval was last on my list, all the way across San Francisco.

Small shul housed in the building of the Humanistic Society. In the pews, elderly, most with numbers tattooed on their arms: Holocaust survivors. They bore an air of invincible desolation, which appealed to me.

The rabbi, Jack Frankel, was an American-born Israeli Army veteran in his late sixties, the former rabbi of Anchorage, Alaska, where he administered last rites to Eskimos and gun-bearing trappers; previous to that had been a rabbi in Reno, Nevada, where he ministered to prison inmates and professional gamblers. He was Jack London meets the Torah, rabbinical rogue and ladies' man. My sort of guy. All the women congregants batted eyes at him and despised his wife, Brue, a toy manufacturing millionaire with a vicious temper.

I sat in back, dressed in my plaid shirt with torn sleeves, long black hair, and gold earring.

At a certain point in the morning ritual, two or three of the elderlies crowded around and one said: "Young man. Would you mind very much to remove the big Torah from the cabinet and carry it up and down the aisles? The poor rabbi has been doing it every week and he's going to give himself a hernia. No one else is strong enough."

"Sure," I said, slightly abashed. Had never carried a Torah before. Seemed like a singular mystical sort of honor. But what if, God forbid, I dropped it? Balancing its handles, hoisted it aloft, walked up and down as congregants pressed the fringes of their talisman to the Torah, planting kisses.

After the service, they said a blessing on the challah, and I readied myself to slip away. I'd had my synagogue experience, didn't plan a return. But as I moved to the exit several of the congregants closed around.

"Young man, would you mind very much to come next week and carry the Torah again?"

They looked up at me with such hope, I couldn't refuse. To stay would be amends for all the times I'd left when I should have stayed. Ended up going to that congregation for four years. Jewish guilt: it works.

Through the synagogue, I heard of a therapy group starting up for children of Holocaust survivors, offered by Jewish Family Services, and decided to enroll. Once a week we met with Yigal, a therapist. My fellow Second Generationers were Gadi, David, and Naomi. Week after week, we revealed to each other ways in which being children of survivors had made us different not only from Gentiles but from other Jews whose parents had not experienced what ours had.

We found amazing similarities to our experiences. The isolation. Distrust of the world. Fear of what people were capable of. A sense of being unable to fully bridge the gap between oneself and the survivors' memories. Most of all, a haunting sense that somehow we must make up for what they suffered—try harder, live more fiercely, take extraordinary risks or, alternatively, none at all; be as inconspicuous as possible, preserve ourselves against risk, suspended over a chasm between crazy gambits and immobilizing caution.

The four of us began to meet outside of therapy, to socialize. We became a close-knit, quirky family, brothers and sisters bound not by blood but by atrocity.

One day, I received an unexpected call from Danny Shot, editor of an East Coast underground lit mag called *Long Shot,* which Danny had founded, in part, with money from Allen Ginsberg and in which writers like Charles Bukowski, Ginsberg, William Burroughs, Gregory Corso appeared alongside younger relative unknowns from the emergent Spoken Word scene, like myself.

"Alan, you're the son of a survivor, aren't you?" said Danny.

"Yeah. Funny you ask. I'm in this therapy group just now for kids of survivors. The Holocaust is on my mind a lot."

"Did you know that I'm the son of a survivor?"

"I had no idea, even, that you're Jewish."

"Listen. Why don't you and I co-edit a special *Long Shot* issue of underground Jewish writers?"

Later we brought in Hershel Silverman, a Beat-era poet, and among us we assembled a definitive compendium of underground Jewish writers and artists that included Ginsberg, Tuli Kupferberg, Wallace Berman, Bob Holman, Adrienne Rich, Jack Micheline, Marge Piercy, and Hal Sirowitz. We titled the issue "It's the Jews! A Celebration of New Jewish Visions" because when something goes wrong in a society, the first thing Gentiles do is blame it on the Jews. In keeping with our irreverent countercultural stance, our avant-garde pledge to shock, the cover displayed a photo of a completely naked muscle man posing on a beach alongside a fully clothed ultra-Orthodox Chasid.

The simultaneous release parties in New York and San Francisco were massively attended—in San Francisco the club so crowded that in the middle of the performance someone had to climb a ladder to remove ceiling panels to let in more air. Ten underground poets read, including Jack Micheline, Julia Vinograd, Jack Hirschman, and myself. The enthusiasm and size of the audience persuaded me that in America, and perhaps around the world, an audience of young unaffiliated Jews did not feel served by the rigidified institutions of the Jewish community and yet longed for some way to be Jewish in a postmodern world. Perhaps pop culture might serve as that bridge: it now was, after all, the true religion of the US. Green Day and Madonna held far more sway over young Jewish American minds than UJA.

I thought, too, of the Jewish magazine itself. Could anything be more moribund, out of step with today's world? *Commentary, Jewish Frontier, Moment, Present Tense, Lilith*—provincial phantoms of an outworn glory, a time when Jewish studies were on the rise in America and Jewish writers like Bellow and Malamud and Roth had staked their claim—successfully—as the new boys on the block.

But that day had come and gone. Most of these writers were now household names. Multiculturalism ruled the roost, and I knew from my experiences in the underground that Jews were not invited to the party. We would have to throw our own.

Consequently, I conceived of a kind of experiment. Had always been interested in Jewish magazines, from the one I published in college, *Jewish Arts Quarterly*, to those I worked for in Israel, including *Shdemot* and *Spectrum,* to my dramatic staging of a live literary magazine at the Israel Museum and my editing of *Jewish Frontier* and serving as an editor on the *Tel Aviv Review.*

What if I used the genre of the Jewish magazine to launch the most transgressive, in-your-face Jewish pop cultural publication imaginable—one that celebrated Jewishness for its inherent outsiderness rather than argue for its centrality, as so many Jewish mags do? What if I pushed the envelope both contentwise and graphicswise, beyond anything that had ever been done or even conceived of in a Jewish magazine?

I had only to share my ideas with my Second Gen friends, Gadi, David, and Naomi, and next I knew I was standing at the head of a conference table in the headquarters of Wells Fargo Bank, for which Gadi worked as a vice president, sharing my vision with some twenty-five young Jewish professionals whom my friends had invited. I spoke of a new kind of mag of pop Jewishness. I called it *Davka: Jewish Cultural Revolution*. *Davka* was an Israeli Hebrew slang word meaning, loosely translated, to defiantly do something in spite of being warned not to. If Michael Lerner's *Tikkun* is the Osbournes, I said, then *Davka* will be the Ramones.

The room buzzed with excitement. Within minutes, I had a full-scale editorial staff and board that included businesspersons, professional graphic designers, photographers, even a CPA to keep track of finances. Flush with hope, I contacted Rabbi Stephen Pierce, head of the progressive and influential Reform congregation Temple Emmanuel, told him my idea, and asked if he would help sponsor it. He gave me a check for a thousand dollars and said that I could include his name in the newly formed board of directors.

Ideas exploded in my head. I couldn't sleep, so I called Allen Ginsberg's office. He faxed a poem for the first issue, along with permission to include him on the editorial board as well. I contacted J. Hoberman of the *Village Voice*, Tuli Kupferberg of the Fugs, Bob Holman of the *Nuyorican*, comedian Josh Kornbluth, Beat poet David Meltzer, novelist Marge Piercy, Street poet Jack Micheline, lesbian feminist juggler Sara Felder, Alicia Ostriker, Hal Sirowitz, Hirsch Silverman, and many, many others, all who contributed to the first issue.

But, as yet, I had no real idea what such a magazine could look like. Naomi knew a designer named Jill Bressler. "Contact her. She's a genius."

She was right. The moment I met Jill, we clicked. She was tall, attractive, plainspoken, and brilliant. I explained the magazine's purpose and produced the thousand-dollar check, which she looked at and laughed.

"Not enough," she said.

"How much do we need?"

"Another two grand at least."

"Okay. What else?"

"What's on the cover? The cover will make or break your first issue."

"I know. But I'm stumped. Won't the contents carry us? Ginsberg is in it."

"The cover image is more important. It's going to visually signal to a new generation what your Jewish Cultural Revolution looks like."

"I know you're right," I said. "Because when Herzl produced his pamphlet 'The Jewish State' he felt that the look of the flag was the most important detail."

"Right! You need to think of your first cover as the banner that others follow."

But what could this be? For days, I agonized. Then prayed to my Higher Power: God, here is a chance to be of service to the Jewish world. The community is losing the young. What am I to do? What should I put on the cover?

I knew: once I turned it over to my Higher Power, an answer would come. He never failed me.

And it came. But not from Him. From Her.

That Saturday, Rabbi Frankel had spoken of the Shekinah—the earthly incarnation of God in Jewish theology. My ears pricked up. I'd never heard of this. Later, at the Jewish Community Library, read as much as I could lay hands on about the Shekinah. She was considered by some Chasidim to be a true incarnation of God in female form. I learned also of Lilith, a rebellious female spirit outlawed by God. As the father of a daughter myself, I loved the idea of a rebellious daughter-spirit causing cosmic mischief. Some of the most interesting, intelligent, and avant-garde writers and artists in America, the ones I most admired, were women, Jews and non-Jews.

Sapphire, Irena Klepfisz, Diane di Prima, Brenda Knight, Kathy Acker, Laurie Anderson, Patti Smith, Annie Sprinkle, just to name a few. In fact, the two artists with whom I felt the greatest creative kinship, most admired, were the poet Sylvia Plath and the photographer Diane Arbus.

In many respects, recovery was, by nature, iconoclastic—a smashing of old and rigid ideas to allow for new life-giving perspectives. So, why not try to pray to the Shekinah as the female incarnation of God, make her my Higher Power?

I prayed with great trepidation: Shekinah, I don't know who you are or if I can trust you, but I am proclaiming you to be my God and asking: What shall I put on the cover of *Davka*?

Nothing.

Closed my eyes, breathed, counting breaths from one to four and back, allowing my thoughts simply to happen without intention.

Shekinah. Show yourself to me.

Out of the recessed darkness behind my closed eyes appeared the tiny silver figure of a female, sleek, slender, perfectly formed, who came backflipping and somersaulting toward me with acrobatic joy and landed on her toes, arms outflung in a posture of girlish exuberance, as though to say: Here I am!

Wordlessly, she commanded me to open my hands, which I did, and she leaped back and forth from one to the other in an adorably playful performance. Then, just like that, she backflipped and somersaulted into the darkness and vanished.

Amazed, I opened my eyes. I knew: I had just met the Shekinah.

That night, before sleep, Lana already dreaming, I lay with eyes only partially closed, gazing out the window at buildings drenched in bluish moonlight. Saw the silvered face of the Shekinah, grown now to immense proportions and floating visibly before my eyes right past my window, ever so slowly, gently, watching, gazing in, meeting my eyes, and then floating on, past, away, out of sight. And again I knew: the Shekinah had left her world to visit mine.

Shekinah, I prayed. What shall I put on the first cover of *Davka* that will inspire young Jews?

And the next day, as I walked down Hyde Street to the supermarket, it came to me: a naked young woman with piercings and tattoos, discreetly covered by only a tallis and a yarmulke.

I called Jill. "I've got our cover."

She arranged for Marcus Hanshen, a rock-and-roll photog who had worked for *Rolling Stone* and other prominent national zines, to do the shoot. He found someone, an ideal model, who happened not to be Jewish but in every way fit the exact image I had in mind. It would be interesting, I thought, to keep people wondering whether or not she was Jewish—call into question some of our visual ideas about what constitutes Jewish identity.

When the first issue of *Davka* appeared it became, literally, a shot heard around the Jewish world. *Davka* received more mass-media coverage than any American Jewish magazine in history. *Good Morning America* did a special report about it. It was featured on CBS's *The Osgood File*. Appeared in magazines and newspapers as diverse as the *Los Angeles Times, Chicago Tribune, Utne Reader,* and *USA Today.* Numerous Jewish newspapers covered it, while articles about *Davka* were featured in the Israeli, German, British, and South American press.

Sounding a clarion call for young Jews to rise and take the helm of Jewish culture, we named ourselves: "Generation J."

Davka only ran to three issues. But each issue carved out some new sector of Jewish pop, such as Queer Yiddishkeit and Jewz in Hip-Hop, Jewish countercultural poetry and iconographies of

Jewish kitsch, that other Jewish magazines, like *Heeb*, continue to mine to this day. Each issue defined a new sphere of Jewish cultural studies. David Mamet and Leonard Nimoy appeared in *Davka*'s pages. Mamet actually contacted me with a note from Vermont: "Good for you, good for the Jews. How can I help?"

Before the release of the third issue—with Annie Sprinkle, the porn star, as our cover girl Hannuka Queen, replete with Star of David pasties—our business board, who had not brought in a single shekel, complained to our editors that their parents threatened to disown them if *Davka* didn't "tone it down." We refused.

Then the ADL attacked, warning us that we stood to inspire an anti-Semitic backlash. We shrugged and pushed harder.

Finally, a Jewish religious software company called Davka threatened us with a trademark infringement lawsuit, which, in effect, shut us down.

69

GRATIFYING THOUGH *DAVKA* WAS, STILL, something unfulfilled remained to be done. What could it be? I asked Old Ray what he thought.

"I've always been under the impression that your great ambition is not to be a poet or a magazine editor but an author of books. Hmmmm? Yes?"

"What makes you say that?"

"It's all you talk about."

I hung my head. "You're right. It's what I really want."

"Well, you have a little problem."

"Which is—?"

"Most book authors have written actual books before they are considered authors. You, like most alcoholics, want it the other way around."

"So what, then?"

"You've stopped yourself from writing a book all these years. Probably, it's one of the reasons you drank. Maybe *the* reason.

Could be? You know the kind of drunk we see in every bar who talks about the books he will write someday? Why don't you avoid that. So you can look yourself in the eye. Wouldn't that be nice? To actually do it? Go write your book, Alan."

"About what?"

"Well, your mom was a survivor. You've been doing all the Jewish activity. Why don't you write about that? You talk about it all the time in that therapy group. Write about it. Write about being the son of a survivor."

As he spoke, I already knew what to call it. *Jew Boy*.

I had never managed to sustain a narrative longer than a short story, poem, or essay. Reading, could blast through books for hours, but couldn't write longer than fifteen minutes at a time. Inspired by the example of Rabbi Allen Lew, known as the "Zen rabbi" for his long immersion in *zazen* meditation practice before attending rabbinical seminary, I started going to the Zen Center. One day, at a Dharma talk, the teacher spoke about meditation's positive impact on focus. I wondered if Zen might not offer a way. If I could learn to sit staring at a blank wall without moving for thirty to forty minutes at a time, I could sit staring at a blank page until words came.

I obtained a teacher, Paul Haller, a Zen Buddhist born in the slums of Belfast. He helped me with my sitting form and taught me to extend my practice by slow degrees until I could sit without moving, eyes open, focus held, lightly, gently.

Old Ray had me make out a writing schedule. Each day I would attend a 12- step meeting, after which I'd sit at a café table—at the same time, in the same place, often at the same table—for three hours. Either I'd write or sit there bored, staring at the wall. But there would be no leaving before the three hours elapsed. Whether I wrote a sentence or thirty pages, I had to remain.

I kept the pact. During my time, I paced the café. Wanted to scream, pound the walls. Rushed out to make frantic phone calls from a pay telephone. Wandered into nearby shops, the local hardware store, to read hair product labels and browse gardening tools before returning to the café. And then, one day, at the top of a page I wrote "Jew Boy" and made a list of the incidents in my life that seemed somehow to pertain to those words. Picked the first episode off the list that excited memory, and began to write.

Three hours later, I had composed the first draft of a chapter of *Jew Boy*. It took six months to produce 1,200 pages. While writing especially difficult passages about my abuse as a child, I'd retreat to the rear of a nearby grocery store, where I stood hidden among the canned peas and mayonnaise jars, crying. Then I would wipe my eyes on my sleeve and return to the writing.

I began to see a therapist to help me with the feelings that came up. Had a fear that *Jew Boy* not only betrayed my mother but made the Jews look bad, would offend survivors. I decided that *Jew Boy* was best left unpublished, and I told Old Ray this.

"Fine," he said. "But first make sure to finish it."

When I had composed the last page, I shut the notebook, gathered up all 1,200 pages, bound them with string, and stored the bundle on a shelf. I had done it, written a book, or at least the first draft of one. I was through.

Old Ray did not agree. "So, what are you going to do with *Jew Boy*?"

"Do? Nothing. What should I do?"

"You've written a book. Don't you think you should get it published?"

"What for?"

"To be of service. Let others read it."

I looked at Old Ray. What did he know about it?

"No one will publish that," I said with absolute certainty, my voice striking a scornful authoritative note. "And I promise you, absolutely no one wants to read about the son of a survivor. They all want to know about the survivors, but not the kids."

"I disagree," said Old Ray.

"You never agree with me," I said.

"Well, I find it hard to agree with your alcoholic thinking. With you playing God and deciding what will and will not be publishable, what people will or will not want to read. We're not allowed to make up our own minds about it—you've decided for all of us. How about getting the book published—which is part of your responsibility as a writer, your job. Huh? Remember? This is not about outcomes. It's about practicing our principles. It's about finishing what we start. Yeah?"

"Okay," I conceded begrudgingly. "So. I type it up. Revise it. Get it into shape..."

"And we'll take it from there. One step at a time. Let's leave the publishing decisions to the publishers. And the decisions about what to read to the readers. You just be the writer. Huh? Yeah?"

"All right, already, fine!" Goddamned old pain in the ass.

"One last thing?"

Ready to kill him, I said: "So?"

"What is a writer?"

"What do you mean?"

"I mean: what is a writer?"

"Someone who portrays the life of his times."

"What is a writer?"

"A person with published books?"

"What is a writer?"

I stared at him. "Call me stupid, Ray. What is a writer?"

"A writer is someone who writes. When you write, when your pen moves over the page, you're a writer. When you talk about writing without doing the work, it's called being a phony. And when you judge what you wrote, it's called being a critic. And when you decide the fate of manuscripts, it's called being an agent or an editor. You be a writer. Okay? The world has some good editors and agents and more than enough phonies and critics. But there are too few real writers. So why don't you be one?"

"Okay. I'll be a writer."

———

70

I TOOK DOWN THE HANDWRITTEN MANUSCRIPT
and began to input it on my old desktop Dell. The work at first went
painfully slow but in a short time quickly accelerated until I had it
all up on screen, 900 double-spaced pages. I'd scroll up and down,
refining sentences, eliminating repetitions, exchanging polysyllabic words for monosyllabic ones, removing needless punctuation,
honing details, introducing greater variety into sentence structure,
sharpening dialogue to show more of a character's verbal tics or
personal flavor. Writing is like pitching in baseball. The reader is
your batter, the sentences your spitballs and curves. To get them
over the plate in the little strike box, hurl with variety, control, and
syntactical surprises.

I cut and slashed through the text, mercilessly eliminating over
300 pages. During the process found myself laughing aloud at
passages, feeling moved by others. It was good. Maybe even better
than good. If you don't like your own work, why should anyone? I
liked my book. Even began to love it.

"Okay," I said to Old Ray when I was done. "Now what?"

"Now get it published."

"How?"

"When you have a legal problem, what do you do?"

"Panic?" I grinned.

"You get a lawyer. When you have a medical problem, what do you do?"

"Presume it's fatal and contemplate suicide."

"That's probably true for you. You're an alcoholic. I don't see why you'd be any different from the rest of us in that regard. But what most sane people would do for the legal matter, what you ought to do, is get a lawyer. For illness, see a doctor. And when you need a book published, get a literary agent. You had a book published back in your drinking days, huh? Yeah? No?"

"Yes."

"Did you have an agent?"

Grimly, I nodded.

"What's the matter?"

"No agent's going to want *Jew Boy*."

My sponsor smiled. "Good title. Catchy."

"I don't know how to get an agent. My last one was given to me by a professor at Columbia."

"So, go to Borders Books. Get a book on 'How to Find a Literary Agent.' Follow the instructions."

I gawked at him in confusion, feeling betrayed. "That's it? That's your great advice at the end of this whole ordeal, nine hundred pages later? 'Get a book on how to find a literary agent and follow the instructions?' Thanks, Ray! That's really very helpful! Shit!"

"I know the idea of following the instructions on the packaging is especially onerous to you, but why don't you just follow the suggestion and see what happens?"

"You don't know anything about this, Ray! I do! Had a book published by Doubleday! I tell you, I know in the pit of my gut that no one will ever want to publish a book called *Jew Boy*."

It was mortifying. I, the great Alan Kaufman, browsing like some wannabe Harlequin Romance–reading aspirant in the reference section of Borders, under "Literary Agents." In shame I brought home a book about how to get a literary agent and hid it from sight under the bed.

One day, I took it out, read it cover to cover, and followed the instructions to the letter. Twelve well-composed inquiries to agents went out in the mail.

In my closet was a mountain of memorabilia that I had collected from the Spoken Word scene—flyers, posters, chapbooks, manuscripts, and so forth. Since 1988 I had belonged to an emergent avant-garde poetry scene that had broken into camps—Slam poets, Punk poets, Spoken Word poets, Performance poets, Unbearables, Nuyoricans, Babarians, Slammers—that had its antecedents in earlier movements, from Beat to Meat and Folk, Rock, Psychedelic, and Protest poets, a massive uncollected history extending to the beginning of the post–World War Two era.

No anthology had ever made the case for such a tradition in a comprehensive, coherent way. Besides, what publisher would ever be crazy enough to issue such a costly book—it would take several hundred pages at least to document: hundreds of poets, historians, editors, critics, plus photos, marginalia. I could see it clearly but didn't believe it could be done.

Nonetheless, remembering Old Ray's words, I decided to try. Ran a proposal past Brenda Knight, legendary editor of the groundbreaking best-selling anthology *Women of the Beat Generation*. Brenda, a true visionary, one of the most imaginative editors

I have ever met, immediately saw it. "What will you call it?" she asked.

Without a thought, I blurted out, off the top of my head: "The Outlaw Bible of American Poetry."

Her face lit up and she smiled. "That's perfect. Let me take it up with some of the houses I'm in touch with and see what happens."

Weeks later, she called to say that I would shortly receive an email from Neil Ortenberg, publisher of Thunder's Mouth Press in New York, with an offer.

"You're kidding."

"No, A.K., it's true. Check your emails. It'll be there."

It came that night. A generous advance to publish "The Outlaw Bible of American Poetry"—a book that was as yet only an idea with a title. I wrote back to say simply: yes.

Next day, Neil Ortenberg and I had our first conversation, one of dozens to come. I told him that I wanted *Outlaw* to be the kind of book that some kid poet stuck in a mall in Topeka could flip open and feel the hair rise on the back of her neck. A book that would make her want to pick up and come to New York or Chicago or San Francisco, become an underground poet, or start a scene in her own community; that would make becoming a poet seem worth the sacrifices and possible heartbreak; a book that possessed the spirit of the all the underground poets who had blazed the way. *Outlaw* would be a transmission to the young. A book that would make a difference. A kind of bible of underground poetry that would reveal a new, previously ignored vein of literary history.

Neil liked that.

Rather than finding the scale of book I had in mind prohibitive, he suggested we expand it to include as many poets, nationally, as fit the outlaw category, and he even presented his own short list of favorites. I said the book needed pictures, should be visual. Done!

Photos of the poets. Done. Extensive bios. Agreed. Mini-essays and introductions written by scholars. Why not? Reproductions of flyers, marginalia. Of course! I think ours may have been the only such cooperative conversations to occur in American publishing at the time. I had never met an editor more willing to foster the production of a beautiful, meaningful book than Neil Ortenberg.

In other ways, he was tough to work with. Always trying to share the bill with me, the contracted client-author. Wanted his name on the cover alongside mine. I refused. He insisted on including a manifesto from the publisher. I agreed but knew that it was rather unusual. He had a savage temper—once, during a phone conversation about whether to include or drop a particular poet, he knocked a computer off his desk.

His assistant came to the phone and said: "Neil just knocked the computer across the room. He's stepped out. Hold the line, Alan. I'll bring him back."

A moment later, he returned. "I'm sorry," he said.

"No problem." And we continued.

As much as Neil wanted to add, he wanted to cut. He went after my lists with lists of his own. I asked Old Ray what to do.

"It's a matter of good generalship," said Old Ray. "These poets are your troops. You've got to get them over the bridge. I think Flaubert said that, about his words. So, make three lists. On the first list put those you don't particularly care about, yeah? Hmmm? Okay? The ones you can live without. Those are the ones you are willing to sacrifice. On the second list put those it would hurt to lose, but you could bear it. Of them, be willing to give up, say, forty percent. High losses but not unreasonable. The third list is those you refuse to give up even if it sinks the book. If your editor goes anywhere near them, you unleash hell. Tell him to back off or you'll walk. Because in this life you have to have a bottom line. In anything you do, there has to be a point at which you're unwilling to compromise your vision, your beliefs, your values, and if it means losing everything to defend that, then lose it. If he doesn't support your vision to that extent, it was not meant to be. Hmmmm? Do you see what I'm saying? No? Yes?"

I nodded. "That's gonna be tough," I said. "I don't know that I can do it."

He grinned. That gloating grin he wore whenever he encountered vanity in himself or another alcoholic. He loved the ways we fool ourselves. Old Ray saw all those things in himself and in some ways delighted in them, even while knowing how deadly they are, how they actually have the power to kill us. Maybe he even loved them a little for their very lethality, the subtle twists and turns they take en route to our annihilation.

"Well, isn't the motto of recovery 'To Thine Own Self Be True'? Huh? What do you think that means? Be true to yourself when there's nothing to lose? But when the stakes are too high, it's okay to betray your values?" He laughed.

"Okay. I see your point. I'll be true to my vision. To myself."

"And most of all, to the poets you believe in and are trying to help."

"Right."

It worked like a charm. Our visions, Neil's and mine, were not that far apart. He always saw things my way in the end. Some poets who might belong to the record, the history, whose presence might have detailed the picture even better, had to be sacrificed, dropped, but none whose work I believed in very strongly.

The one poet whose work would have truly garlanded the collection was Charles Bukowski, alongside whom I had published in such mags as *Long Shot* and Mike Daly's *Stovepiper*. But for trifling reasons that continue to baffle to this day, and despite overtures Neil and I made to Bukowski's widow, Linda, in the form of conversations, letters, and emails, she refused to allow it. And the shame of it is that Bukowski would have loved to be included in the book.

As I continued to work on *Outlaw* and simultaneously on the marketing to agents of *Jew Boy,* I flew on faith alone.

"Doesn't matter what you believe," a recovery old-timer named Si told me when I confided my doubts. "Just so long as you don't take yourself seriously."

And Ray: "Take the action. Turn over the results." He added: "By which I mean: turn it over to God. Remember? The one who got you sober?"

And I'd nod, smiling with chagrin, for Old Ray well understood: I felt stretched to the very limits of my capacity to absorb all the good that trust in a Higher Power was creating in my life. What I most feared as an alcoholic was not failure—at which I was something of an expert—but the far more terrifying prospect of achieving genuine success.

71

TO CELEBRATE THE PUBLICATION OF *THE OUTLAW Bible of American Poetry* Thunder's Mouth Press obtained use of the historic St. Mark's Poetry Project in Greenwich Village, and we invited as many of the still living poets, editors, and writers in the book as could come, including Barney Rosset, Tuli Kupferberg, Hettie Jones, Ron Kolm, Jim Feast, Eileen Myles, Daniel Higgs, and dozens of others. Brenda Knight, heading up the prestigious San Francisco Book Festival, arranged for a special stage presentation of *Outlaw* in the main auditorium, where such prominent poets as Sapphire, Harold Norse, and Michael McClure took the stage and performed to a large and adulatory crowd.

For the New York event, Gary Shapiro of the *Jewish Daily Forward* arranged for Lana and me to stay at the Harvard Club. One morning, out for a stroll, we stopped by an international newsstand and found that two different papers had run features about me, including the *Jewish Daily Forward* and *Jewish Week*.

The next day, with Lana in our room at the club, I received a call from my literary agent, June Clark at Peter Rubie Associates, advising me that the legendary editor Fred Jordan, who had worked with Barney Rosset at Grove Press and helped to make Rosset's eclectically tasteful house one of the most important in history, wanted to see me.

As a book-starved teen in the Bronx, I had devoured Grove Press books and issues of *Evergreen* whenever I could lay hands on them. At sixteen, I knew the names of Barney Rosset and Fred Jordan before I had ever heard of most contemporary American authors, like Philip Roth, John Updike, or Saul Bellow. Rosset was my hero.

Jordan now had his own imprint called Fromm International, part of Farrar, Straus and Giroux, and this was the same Barney Rosset, I knew, who had fought his way to the Supreme Court three times, and won, for the right to issue such controversial master-pieces as Henry Miller's *Tropic of Cancer*, William Burroughs's *Naked Lunch*, and D.H. Lawrence's *Lady Chatterley's Lover*.

"When does Jordan want to see me?" I asked my agent.

"Now!"

Jumped into a cab, rushed to his offices in a Lexington Avenue skyscraper. As the taxi raced through traffic, I became the little Bronx boy in front of the stationery store paperback rack, running his fingers over the spines of books by Kerouac and Selby Jr., vowing someday to see such books bearing my own name, under K, sandwiched between Kafka and Kerouac. Recalled the painful years of drunken trying, pounding typewriters as I swilled from bottles for inspiration, courage to achieve what no one had ever equipped me for and had even gone out of their way to discourage. Remembered my father's jeer when I showed him the copy of *Magpie*, the literary mag I edited at DeWitt Clinton High; the way my good friend George had attacked and pontificated about my grandiosity when I told him I wanted to become a book author.

Please God, I prayed in the cab, silently, to myself, I need you now as I have never needed you before except to get sober. At the heart of the book that I have written lies the blackest and deepest of holes, a pit, an abyss: the Holocaust. I am here because of a book I've written about what it felt like to grow up as the son of a survivor. It is my truth.

The receptionist led me to an office off a large suite. From behind the desk Fred Jordan, elderly, distinguished, such a man as you would hope your editor to look like, dressed in a handsome suit and with black-framed glasses riding the tip of his aristocratic nose, held out his hand and said: "Alan. Thank you for coming on such short notice."

"Sir," I said, taking his warm hand, shaking it. "I am so honored to meet you."

I sat. He had the manuscript of *Jew Boy* before him on his desk. It had traveled from conversations with Old Ray to notebooks that I filled with my handwriting to the agent in New York and now, here, to the desk of an editorial legend.

"Let me get right to the point, so as not to waste your time. I like *Jew Boy* very much. But it's too big. I told your agent that you are the sort of highly original writer who might not agree to cut his manuscript or accept suggestions for changes. Samuel Beckett was such a writer. When I worked with him he would not permit me to change a comma. So my concern is, will you let this manuscript to be reduced in size? Because as is, it's too large to publish. But I could do one that is, say, four hundred or so pages. What do you think, Alan?"

"Fred, I already know that it's too big. I told that to my agent and want you to know that I am more than willing to reduce its size. In fact, I think that, shorter, it would make for a better book."

"Oh." Fred smiled, pleased and visibly relieved. "Well, do you know where you'd make the cuts?"

"Absolutely. May I?"

I came around his desk, leaned over the manuscript, pulled out the table of contents, and in a matter of less than a minute drew lines through the chapters that were nonessential.

He was impressed.

"Well," he said, looking over my handiwork. "That brings it down to something workable. Tell you what. Let me take *Jew Boy* home tonight, read it through one more time with the cuts you've made, and get a sense of how it works."

"Of course," I said, bravely hiding my dread of having to endure twenty-four hours more of uncertainty.

"I'll call you first thing in the morning to set a meeting. Good?"

"Wonderful!"

We shook hands. I left.

The interior of my skull seemed to crawl with little insects that hatched others in increasing numbers, swarms, armies. A cylinder of volatile black liquid despair jangled mercurially in the central cavity where my heart had once been. I wanted to lie down on some sidewalk, as I used to when drunk. The gutter was my mother, and I wanted her cold cement to embrace me. Or find some urine-soaked stairwell to curl under, fetal, sleep the black sleep of unbearable living death. My moving feet carried me south. I didn't know where to. Phoned my girlfriend. Told her what had happened.

"Let's go to a meeting," she said.

We did, and it helped, but it remained difficult for me to properly breathe, think, exist. Had there been a pill at hand to provide painless instant death I might have taken it. We went into a store to buy food. I stood there, staring at the steam counter, appetite gone.

"I can't take it," I said. "The waiting. I'm terrified. So close! What's going to happen?" Lana put her arms around me. I looked into her eyes. "You know better than anyone what this means to me. My whole life I've waited for this moment. And now it's here and I wish I were dead. I won't make it through the next twenty-four hours."

"Yes, you will," she said. "You'll see. You have a great Higher Power. Have faith. You've done all you can. It's up to God now."

I made it to midnight by attending as many 12-step meetings as I could pack in. But there was still the night. I barely slept. By morning was so spent that when I did doze I fell into comatose unconsciousness. But when I awoke, despite my grogginess, I forced myself to fashion a meditation spot out of some sofa pillows and sat for as long as I could. For I knew that it's in times like these that you need your program most. As I prayed I felt a sense of equanimity flow through me, of protection and balance, warmth, gratitude, and guidance.

On the other hand, I wouldn't leave the room, determined to sit and wait, to be there when the call came.

It came in the late morning. Fred's receptionist asking would I please come by at 2:00 p.m.?

I brought Lana along. We put on nice clothes and calmly cabbed over, holding hands. Felt resigned, neither hopeful nor hopeless but simply willing to accept God's choice for me. I was a champion at defeat. Could not really imagine the other thing—victory. In my heart, I knew: I am a writer. God put that in me. I would do it, regardless of Mr. Jordan's decision, regardless of any outcome, even if no one ever consented to publish the books that I would write.

Cordially, in a relaxed fashion, Fred met us. I introduced Lana. Warmly he shook her hand and with Old World charm showed us to our seats.

He had the manuscript before him.

"I read it completely through last night, until quite late, because as you cut it I found that I couldn't stop reading. I also found that I wished it would go further, into your later experiences, touch briefly on them, bring them up to date, to the current day, even. Do you think that if I asked you to, you could write a few more chapters, to wind it up?"

"Yes," I said, knowing that I could do so easily.

"Then I want to make you an offer. Or would you prefer that I wait to make it directly to your agent? We can put her on speakerphone, if you like."

"Let's put her on speakerphone."

He got the agency on the line. June Clark came on.

Fred said that he had Lana and me in his office and was calling to make an offer on *Jew Boy*. Lana took my hand. The agent said: "Okay! What is it?"

He quoted a five-figure offer. Had he offered two free copies of the book and a catalogue, I would have been thrilled. But a five-figure book advance offer!

June said: "Let me get back to you on that."

"Fine," said Fred.

"Hold on!" I spoke up. Looked Fred in the eyes. "I've waited my entire life for this moment. Honestly, I don't really care about the money. Your offer is more than generous. I don't want to wait a moment more on this." I extended my hand. "I accept your offer."

"Uh, WAIT!" June called out.

"I'm so pleased," said Fred, taking my hand. "*Jew Boy* is a great book and I'm proud to be its publisher."

Lana and I hugged Fred, who said he'd have the contract drawn up and sent to June for review and signature.

★ ★ ★

We walked and wandered, hand in hand, ecstatic, embracing, kissing long and hard, like figures in a romantic ad. No city in the world is more beautiful than New York to an author who has just landed a book contract with a serious publishing house and is walking side by side with a woman he loves. The city welcomes you to its history, opens wide its doors. The sun dotes on you, the autumnal air sharp and clear, a brisk urban perfume. Passersby smile as normally they never do, and every clothing store is your personal tailor, formerly aloof and unattainable outfits now beg to be worn by you. You are not a stranger but welcomed behind the windows of the most fabulous flats and lofts. You are the equal of any famed personage advertised on huge billboards and marquees. Between you and Leonard Cohen, Madonna, or Don DeLillo, the distance has shrunk. You hold your head differently.

I stopped with Lana at the hotel to make love. And that evening, while she slept, walked alone the length and breadth of Manhattan, arriving at the gray granite mortuary of the General Post Office at 33rd Street and Ninth Avenue, where as a teen I had stood waiting for my father to emerge from the employees' exit, to borrow a few dollars from his gambler's earnings, if I could, and maybe walk with him up to Times Square to share a breakfast of greasy hamburger patties and Orange Julius. Now, as I stood there looking at the enormous building, tears of such sorrow and joy, such longing and loss, filled my eyes. Even this moment, the most important in my life, I knew could not be shared with him because he would not really care. "Oh, yeah," I could imagine him saying. "So, they're publishing your book? That's good. That's good. So, uh, what else is new?"

Turned away, walked the few blocks to Times Square, so different now, a tourist trap. A Disney corporate emporium. But a few of the old shooting galleries and novelty shops that Howie and

I had explored as children, when we came down here to learn to sing, still stood, and I wandered through them, touching, remembering, tears in my eyes. Would they ever stop flowing? The manifestations of my past, as if memory itself wept. But now I was someone else too.

And I walked, hard and long, downtown to Twenty-Third Street, to the Chelsea Hotel, to read the bronze inscriptions on the wall plaques about how Dylan Thomas and Arthur Miller and Thomas Wolfe had all resided here, wrote masterpieces. Remembered standing here as a teen, vowing that someday, someday—and now that day had come. Someday had lost the cheap barroom sheen of hopeless and empty promises that Old Ray had warned about. Someday had come, my bright and shining reality, and I thanked God and sobriety and recovery from the bottom of my heart, for I had now become the man that I had always dreamed of being.

I had one of those epiphanies of almost mystical clarity when the veils part to reveal, just for an instant, the scale of miracle occurring as the result of my recovery from alcoholism. I was in my hometown, New York, the city of my birth, with an anthology just published and a book contract for my memoir in hand, and my name, if just for now, buzzing around Manhattan. I had left a homeless drunk and returned in sober triumph.

How had this happened? Stood on a Manhattan sidewalk, riveted by my extraordinary blessings. It was not just my dream come true but better than anything I had ever imagined. I had not dared really to believe this possible for myself. But others had, like Old Ray and Carl Little Crow and Eugene and Si. Just blocks from here, in Tompkins Square Park, I had lain dying. In my bones knew: a power greater than myself had lifted me from a grave, set me walking, and rid me of the merciless obsession to destroy myself with alcohol.

"Don't quit before the miracle," the recovery old-timers had told me. "Have faith and hang in there. It'll be beyond your wildest dreams."

I now knew what they meant.

When I was a little boy, my arms covered with bruises and welts from my mother's blows, I would fantasize that a grown-up, some kind stranger, would knock on the door, enter, and look around at us, my father and mother and brother and me, see our bewildering anguish and pain, and ask: "Good people. What in the name of God is going on in here?"

But no such stranger ever came. After a hellish term served in the galleys of alcoholism, I was rehabilitated and became, myself, the kind stranger. *Jew Boy* was my answer.

72

ON THE NIGHT OF THE EVENT FOR *THE OUTLAW Bible of American Poetry*, I met Barney Rosset, Fred's old Grove Press boss, and Astrid Meyers, Barney's lovely partner. Barney invited Lana and me to come by before the St. Mark's reading, and we went over to their 4th Avenue Greenwich Village loft.

When the door opened, there he was, exactly as he looked in history books. Now in his late seventies, he was still spry, sharp, imposing.

"Mr. Rosset," I said humbly.

"Come in, come in," he said, smiling.

We all sat around in the spacious loft living room, which held a pool table, comfortable sofa, and deep chairs. On the walls hung original art by Henry Miller and a blowup of a photo of Barney seated with his most famous author, Samuel Beckett. Scores of binders contained correspondence with Grove Press authors, some of the most famous in world literature. Barney showed me letters from Maurice Girodias, publisher of Olympia Press in Paris, from

Miller, from Beckett. He told me about hosting Genet in his home. Genet, an inveterate thief, notorious for stealing from his friends, stole from Barney as well. Barney said he didn't mind; Genet was his author and a great one. He spoke fondly of making a film called *Moonstone*, with Normal Mailer directing. Said it was one of the most interesting projects he'd ever participated in—everything was completely improvised.

As Barney fielded my awestruck questions about his relations with Samuel Beckett and Henry Miller, Lana and Astrid, who had in common having worked at one time or another as kindergarten teachers, shared their experiences. They looked beautiful and happy on the sofa, deep in conversation. I felt blessed.

Barney described how Beckett was a kind of saint, in his way, one of the kindest men he had ever met, but also so steeled in his resolve to preserve the original vision of his work that he would not permit anyone to alter his text. Told me about the film Beckett had made with Buster Keaton, a copy of which Barney gave me, signed. And he spoke about Henry Miller's initial reluctance to let him issue *Tropic of Cancer* in the United States, fearing the backlash. "But that was going to come, of course. I knew that." Barney grinned. "I knew that the controversy would blow him up into a public figure beyond anything he could imagine. Miller didn't like to draw fire to himself. But I was persistent, and when *Tropic of Cancer* was published, it became a cause célèbre because of the Supreme Court. Miller's reputation shot through the roof and with a happy outcome. He became a rich legend." Barney laughed. "And what's wrong with that?"

In Barney's estimation, though, Miller had been a far better writer in his Paris years, before he began to dabble in Eastern religion. The change occurred after Miller settled at Big Sur. His Buddhist delvings had weakened his once razor-sharp sense of humor and language, his eye for rendering people and experience with sometimes cruel accuracy. Buddhism, thought Barney, had made Miller somewhat sloppy as an artist and didactically opinionated. The same, he thought, went for Kerouac, and for Ginsberg too.

Before leaving New York, we visited once more with Barney, who has an inexhaustible passion for literature and ideas, an unquenchable questing belief in the importance of writers, the mission of writing. His wife, Astrid, shares this, and together they still edit the *Evergreen Review* in an online version. In time, Barney and I would co-edit *The Outlaw Bible of American Literature*—a volume that reflects, across generations, our conjoined faith in those books that go against the grain with artistry and daring. *Outlaw* was reviewed on the front cover of the *New York Times Book Review*—unprecedented for a compilation of underground and for the most part unknown writers.

Barney asked me: "Have you ever been involved in a tragic love affair?" And proceeded to tell me about his once fierce love for the abstract expressionist painter Joan Mitchell, how he had followed her to Paris, where she introduced him to the avant-garde and suggested that he go see an odd little play running at that time in a small theater and causing something of a stir called *Waiting for Godot*, authored by an Irishman named Samuel Beckett. He went. The rest is history.

I, in turn, told the story of my shattering love affair with Anna during the Lebanon war, my Israeli Army service in Gaza, the way our adultery brought us each to the brink of ruin. Barney said: "That's a terrific story. You ought to write that someday." Four years later, with Barney's words still ringing in my soul, I did. Little, Brown published it as a novel titled *Matches*.

BOOK TEN

73

WHEN *JEW BOY* WAS PUBLISHED IN NOVEMBER 2000, the publisher sent a box of twenty copies to my home. I held the first copy in my hands—a sleek, elegant hardcover edition of 420 pages with back-cover quotes from Hubert Selby Jr., Howard Fast, and Ruth Prawer Jhabvala, among others.

Hubert Selby Jr.'s quote thrilled me. Not so much for what he said but simply the fact of his having said anything at all. When Fred had asked for a wish list of authors to approach for quotes, Selby Jr.'s name headed my list. Author of *Last Exit to Brooklyn*, a novel published by Barney Rosset which I regard as the greatest masterpiece of the postwar era, Hubert had been a literary hero since before my teens, when I had first read *Last Exit* in the Bronx. The impact of his book remains with me to this day. More than any other book, it confirmed my decision to write; more than any other writer, more than Kerouac, Hemingway, Wolfe, Selby wrote about life in a way I could recognize my own experience in. After reading *Last Exit*, I thought, if a writer could reveal life to that depth and degree of rawness, then I wanted in. It was the same with Diane Arbus's photographs, the short stories of Isaac Babel and Tadeusz Borowski, the paintings of Mark Rothko and Willem de Kooning, the plays of Samuel Beckett, and the poetry of Sylvia Plath. Each shocked me into an awareness of the possibilities of self-expression, the extreme lengths that one could go to give identity a voice.

Fred Jordan wrote to Hubert Selby and sent him a copy of my book. A letter returned with a rave quote. It also bore his phone number.

Did Fred think that Hubert would mind if I called to thank him?

"Knowing Cubby," said Fred, "I'm sure he'd love it."

"Cubby?"

"That's what friends call him."

I phoned that night to LA. A soft, raspy, Brooklyn-inflected voice answered—frail but infused with steel.

I introduced myself, and he said: "Sure. I know who you are. That was some book. Thank you for *Jew Boy*. The stuff about the mother knocked me out. I mean, I know what you went through. Had a similar kind of thing."

"That means a lot to me."

"Can I ask you, something, Alan?"

"Sir. Anything."

He chuckled. "No sirs here. Just Cubby. All my friends call me Cubby. You too, since we're now friends, because anyone wrote a book that good, that honest, I call friend. So, here's my question. Are you by any chance involved in twelve-step programs?"

"I am. I've got ten years clean and sober."

"I thought so. You can usually tell. There's a certain lingo. And all that stuff in the chapter about Carl Little Crow. I got a real kick outta that. Well, uh, I'm also in the program."

Floored, I said: "You're kidding!"

"Nah. I kid you not. Got double-digit years."

"Cubby, I'm having a hard time wrapping my brain around this. You're my hero, man. Your quote's on the back of my book. And now I find out that my hero is also in recovery? That's nuts!"

"What are the odds?" He laughed.

"What are the odds," I agreed.

There are moments in recovery when the circle of one's life opens out into some vast expanse of possibility beyond anything imaginable, when the larger pictures gel for just an instant, held in your heart and mind with reverent gratitude, glimpses of God, of eternity, of some transcendent design in which the events and circumstances of our lives are but signposts, signifiers, clues, crumbs dropped on the forest floor leading to vistas of ultimate freedom, and this was such a moment, when everything seemed to click and round out, from Old Ray to Fred to Barney to Hubert Selby Jr.

Fromm International's publicist produced a book tour that took me from San Francisco to Palo Alto, Berkeley, Los Angeles, Seattle, Detroit, and New York. When Fred asked my hotel preference for the New York leg of the trip, my choice was obvious: the Chelsea.

"I should have known you'd ask for that. All my best authors stay there," he said.

Since the age of sixteen, when I first stood outside its doors reading the wall-mounted plaques honoring its most famed author-residents, from Dylan Thomas to Thomas Wolfe, I had fantasized that someday, perhaps, I too would be among the authors to reside at the Chelsea, engaged in literary work. Fred was of an era, unlike now, that treated authors with deference, as though they yet mattered. He had limos sent to transport me to and from each airport and my hotels.

I rode my first limo from LAX to Wilshire Boulevard, where I was booked to read in the Jewish Community Library. My publicist had advised me that my audience would consist, largely, of Holocaust survivors and their children. It had occurred to me that a nakedly honest portrait of my particular experience might incite survivors and their children against me. I knew it was possible that by daring to tell my particular truth in such harsh detail I opened myself to charges of betrayal.

In fact, the audiences thanked me for my frankness. Some of the Second Generationers said that though my particular experience appeared to represent the extreme edge of the curve, still, *Jew Boy* accurately brushed up against their own experiences. They liked that I had presented my upbringing without blame, even, at times, with humor, and they hailed *Jew Boy* as a breakthrough work of Second Generation Lit, a still relatively new genre. Because I shared myself as I am, others found light for their own dark corners.

The honesty of *Jew Boy* reaped other, unsuspected benefits. At one of the readings a Latina social worker whose client base was chiefly Cambodian, children of the survivors of the Khmer Rouge genocide under Pol Pot, said that *Jew Boy* gave her the first real insight into the traumatized Cambodians, the complex fabric of their family life. "Your book will benefit another community that it was not intended for," she said. "I came tonight to tell you that."

My deep wish to be of service through my writing had come true.

I spoke to large appreciative audiences at the Seattle Book Fair and the Detroit Jewish Book Fair. In New York, in residence at the Chelsea Hotel, met with the hotel manager in his office and presented him with inscribed copies of *Jew Boy* and *The Outlaw Bible of American Poetry*. He very ceremoniously opened a special

cabinet and stood my book alongside autographed copies of books
by Arthur Miller, Thomas Wolfe, Dylan Thomas. The Bronx kid
who grew up feeling doomed as an outsider, had once gawked at
this hotel from the street, now had books stored within its innermost heart.

74

NOW ENSUED ONE OF THE STRANGEST PERIODS OF my life. *Jew Boy* received splendid reviews. Editions appeared in American paperback and British paperback. Holland bought it and issued *Jew Boy* in a Dutch translation. In a front-page review in the *San Francisco Chronicle,* James Sullivan called it "a classic American coming of age story." I now had more "game" and money than I'd ever known before. In 12-step meetings, I became a kind of hero. People all over the world contacted me. I flew to England on a book tour. In San Francisco, my profile jumped into prominence and I was stopped on the street, even asked for autographs. I was a "known" author. Fred Jordan and Barney Rosset teamed up to nominate me for membership in PEN American, the authors' organization that included among its ranks almost every major American writer.

In response to all this success, my sponsor smiled wryly and said: "Do you know what's even harder for an alcoholic to deal with than failure?"

"No, what's that?"

"Success."

"Leave it to you to piss on my parade."

One day, I encountered an exquisite, heart-stopping woman in her thirties, blonde, blue-eyed, with a face like Candice Bergen and a figure like Joey Heatherton: Pia.

She was new in the building, riding the elevator to the third floor. Not one word passed between us and I fell in love with her. By the way she smiled at me as she exited I knew that I had made an impression on her as well. Even in that first brief wordless exchange, there was palpable fire between us.

As Lana slept beside me, I lay awake thinking of Pia. Lived for our chance encounters. She was a Vargas girl stepped out of the pages of *Playboy*, circa 1967. Wore her blonde hair drawn back in big Viking knots, stood in a miniskirt on tall thigh-high heeled boots, body sheathed in a stretch pullover that contoured her breasts like plastic injection molding. Pia. Just the sound of her name made me tumescent. Filliped me from this dimension through the walls into her room, where I nailed her pink-white body to the mattress with ruthless excited thrusts. My libido was turning into a cheap paperback. I wrote my sexual narratives in hack prose.

Just by existing in proximity to me, Pia made me see that I needed out of my life with Lana, which had grown into a well-furnished rut. The way Pia smiled at me. Lust. Amusement. Tenderness. Vitality. By contrast, Lana returned home from kindergarten depleted, sexless. We were fast becoming like an old couple. Soon we'd be sleeping in separate beds. When we made love, we paused to chat, exchange jokes and pleasantries, but then repaired to our separate solitudes where we each grunted and sweated our way to orgasm without any real dance to it. And when we finished we forgot about each other altogether, turning away on a shoulder or rising and going to another room. We were not even good friends anymore. Barely spoke. We were each other's loneliness Band-Aid.

75

I TOLD LANA IN THE NICEST POSSIBLE WAY THAT after long reflection I'd decided to separate our households. I cited her long-standing wish to live someplace that was spanking brand-new, flawlessly clean. That was certainly not the shambling, comfortable, but well-worn bookish flat that we occupied, with its painted bathtub and cracked walls. I told her that as a writer I felt a need for greater solitude. That I now saw the years ahead, given my late start and advancing age, as years of continual literary production with little or no time for personal involvements. I told her that, to be perfectly honest, I really didn't have time any longer for love.

She cried and agreed. She too had thought that we needed a break but hadn't imagined something permanent.

I agreed to see a couples counselor once a week, to air issues that were keeping us apart.

In each session Lana sat helplessly, watching it all crumble, as the therapist and I bandied mutual agreements back and forth, mostly confirming the health of my decision to exit. Lana, still hopeful, was willing to work on it. I, disinterested, wasn't. For a time we did develop a nice little routine after therapy, shopping together in a Chinese supermarket, which served to reassure her, I think, far more than therapy. Her school health insurance covered the sessions.

Alone, secured in my new fortress, I began planning the conquest of Mount Pia. All sense of aimless existential angst was gone. I had a mission: to win for myself the sort of Playboy pinup blonde who had fueled my masturbating fist as a sex-starved impoverished Bronx adolescent dreaming of future literary fame. That day had come, if much later than I'd thought and by a route that I could never have imagined. I was a somewhat mangy, flea-bitten literary lion, to be sure, but my lust batteries were still fully charged and I would have Pia for myself if it was the last thing I'd ever do.

It quite nearly was.

Placed a note in the door of her third floor studio.

Hi Pia! Alan here. Your neighbor in 605. May I invite you to my home for tea and cakes? Sunday afternoon, from 2–4 p.m. It would be so nice to have the opportunity to know you. One should know one's neighbors, don't you think?

Sincerely,

Alan

Left my phone number for her to call. She did. Her voice high-pitched, giggly, anxious. Did my best to sound reassuring, as though the note were a summons to appear at Buckingham Palace, not at the bachelorized flat of a lusting middle-aged letch intoxicated with his first important authorial breakthrough and feeling entitled to plunder as many delectable blondes as he could get his hands on.

She readily accepted the invitation.

I had never "courted" a woman before. In the past, my approach had been, typically, to wait around until they made the first move. Or else to say: "Hi. Let's have sex and move in together." Sensed that Pia would require more. The prospect of the chase excited me. She had an aristocratic look. I learned that she worked as a librarian. A book lover! I saw the hand of destiny in this, my chance for success rising incrementally—and with that thought, something else rose too. I had the powerful sense that she was already mine, that all this was predestined. Still, to reinforce the feeling, I did something I'd learned about setting goals from a self-help book. I cut out pictures of beautiful bikini blondes from magazines, glued them onto a big piece of white construction paper, and wrote in banner-sized block letters affirmations like:

PIA CAN'T KEEP HER HANDS OFF ME!

I AM EVERYTHING PIA HAS EVER DREAMED OF HAVING IN A MAN!

BLONDES FIND ME IRRESISTIBLE BECAUSE I AM TALL, DARK, AND MYSTERIOUS!

I AM A BROODING BYRONIC TYPE!

And so forth.

Every morning, as part of my prayers and meditations, I sat gazing at this visual affirmation aid, a sandwich board for my lust, letting it soak deep down into my unconscious, until it was not something I hoped for but something I already had. And all through the day I recited to myself: PIA IS MINE! I AM IRRESISTIBLE TO PIA. PIA IS LIKE PUTTY IN MY HANDS!

Convinced myself that God must be in full accord with all this. Look how enthusiastic I felt! My joyous sense of anticipation. My bursting energy and single-minded determination to possess her. I must be in love. Of course, I mentioned not a word of this to Old Ray or anyone in the meetings.

Went to a large purveyor of foreign home furnishings and hung exotic draperies depicting elephant trains and Hindu gods. Put around huge vases with bas-reliefs of mysterious Third World entities. Tossed velvet throw blankets over chairs, black and emerald, green and crimson, pillowy erotic colors, and throw cushions with cute kitty faces, rugs of subtle minimalist design. I bought a ceramic tea set from Provence, complete with Provençal cart and several varieties of the costliest tea blends on the market; went to the bakery at Whole Foods to purchase exquisite little confections with precious names like "Mozart nipples" and "Klee cupcakes." She would think, seeing the homey tea set, that I did this sort of thing all the time. Would never suspect that I was setting the stage for a seduction that would grow more elaborately bizarre as it proceeded.

On the day, at the appointed hour, there came a faint knock on my door.

76

HER HAIR WAS COIFFED IN A TALL GOLDEN KNOT
from the back of which protruded a long silken pony tail exten-
sion that draped over one shoulder, the way foxes arrange themselves when cozy in their lair. Her high perfect breasts swelled a
tight autumnal sweater flecked with soft gold hints. Her slender legs
in tight black miniskirt and tall brown leather lace-up high-heel
boots. Her only jewelry demure silver earrings. I took note of this:
she likes earrings.

The flat was scrubbed spotless. Had removed every book
from its shelf and wiped free years of dust. One prominent wall
contained my published works, my books as well as anthologies,
magazines, and newspapers in which my writing had appeared.
It looked impressive, even if it really wasn't. I positioned us in
the living room, she on a small love seat, I in an armchair that
I'd stationed in front of the bookshelf containing my works. I sat
there smiling in what I imagined must be baronial splendor. Had
placed, strategically, on a coffee table directly in front of her lovely

knees two newly purchased and exotic looking volumes of tasteful erotica: Richard Kern's *New York Girls*, in which astonishingly hot naked New York women are posed in every conceivable kind of bondage kink, and a manual, published by Taschen, illustrating every form of sexual perversity known to humankind. So placed, they seemed like favorite perusal items of a well-heeled connoisseur. In fact, they were part of the seduction scheme—intentionally transparent conversational pieces to get us moving in the right direction from the get-go. It must seem at once an elaborately staged seduction and an innocuously safe landing pad for a nice girl's hovering erotic urges.

"I was surprised by your note," she said with a gently disconcerted smile in which the palest hint of coyness signaled unmistakable encouragement.

"I admit," I said with boyish shyness, "in this day and age it's not really done, as a rule."

"But an invitation to tea?" she teased with borderline disdain, and something inside me moved. I had experienced this with women before, recognized provocation but never answered the challenge to be a steel fist in a velvet glove, firmly show who's boss, in bed at least. This time, I would not fail. Felt a stirring in my privates, the snake aroused by the nearness of prey.

My face composed itself into an expression of noble detachment. I said: "It may seem strange, perhaps even socially archaic, but I strongly believe that people ought to reach out to each other in this way, neighbor to neighbor, stranger to stranger, because our failure to do so has warped the social fabric into one of conjoined loneliness and all its attached sufferings."

She looked riveted. "Conjoined loneliness. Attached sufferings. That's so beautiful!"

"Thank you."

DRUNKEN ANGEL

Pia looked around at my extensive library. "So many books. What do you do?"

"I'm an author," I said grandly.

"A writer? A real writer?"

"As opposed to a fake writer, yes."

"You've published?"

I waved my hand at the shelf directly behind me, containing all my published works. She stood up. "Those are yours?"

"Yes."

"I've never met—I mean—I've met many authors—I'm a university art librarian and I'm always invited to their release parties, but they don't write—your books look like real literature. The ones I've known are mainly academics. I've never known a real out-in-the-world writer personally."

"You now do," I said handsomely. "Out in the world, and would you like some out-of-this-world tea and crumpets? And some other confections?"

"I would!"

Her eyes, as I wheeled out the tea tray with the beautiful tea set and the crumpets and other confections with extraordinary names and a jam server with many different and exotic jams, told beyond all doubt that I had her.

After the expected oohing and aahing and polite little gasps of surprised pleasure as she ate and drank, she saw the erotic books— actually, she had first noted them when seating herself—and, leaning over while majestically masticating a piece of tea-dunked crumpet, she carefully turned the pages of the Richard Kern book, eyes widening, a high rosy hue warming her cheeks.

"You're looking at my favorite photographer right now," I said. (A complete lie. Before two days ago, I'd never heard of him.) "Let me come over there next to you and we'll have a look together."

ALAN KAUFMAN419

Before she could object, I slipped down beside her, which caused the cushions to sag into a little valley into which we both slid. We were pressed close, thigh to thigh.

"Old sofa," I said. Smiled. "Well, let's have a look."

I smoldered with lust as she paused, spellbound, at the photo of a woman tied spread-eagled on a bed.

"Interesting," I said in a voice of cool detachment. "Nice composition. I love Kern's use of a limited light palette."

She turned to other photos. Her cheeks flushed a deeper rose color.

"Here," I said, handing her a fat book of lurid images printed on glossy stock. This is a really interesting little volume. From the standpoint of art, I mean. It shows how certain forms of kink played a key role in surrealism and later art movements." I flipped through the pages like someone shuffling a deck of porn. "Which image... appeals to you, frankly? We each have our erotic side. We're in San Francisco. It's almost an expected conversation to have."

She stared at the book, not knowing what to say.

I turned to a drawing of a young piano student fellating her mustached teacher on a piano stool. "This?"

She swallowed hard but gave no sign.

"This?" A woman dressed in a dominatrix costume, all black leather and skin, rode a submissive man around like a pony.

"No!" She laughed. "Never that!" she said firmly, to my great relief.

I turned the pages for her slowly until we came to a voluptuous illustration of a buxom woman in a maid's outfit, her bare rosy bottom crosshatched by whip marks.

"This," she whispered.

77

WE SET A DATE. SHE WOULD COME BY. NOTHING
more planned. We both understood what the absence of specifics
meant: sex.

About S/M or bondage I knew nothing beyond what the lurid
stag mags of my youth had offered. So I assembled my "dungeon"
from fantasy. Found a large sturdy table with collapsible legs that
could be easily stored and quickly brought out of my closet on
a moment's whim; hauled it up six interminable flights. It stood
in the living room with the bizarre air of a serial killer's para-
phernalia. Looked at it and realized that I was crossing some line
into fetish, an outlaw realm of libidinous darkness that could prove
to be an innocuous sexual experiment or a portal into unspeakable depravity. Wasn't this how serial killers got their start? First
a single fly's wings plucked. Next a cat strangled. Then a human
"harvested." What would follow the first welt to bloom across Pia's
lovely ass? An abused child, would I explode into savage violence
at the first blow? What about my old stabbing phobias? Would

they return? Did I possess the instincts and wherewithal to be a proper Dom? All my life, I'd fantasized about it. It was time to give it a try.

She appeared at the appointed time wearing a formfitting black dress, black high heels, rope pearls. There was nothing to say. I kissed her in the doorway. She took my hand. Led her into the living room, stepped behind her, and encircling her waist with my left arm, pressed her to me, lifted her blonde hair with my right hand and inhaled the fragrance of her skin. Her hand folded over mine as she pressed against me harder.

"Close your eyes," I said. She did. I stepped away. "Don't move." She remained still, arms obediently at her sides. Returned with a blindfold. "I'm shutting off one of your senses," I said in a low, sleazy voice, "because it is the sense that judges and most induces fear. But you have nothing to fear. Do you believe that?"

She giggled nervously. "I hope so."

I lifted the dress over her head. Underneath, pure creamy skin in black bra and panties. I left these on for now, to enhance anticipation. My fingertips played peekaboo with the panty line, probing but not entering, feeling, exploring, skirting the edge, floating over the crotch, which grew increasingly warm-soaked. Now and then pressed up against her from behind, and ran my hands along her face, neck, breasts, pausing at the cups to calmly, firmly pinch her nipples through the cloth, then placed my hands between her thighs and spread her legs.

"Are you wet enough? Let's see?" I checked. "Yes," I said. "That's very good. You're almost ready. Don't move." Returned with two neckties, pulled her hands a little roughly behind her, bound her wrists. Came around to the front of her to examine what I had.

Removed her bra and panties. Stepped back.

DRUNKEN ANGEL

There she stood, pinkish white, naked blondness strapped into black high heels, sensual, lovely, to do with as I pleased.

Thank you, sobriety!

I climaxed with her two, three, four times a session. When she orgasmed upright her knees folded and she lost the power to stand. Her entire body shuddered, trembled.

Her eyes showed no love at first. They showed mischief, surprise, uncertainty, fear, doubt, greed, authority, submission, admiration, even veneration, but not love. All we did, initially, for several encounters, is have sex, with ropes and spanking integral to our exchange. But by the seventh encounter, all devices fell away. We made straightforward love, which I preferred. Sex the other way, with ropes, cuffs, blindfold, paddles, operating table, rosewater body wash, felt grotesque, preparations for a vestal stag-mag sacrifice to a bloodthirsty newsprint religious fantasy sprung from the masturbating minds of pulp writers long dead and in their graves. Nonetheless, she was the dream of my adolescent libido, the Vargas girl I had prayed to someday have in my Bronx bedroom reveries of future literary fame.

A woman introducing herself as Sandra appeared in the café where I wrote one day and struck up a conversation. Short, pretty, with a thick mane of jet-black hair, large breasts, and a slender waist, she came from Texas and made her living as an artist. We arranged to take a stroll through the Botanical Garden. Then I took her to dinner at Le Colonial. After, we went straight to my place. Had no idea what might turn her on. I soon learned.

"I'm into S and M," she said flat-out, giving barely a glance at my coffee-table quick-reference guide to kink.

"Oh," I said, acting surprised. I was, in a way. Is this what happened once you tried it? Candidates appeared? Out came the table. Ropes. Blindfold. Etcetera.

Unlike Pia, Sandra brought out my severity, if not cruelty. She panted gratefully, slavishly, as I undressed her. Stood there blindfolded, hands bound behind, in high heels, my leather belt clasped in her teeth, imploring me to belt her.

Chuckling to myself, I barked: "Down on your knees!"

"Yes, Sir," she barely garbled out.

I made her crawl on all fours like a dog with the belt in her mouth. Hoisted her onto the table and banged her bluntly, face to face, and dragged her over to an armchair where I sprawled with limbs akimbo as she sucked me off. Then back onto the table with her, splayed, hands and feet secured, a stack of cushions under her little buttocks as I teased her clit with my bobbing tongue, lathered her vaginal lips, one finger hooked into her G-spot, stroking. She wriggled like a fish, had so many orgasms, one after another, that she nearly fainted. She never giggled, joked, or laughed. Called me "Master" with complete seriousness. I half took it seriously myself. Sometimes left her there on the table moaning and writhing and walked into the kitchen to make myself some tea and peruse the day's unopened mail, skim through the week's issue of the *New Yorker*.

She took cabs to my home dressed in fishnet body sleeves, high heels, and a tan belted raincoat. I liked the look. French Existentialist. She also knew more about literature than Pia, who, I was learning, was not especially bright, all pose and seduction but hardly any substance. Pia shelved books but didn't read them. The only literature in her room was copies of *Cosmo* and *Vanity Fair*.

In many ways, Sandra was more fun—demanded nothing and could discourse brightly on almost anything from Dickens to the Cold War. But Pia commanded my full attention. She was the main act—Sandra a sideshow. Hard to say why. In a radical effort at complete honesty, I told both women about each other. Both claimed not to care. I believed Sandra but not Pia. Sometimes cruelly went down to Pia's studio still smelling of Sandra and entered her. She received my thrusts with a concentration and solemnity that showed me that she knew I'd been with Sandra only minutes before. It was touching. But there was as yet no love in her eyes. And until it was there—and I was, for reasons unknown to me to this day, determined that it would be—I was prepared to hurt her into loving me.

But Pia launched her own campaign to make me jealous. She succeeded. I became like a madman. The truth is, I was in love with her. Once, I caught her embracing a fat pimply man named Erik in front of our building and walked past, indignant, pretending not to see. I couldn't sleep for days after that. Another time, she told me that she was going to a reunion dance at her alma mater and later that evening I saw her well-spanked behind sheathed in an evening gown vanish sparkling into the depths of a black stretch limo parked at the curb. Peering in as I passed, saw a tuxedoed older man in the gloom, waiting. Should have felt amused; was instead outraged.

Sandra, by contrast, never provoked so much as a single snappish remark from me; though she too tried the jealousy route, at all times I was winsome smiles and chuckling pleasantries. Pia had tapped into my central nervous system, and it felt to me like terror. Oddly, my physical pleasure with Pia never equaled that with Sandra—in every way, Sandra was the better lover—but with Sandra there simply wasn't the depth of emotion or even arousal that I experienced with Pia. Pia had a lock on my libido.

When I came in Pia, a world of emotion fueled my ejaculation. There was love, pride, hope, but also hatred, distrust, sheer incomprehension. She ruled my lust like a fickle deity, not really even trying. I was as helpless before her as Van Gogh before nature;

ate her pussy the way Vincent devoured the paints that poisoned and drove him mad. Tried to push her flesh into love, the way Van Gogh tried to make colors perform beyond their capacity.

He succeeded. I failed. In some strange way, she was dead inside. In the way that Van Gogh quite literally painted himself to death, I almost succeeded, with Pia, at killing myself banging her. But where he left behind masterpieces, I produced only suicided spermatozoa and ashen emotions.

Sandra left town to spend a weekend in Chicago with an old flame. Would she sleep with him, I wondered aloud. Absolutely not, she said. They were just good friends. I searched my feelings, wondered if I cared one way or another. Didn't.

When she returned, she cabbed over dressed in the usual fishnet body stocking and belted tan raincoat. Seemed a bit distraught, paler than usual, eyes sleepless. Threw her arms around my neck. "I missed you so much!" she announced. Kissed my neck, cheeks, eyes, and we made love, forgoing the table. I went down on her. She tasted funny. The smell different. Alien, another person's.

Lifted my face, a bit dismayed, and said: "You slept with him."

"Yes, Sir," she said.

"Oh, drop all that Sir stuff! I thought you didn't plan to."

"I didn't. It was unplanned. Just happened."

"More than once, I would say?"

"Yes, more than once."

"Huh!" Came to my feet, retired to an armchair to think. She crawled over and took my member in her mouth, began pulling on it with little kitten mewlings. I let her. Stroked her face. But couldn't rid my mouth and nose of that brassy alien taste. My erection wilted.

"What's wrong?" she asked.

"I don't know. It's strange. But I feel not only a complete lack of jealousy but an equal sexual disgust. I don't want our bodies to touch."

She froze, tears in her eyes.

"Sweetheart," I said sincerely, "I don't wish to hurt your feelings. But it feels like there's a third in bed with us, some man, and it turns me off. Turns my stomach, actually."

She stood up and dressed. "Will you call me a taxi, please?" Said with great dignity.

"Of course."

Now all my focus was on Pia. A mistake. Unknown to me, Sandra had served as a buffer against the feelings that now erupted. I was madly in love with Pia, insanely jealous, and she was in love with me, a condition that I soon learned rendered her monstrous.

78

AT FIRST, BECAUSE SHE DID NOT ACTUALLY SAY SO, I was able to tell that Pia loved me by a certain doelike gentling of her eyes during sex, each time I penetrated her. Her face softened, grew focused and watchful and sad with pleasure.

To compensate for her new vulnerability, she became workaholic. Pulled long shifts at the job and came home and worked more on her computer. I didn't see her for days at a time.

"You're terrified of chaos," I said.

"Yes. How do you know?"

"Your strict routine makes no allowance for fun. Work, work, work, and more work."

"That's not true. I spend time with you."

"We don't even sleep together. I ball and leave. Or you ball and go. It's more like we're hygiene partners. Getting our biweekly sex. A pedicure for your pussy."

She laughed. "I like that!"

"Fine with me," I lied. "But you love me and you're terrified."

★ ★ ★

Her liaisons with other men continued. Each time, I swore to leave, and stayed.

Once, at the Yerba Buena Center for the Arts, by the Martin Luther King waterfall, in a violent display of feeling I berated her as a pathological liar because I had caught her out in a lie. I insisted that she remove a ring I had bought her and hurled it across the grass knolls, sailing over sunbathers' heads and into traffic, where it vanished, crushed under wheels. She wept. I left. Days later, passing her door as I descended the stairs to the lobby, glimpsed her standing at her open door, as if she'd been waiting for me, wearing a look of despair so abject that I next found myself lodged firmly inside her, all thought of desertion gone.

When I mentioned this to my sponsor, he said, simply: "You're addicted to her."

"How?"

By now, Old Ray had learned the whole sordid score. He leaned forward, hands clasped, lips set in a bemused smile. "You've just told me that everything inside you screams that she's no good for you, yet you can't seem to stay away. Isn't that what happens to the alcoholic around alcohol, the drug addict around drugs? The head telling you to stop even as the bottle goes to your lips and you swallow enough to paralyze ten normal men. And then drink some more. Has the frequency of your sex escalated?"

"Yes," I admitted, ashamed.

"How often are you having sex?"

"A better question would be, when am I not having sex?"

"Are you seeing friends?"

"No."

"How's the writing?"

I laughed sadly. "I live to have her."

"It feels good."

"Yeah. I guess. Not always."

"Like drinking. It's not the pleasure that increases but the compulsivity, the frequency, in direct proportion to which the pleasure actually decreases."

"Oh, shit!" I said solemnly. "You're right! I'm hooked."

"Just keep in mind," Old Ray said, "knowing that you're hooked won't necessarily help. You'll know it and still return for more."

"What will help?"

"Only your Higher Power."

And now ensued an anguish and torment such as I had never experienced except in the throes of my worst PTSD paranoia—somehow even worse, since I had no alcohol or drugs to lessen the pain. This was not terror unfolding in complex patterns of fantastical plots but a mounting wave of inconsolable grief and shame. I cried continually. It must have been some form of nervous breakdown. A mere inquiry after my welfare reduced me to a sobbing, quivering mess of indescribable sorrow. My friends were deeply concerned. No one seemed to understand except Mel, a cab driver acquaintance, who would appear at my door with the cab left running downstairs, drag me out, and haul me, off the meter, to 12-step meetings where I sat in the back rows, an unremarked wall speck unable to hear, see, speak, or think, a raw, exposed nerve ending sensitized to a level of intensity that no human was meant to endure, let alone survive. I swore now that I must not see her.

All of me at every moment hungered to copulate with her, just one more time.

She wouldn't leave me alone. Once came up to me outside her door as I descended the stairs, took me in her arms, and squeezing my buttocks said, smiling lecherously: "We don't have to be in a relationship just to do this. We can still have our fun."

I pulled her hands off, left, crushed. Thought that night of sleeping outdoors in the streets. Homelessness beckoned. Madness. Anywhere I walked I scanned streets for outdoor nooks to colonize. Under a stairwell downtown, an alley that looked safe and inviting, a bench in a deserted part of the park. And yet, the one ingredient that would propel me into the gutter for good, alcohol, never even crossed my thoughts. Miraculously, I felt not a single urge to drink, only to die.

Finally, it came down to suicide. I decided, calmly, that I could not endure a single day more of such anguish. Calmly, en route home from a 12-step meeting, knew that I would simply climb to the roof of my building that evening and jump off. Smiled at the thought. Felt no fear at all, just relief. One knows when one has reached the absolute limits of endurance: I had reached mine.

I paused on the sidewalk, closed my eyes. Listened to the night. My last on earth.

A single thought entered my suicidal mind. Flew about my skull like a silver sprite. Touched my crippled brain with a lovely wand. The Shekinah. "What if," she whispered, ever so softly, "you somehow managed to survive this ordeal? Think of the great strength of experience you'll have to share with others. Think of how much service you can bring. Survive, so that you can pass it on, so that others may live. By saving them, you can save yourself."

I stood on the dark, empty street and laughed aloud. Called out to the sky: "Don't I even get to kill myself in peace?" And the quiet voice of the Shekinah whispered: "You tried to do that for twenty-two years. Now you have only the right to live as best and meaningfully as you can."

By the time I reached my door, all thought of death was gone.

★ ★ ★

I would see Pia now and then, in the corridors, the street. I made the request that she move. Explained that I'd resided in the building all these years, the only stable home I'd ever known, rent-controlled, and would she consider changing residences?

To my amazement, she agreed.

Shortly after, I began to meet, all in a row, one recovering alcoholic man after another who was broken-hearted over a blonde, owned a gun, and struggled desperately against an overpowering urge to put the barrel in his mouth. In time, I worked the steps with some of these, befriended others, and tried to set an example based on my experience. I reminded them that years ten to twelve in recovery were for some reason a period notorious for sober suicides, but somehow we'd been spared.

Grateful, we formed a little coterie that we called the "Guns and Blondes Club." Now and then, drove cars to a local firing range, where we discharged weapons at paper silhouettes rather than ourselves. Afterward, over lunch, we recalled our survival of what each of us agreed was the worst pain we had ever endured sober: withdrawal from sex and love addiction.

79

IN 2002 IT SEEMED AS IF EACH TIME I WENT ONLINE to scan for news, another bus bombing had taken place in Israel's major cities, Jerusalem or Tel Aviv, or at a bus stop near an army base or in a café. The Internet was filled with photographs of the decimated hulks of destroyed buses. I found on one website a sequence that displayed a bus, its roof blown off and inside a tangle of metal, Israeli passengers slumped in their seats, eyes closed, with chalky faces snuffed by the concussive blast. Not all the seats were filled, though the bus would have been packed tight, as Israeli buses are—the missing passengers blown to pieces or hurled with the roof in a hundred directions, a head impaled on a lamppost, a hand lying in the road.

The frequency of the attacks took a toll on my nerves. Tried to call Isadora, but Esther refused to let us speak to her or even to provide details of how she was. By the time summer came, I was distraught.

I asked my Higher Power what to do.

And one day, during meditation, came a calm whispery voice: Go to the Wailing Wall in Jerusalem, offer prayers there.

I set about making arrangements with an editor at the *San Francisco Chronicle* to obtain a letter from the paper appointing me as a correspondent and requesting of the Israeli government foreign press credentials. This would give me a free hand to enter trouble zones and hot spots from which the bombings emanated—and perhaps generate articles, for I intended not only to see Isadora but to say something about the human cost of these murderous attacks.

On arriving in Jerusalem my first act was to attend a 12-step meeting that evening. Many of the same faces who had welcomed me during my last visit welcomed me now. Warm outstretched hands shook mine all around. Isadora was asked after: they remembered. I explained my purpose in coming. Their faces saddened.

"You will find the city much changed since you've last been here," one said.

"How so?"

"You'll see."

Being among them gave me the sense that I belonged, reminded me that before all things I am an alcoholic and the bottle but a symptom of a deeper underlying malaise, which, in my case— having sought and tried innumerable remedies and panaceas, from psychotherapy to sex, ambition to physical exertion—was answerable in the final analysis only by a spiritual solution. As my friend Si, an old-timer, would say: "The solution is simple. The solution is spiritual. And the solution has nothing to do with the problem."

Strange to realize here, in the seat of three world religions, that even religion could not suffice to answer the need within me.

As I walked that evening through Jerusalem, I thought of what a strange path mine had been—a Jew who found his best approach to YHWH or the Shekinah through nonsecular prayers such as the Serenity Prayer or through the diligent practice of Zen meditation, a persistent mindfulness; who had reached new visions of his role in Jewish life and the world at large through helping drunks, only some of whom, a mere handful, were Jews, who might come from every conceivable background and belief system and included desperate former criminals, fallen neo-Nazis, motorcycle gang members, ex-gangbangers, reformed stickup men, and muggers. Anyone who reached a hand out asking for help with drinking, I must freely help. Only together could we survive and transcend a fatal and incurable disease. I needed them as much as they me.

But the 12 steps cannot save the world, only drunks and addicts. For the steps to work, one must be in serious pain and ready, at all costs, to change.

In the morning, I rose early and went down to Ben Yehuda Street, a busy main thoroughfare of shops situated between King George Street and Jaffa Road. The cafés here were sure to be overflowing with all manner of Jerusalemites, crowding into cafés for their early-morning coffee and strudel.

Instead, I found deserted streets and empty shops with aproned storekeepers standing in the doorways looking forlorn, and in front of the cafés stood plastic bubble tents with posted armed guards who frisked you and inspected your ID before granting entrance. Up and down the street cruised border guard jeeps and a new type of antiterrorism motorcycle cop like something from a futuristic graphic novel: pistols holstered at their chests, wearing black bubble helmets that obscured their faces as they cruised slowly, scanning every nook, each set of eyes, prepared at a moment's reflex to dart off after suspects and bombs.

I got frisked and admitted to a favorite café spot, only to find it completely deserted, with only a single pair of elderly women gabbing over transparent glasses of steaming hot tea.

When I sat at a table nearby they turned heavily rouged faces to me and said: "You are a tourist?"

"No. I'm an Israeli American from San Francisco, visiting."

"But still, you are visiting?"

"Yes, I'm here to do some journalism work and to see my daughter."

"Where lives the daughter?"

"In Ashdod."

"But still, you've come from outside Israel. Do you see what's going on here?"

"I'm beginning to."

The waiter came. I ordered a Turkish coffee, or "mud coffee," as we used to call it in the army. It has caffeine enough to keep one going for days with little sleep, which soldiers often must do.

"Young man, you should be very proud of yourself to come now when you do. There's no tourism. People are afraid. We beg the world's Jews to come but they stay away. It's never been so bad."

"I didn't feel I have a choice. For one thing, I have a daughter here. For another, Israel is my center of gravity. I don't want to live in a world without Israel."

In Beit Agron, the Government Press Office had the pitched grimness of a command bunker at the height of a siege. I didn't like the new government spokesman even a little. He exuded a feeling of shrillness and incompetence. Nonetheless, I presented my Israeli and American passports, the letter from the *Chronicle*, and while these were examined and my application for a press credential processed, I recalled the trysts with Anna and Edna, the crazy days of shuttling around with a sidearm and officer tags. They made for good stories, no more. But alcohol had linked them to a fatal and progressive descent into hell.

A harried young woman sat me in front of one of those camera ID-making machines, shot my face, and issued me a press card. It showed me as a correspondent for the *Chronicle* and listed me as an Israeli citizen. I was now free to go out and get myself killed any way I pleased.

I then sat with a spokeswoman. "I want to write something about the war that no one talks about, no one sees," I said.

She thought. Then reached for a desk drawer and pulled a file. "I have something. As a matter of principle, I offer it to each reporter. They all say no. They want to see soldiers, guns. They don't want to see what's inside. Deeper. The uncomfortable place."

"What have you got?"

She put the file before me. "Two mothers. Their teenage daughters, fifteen, best friends, blown up together by a Hamas suicide bomber in a downtown Jerusalem pizzeria. There have been a few minor stories but no one has told the whole story, as it should be told. No one has let these women really speak. Too painful. What do you think?"

There was no question that to go and, if nothing else, just sit and listen to these ignored women, their grief, was what my Higher Power intended for me.

"I'll do it."

Astonished and pleased, the spokeswoman said: "You're the first not to push it away with a face." Then added: "The odds against your paper running this are high."

"Worth a try," I said, taking the file. I rose. We shook hands.

"Will they talk to me?"

"I'll call to let them know you'll be in touch."

★ ★ ★

The two mothers agreed to see me. They lived in an ugly white housing complex in an area regarded by some as disputed territory: a bus ride of several minutes from the center of town, where the girls had been blown up.

The two mothers lived just doors apart. The first, Frimet Roth, an American Jew from Queens, had immigrated to Israel, changed denomination to Orthodox, and married. The house was filled with children, scruffy little boys with earlocks and yarmulkes and jam-stained mouths. Little girls in long-sleeved dresses shuffled around, fingers hooked in their cherubic mouths, dragging dolls along the ground. Frimet sent them outdoors to play, sat me down. The place was as gloomy as a cave, disheveled, filled with unsorted laundry, toys—a typical motherhood battleground. It was not a cold gloom, though, more like a warm ovarian cave in which we sat at a big wooden table covered with alphabet blocks, notepads, dreidels, coloring books, crayons. She pushed these to the side, made space for our tea and elbows. Set down a plate of hard-looking homemade cookies dusted with confectioners' sugar.

"I'd like to show you something," she said.

"Of course. Do you mind the tape recorder?"

"No. Go ahead."

She returned with a stack of photo albums. Placed a photo before me. "This is them."

"Your daughter's on the left?"

She nodded. "Malki. And the other, of course, is Michal. Both fifteen."

They appeared like so many girlfriends of that age, complementary—Malki, the fair-haired dreamer, Michal more down to earth. Each smiling brightly, as if dazzled by all the promise they embodied.

"They're beautiful," I said.

"Were beautiful."

"Yes, of course."

"Michal was Malki's best friend. I never saw two girls so close. More than sisters. They did everything together. Michal was like my other oldest daughter. I still can't believe they're gone. On some mornings I wake up thinking she'll be here. You never saw such a child."

"I have a daughter," I said.

She looked at me vacantly. "Oh? Where?"

"Ashdod."

"An Israeli?"

"Yes. Like me. I also emigrated years ago. I served in the army too."

"But she doesn't live with you. You're from San Francisco. The *Chronicle,* you said. You're in California."

"It's a long story."

"I see. How old is she?"

"Isadora is fifteen."

She nodded. "The girls' age."

"I'm just telling you so you'll know I'm not here only as a reporter but as a father."

She nodded. "Thank you for saying that. I've spoken to reporters. But the way they twist the story, it never gets told."

"On the day, what happened?"

She spoke as those do who live in the presence of their worst tragedy every waking minute, entranced by it, benumbed, even in dreams; who as they speak lean close to the sound of their own voice, listening with their heart to their recounting, hoping to pluck from it some shred of déjà vu so evocative that for an instant the world will again seem as it was before the loss occurred.

The girls, she said, were inseparable. In their circle Malki was the leading light. During the year preceding her death she had suffered frequent nightmares due to the incessant blowing up of buses. The bombers hit hardest the bus lines that she and Michal rode to and from school and other destinations important to their sense of normalcy, of life's routines. So, for these two girls, the effort to live normally was fraught with peril.

"Malki had so many plans. She was going to volunteer that summer to a camp for mentally disabled children. Michal planned to join her. Both girls loved to play the guitar. Malki had a special gift. She was extremely talented. They had guitars with them when they were killed. And do you know what the irony is?"

"No, what?"

"That the terrorist who killed them carried his bomb in a guitar case! He was standing right next to Malki at the pizza shop when the bomb detonated. Hamas had made him to look like a normal teenager."

"Was the terrorist a teenager too?"

"Yes."

She said more. Then we sat quietly for a time. I thought that perhaps she'd said everything there was to tell.

But there was more. There is always more.

"I want to show you something."

She went into another room. I could see her through a doorway looking at a small picture in her hand. She wiped her eyes. I snapped my head around, pretended to gaze dumbly ahead, the way New York subway riders do, sealed in waiting. She sat down, the photo cupped in her right hand. Gingerly, laid it down before me. It could have been Isadora's photo, or any Israeli girl's, but I thanked God that it was not my daughter and grieved that it was Frimet's.

"This was the last photo taken of Malki in the hospital morgue.

You can see, her features are unmarked. But the whole of her face had been completely flattened. At the moment of detonation, she stood right next to the bomber. The explosive concussion completely flattened her face, her body. The victims who stood or sat further away were shredded by nails and ball bearings and burned by fire. It's amazing, isn't it? Except for the flattening, she seems unscathed."

It was as though a giant boot had crushed her. She seemed scathed enough for me.

"And Michal?" I asked.

"Not like this. Much worse to look at."

I nodded.

She leaned forward. Lifted the snapshot. It was passport sized. "They give you this to help with identification. On the clipboard on the table where she lay. I took it off, kept it. And you know what?"

I waited.

"I love her in this picture as much as any picture ever taken of her. She's still my daughter in this photo. The blast that killed her did not turn her into something that is not my little girl. She is still my little girl. She'll always be my little girl."

And then she spoke politics. Her rage at Hamas. The world's indifference. As she spoke, the shadows grew. She needed to talk. I sat quietly listening, opening my heart to her with a wordless, focused gaze.

I then went to visit Rivka, the other mother.

She was slender, pretty, brunette, nonreligious, a modern nonsecular Israeli woman formerly from South Africa, with dark gentle eyes and a soft-spoken manner. I could tell: the interview would be brief.

"What is there to say?" She smiled sadly. "The girls went out to the center of town for pizza. A young man came in with bombs and blew them up. I should make sense from this? Only those whose own children have not died in this way can make sense of such things. The rest of us, like me..." She shrugged.

"What?"

"What? Nothing. That's what. Every day that I wake up, she is gone. I wake up to nothing."

"How did you find out?"

"On the radio they said there was a bombing in the center of town, where they had gone. I tried to call on her cell. It went to message because her phone was destroyed. That's when I knew. When it went to message, I knew."

80

THE NEXT DAY, A RECOVERY CONTACT PUT ME IN
touch with a woman named Helene, who invited me to meet her
at Café Cafit, an upscale German Colony hangout in Jerusalem.
Just months earlier, an explosive-packed suicide bomber with wires
poking out everywhere had visited the café, took his seat, broke out
in a cold sweat, behaved weirdly in general, and my guess is, lost
his nerve to hit the trigger. Overwhelmed by suspicious waiters and
patrons, he was dragged into the street, his wires ripped out, and
he was turned over, defused, to the police. Shortly after, another
bomber entered the Moment Café, in nearby Rahavia, and detonated himself, along with eleven young Israeli patrons.

Helene, who was born in Northern Ireland and was a registered
nurse and paramedic with a local hospital, was in 12-step recovery.
She invited me along on her secret route through the deadly corridor
between Gilo and Beit Jalla, smuggling illegal medical supplies to
Arab infants. A woman not much given to fuss, Helene waved me
into her dusty vehicle, a generic car so unassuming that I failed to

note its make. Within minutes, the boutique-lined relative sanc-
tuary of the German Colony gave way to rocky, terraced hilltops
covered with Jewish settlements and Arab villages.

For the past eighteen months, the area had been the site of an
ongoing firefight between the IDF and Palestinian snipers that had
escalated—in response to the Palestinians' use of armor-piercing
bullets to fire on Jewish homes—into full-scale warfare. The battles
involved tanks, Cobra helicopters armed with Vulcan machine guns,
and, it was rumored, shoulder-held Stinger-like antiaircraft missiles
deployed by the terrorists. The snipers were not targeting military
installations but the kitchen, bathroom, and bedroom windows of
a defenseless block of apartment buildings that strikingly resembled
any average one-bedroom community in America. As we drove
past I imagined the armor-piercing rounds smashing into shower
stalls and piggy banks, and it made me shrink a little in my seat.

The buses that traveled this route, said Helene, were bulletproof,
yet for the most part the road stayed empty—even the orneriest
residents preferred alternative routes to this road. The sniping here
had been continuous and accurate.

"There on your left," she said quickly. "The Church of Saint
Elijah, Palestinian militia meeting place."

We now entered a tunnel. "There was sniping in here just
yesterday."

"Here where?"

"Right here in the tunnel. They drove past and fired shots. No
one was hit, I think."

We charged at high speed. The only other vehicles in the tunnel
were a Land Rover black-taped with the word *TV*, a U.N. Forces
military jeep, and an IDF armor-plated truck. Helene's fragile no-
name car rattled among these like a tenacious beetle as the speed-
ometer climbed. Then we burst into light, and on the left rose a

haunting row of sniper barriers. "These are new, put up in the last two months. Not perfect, no, but better than nothing."

We entered a second tunnel, the only ones traveling in it, and emerged on a curving stretch of sun-hammered blacktop that branched to the left and right. "There, to the left, the army checkpoint to Beit Jalla," she said, bearing away to the right. She slowed to let me absorb the immense tank cannon pointed straight at the road, then sped up. "We don't want to enter there with what I've got in the trunk."

"What is it?" I asked nervously.

"Baby food. Medicines."

"What will the IDF do if they find it?"

"Nothing," she said. "They actually turn a blind eye to what I do, though they always search, which is a pain. The Palestinian militias are the ones I worry about." She navigated the car through narrow dusty streets and up inclines, approaching her secret drop-off point. "Until 1995, my Palestinian patients and their kids all had Israeli medical insurance, and were under my care. But since then they have been under the jurisdiction of the Palestinians, who get their health care money from the EU, who have given over, in good faith, a fortune in funds. I tracked my baby patients through the new situations. Their conditions were now declining. And year after year, I wondered, why are they not receiving their medications? What supplies there were got stockpiled in warehouses but remained undistributed; or if they were ever given out, it was grab what you can. And my patients just did not receive the specific medical help they required, like powdered breast milk formula, special baby foods, eardrops, such things."

"Why not?"

She didn't admit it easily. Up ahead was a gate. She stopped the car. Before getting out, she said: "Because the militias used the EU health care funding and the medical supplies that got brought in, used all of it, it all went—they bought guns with it. It all went to buy weapons."

We were in what Helene called Area C, a West Bank Arab zone, at the gated entrance of a local institution. She exited the car, spoke through an intercom. A buzzer sounded and the locked gates parted just enough for Helene to swing them wide, then shut them behind us. She drove quickly through the grounds to a rear area of dense woods and up a road to a house. There, behind a low stone wall with a rusty metal door, lay Beit Jalla under curfew.

We entered the woods and, following the barrier wall, mounted a small hill that afforded us a panoramic view of the entire city. It spread before me, white and hot, miragelike.

"Listen," she said. It was the muezzin in his tower, sending the faithful a mournful, lilting summons to prayer. Then out came a cell phone. "I'm calling Sami," she said. "He's the contact. I'll leave out supplies. He'll come get them when it's safe."

We descended to the car. Helene popped open the trunk and began lifting out transparent pink grocery bags filled with jars of baby food, cans of powdered breast milk, and medicines of all sorts. These she left in a small pile by a wall at the side of the house. "I've treated some of these children since the day they were born. Some of them need special medications, foods. I know their cases. The authorities can't be trusted to get them what they need, so I bring it myself. It's my money."

In the US you could find this pathetic little pile of goods on the shelves of any pharmacy. Looking at it, I wondered how many jars of baby food went to buy a clip's worth of armor-piercing incendiary rounds. How many cans of powdered breast milk formula, how many children's-strength antibiotics, how many bottles of ear and nose drops and packs of cotton swabs went to underwrite a suicide bomber's belt?

81

ESTHER AGREED TO LET ME SEE ISADORA. MY daughter's appearance shocked me. She didn't look herself—had grown taller but her gaze seemed listless, face puffy, flat, withdrawn. While Esther talked nonstop in her usual manic high-pitched mock-theatrical English stage voice, Isadora's eyes rarely met mine. After a time together, she withdrew into her room, where I glimpsed her lying on her stomach on the bed, reading *Prozac Nation*.

"Is she on meds?" I asked Esther.

"No, no, no, no, no!" she said dismissively, but by her eyes, her manner, I sensed deceit.

"The reason I ask is because in recovery I've had occasion to see a lot of people on meds, and Isadora has the same…how shall I say? She's withdrawn. Listless. Her face is puffy. She's reading *Prozac Nation*."

"She's not on meds."

"Has she ever been?"

Esther's eyes searched the ground for how to frame an answer.

"No," she said. And then: "Well, yes. A while ago."

"Tell me about it."

"Look," Esther said angrily. "You abandoned your daugh-ter! So, don't get high-minded with me! I know who you are. Don't come here like the great man in recovery. I saw you once upon a time. I know."

"I apologize if I'm coming across to you that way. That's not my intention. I'm just surprised by the changes in her. She's not the girl I last saw."

"Of course not! She's older. She's a teenager. They're always moody and withdrawn like that."

"But she was such a happy little kid."

Esther's face flushed, her eyes turned guilty. "Having no father does that to a little girl."

I didn't respond. Could tell that my silence unnerved her. I was after the truth.

Finally, she blurted out. "She has a problem with violence!"

"Violence?"

"She's emotionally disturbed. I had to take her to see psychia-trists."

"When?"

"She's still seeing someone."

"When did this first happen?"

"After your first trip to see her. It's why I had to cut off any further access. After you left, she became insane."

Tears filled my eyes. I hung my face sadly, open to hear it all.

"She cried all the time. She yelled. Her grades fell. She couldn't understand why you had to go. She began to attack me."

"Attack?"

"She hit me."

"Hit?"

"Yes! HIT!" Esther sneered. "Your daugh-ter began to attack me with her fists."

"Well, what did Yaacov think? I mean, did he try talking with Izzy?"

Her eyes grew shifty. "I dropped him."

"Why? He seemed nice enough."

"He was a shiftless loser."

"Okay. So, no Yaacov. But still, I mean, she was nine. Were you afraid she was going to hurt you?" I grinned. "Like those horror movies where some kid becomes demonic—*The Exorcist*, or something?"

"LAWF!" she blared out in her most stentorian stage voice. "LAWF! Because you're a man and after all, what does it mat-ter to you if a little girl, your own daugh-ter, violently assaults her own MO-THER!" She leaned forward. "But I am her MO-THER! She is supposed to have respect. She has none."

"Okay, but you don't send someone to shrinks because they don't respect you. You become worthy of respect."

She deflated. "You don't understand," she said tiredly. "She was completely out of control."

I looked around me at the squalid conditions of the flat—the trash pile in the corner of the porch, still there after all these years, the shabby thrown-together furnishings over which hung the awful smell of cat urine, sardines, and ammonia. Considered what it must feel like to awaken daily to someone like Esther ruling your world. Hell, I'd take a swing at her myself, I thought.

"So, what did the shrinks have to say?"

"She's emotionally disturbed."

It's not that I didn't want to believe this about my daughter, couldn't bear the truth about some shameful fact that I'd wish to hide from others and myself. It's that I sensed, intuited, objectively, that there was absolutely nothing wrong with Isadora that sane parenting wouldn't remedy.

If Isadora was striking out, as Esther claimed, she did so with good reason. Her mother was mad but she was the adult in charge nonetheless. She had used her position to emotionally blackmail me for years, barring me from contact with Isadora. Now she was spinning a narrative about Izzy that was false, destructive, and unsparing.

Needing to know all the facts, aware that Esther still stood between me and my daughter, I played along.

"Well, what sort of remedy did the psychiatrists prescribe?"

She paused, looked down, away, trying to sort out from her racing thoughts how exactly to frame it.

"Institutionalization," she said flatly.

Stunned, I whispered: "How long?"

"A year," she said.

Fury leaped in my chest like a hooked marlin, writhed and twisted before crashing back beneath the surface calm. In my face it may have flashed from angry eyes but just as quickly sank. A perfectly beautiful child was undergoing legal torments orchestrated by a lunatic mother, and I, a visitor, here by her permission only, could do absolutely nothing about it.

"And so, she did the year?"

"Yes" is all Esther said.

"And she got a clean bill of health?"

"Yes."

I let it go at that. Asked no further questions. It was all plain enough to see. I would need the faith and perseverance to wait until Isadora was of legal age. Only then could I finally reach out, once she was free of Esther.

But there was one moment that even Esther could not suppress, when I saw Isadora as she truly was.

★ ★ ★

My friend the Israeli author Etgar Keret organized a poetry reading for me in a Tel Aviv nightclub. I asked if it would be all right for Isadora to join me onstage. Of course, said Etgar. I asked Isadora if she would read some of her poems onstage with me. She smiled and agreed.

The club was packed with young people. Isadora and I took the stage, stood side by side. We took turns introducing ourselves, I in English, she in Hebrew. I said that I was her father, I was in recovery, and we lived apart, I in San Francisco, she in Israel. But we were trying to be together, to know each other better, she said. And because we were both poets we were reading poems together for the first time.

The audience clapped and whistled appreciatively.

Onstage, she was transformed. She is beautiful, has a quiet authority and naturally likable disposition. She is also a born performer. I asked her to read first, and without hesitation she ran through a poem of great power and insight that earned thunderous applause. I followed and got a big hand too, whereupon Isadora and I bantered a little between us, and then she read, and then I, each discerning the audience's mood, picking our poems accordingly, like a couple of old pros who'd been reading together on the circuit for years.

Between us flowed a natural performing symbiosis: poetry and performance are in our blood. At one point, as she belted out a terrifically moving piece about what it felt like to grow up without a dad, I thought: God, thank you. She's my flesh and blood, reading poems onstage with me. This is an absolute miracle. I can't believe it! The Shekinah smiled and whispered: "Believe it."

Then I read a poem about my sadness at not being with my daughter all those years. And felt some great healing take place in both of us on that stage, an unbreakable bond forged by a moment of truth. We were conducting, with poetry, before a public, the kind of conversation that we had desperately needed to have and couldn't for all those years. It wouldn't make up for her losses. But it was a start at reclaiming our love. And to the audience, we were an example. They felt us and understood. We were frail, imperfect, trying as best as we knew how, with poetry, to forge our father–daughter love, and asking the audience to be our community of witness. We got a standing ovation from the crowd.

When it was over, Etgar said. "That was absolutely amazing."

BOOK ELEVEN

82

WHY AN ANGEL? BECAUSE I BELIEVE THAT, IN TIME, that is what we become in sobriety, if we last long enough, to the end. Not the winged kind, no. Not some haloed cupid or sword swinger but a kind of flawed angel, without wings, that belongs to no religion but rather to a species of human heartbreak unlike any other known.

Alcoholics and addicts are unlike any other people I've ever met. I am unlike most people. A blazing mutant of some kind. A wondrous freak. In my mind lurks an urge that will be with me to the end, to put a bottle to my lips and drink myself to death. A judge and jury that I wake up to each morning has pronounced a verdict of guilt on me for no crime that I have committed, just for being alive, and has sentenced me to death, not by guillotine or rope but by a single drink.

It is the strangest thing, this sentence of death, this disease I have which tests me to the max and each day holds my existence accountable to the very universe, a god no religion can

know as we drunks know it.

A god of drunks who goes with us into our prisons and gutters, bedrooms and businesses, flophouses and alleys, hospitals and mansions, and patiently waits with hand on our shivering shoulders as we groan through yet one more night of near death, waits to see if maybe this time we've had pain enough, loss enough, enough hangover, illness, fear, to ask for help.

And yet many cannot ask, and die right before the god of drunks, who I think must weep helplessly when this occurs.

So many lose heart and fall. I have seen so many of my brothers and sisters in recovery fall. I have seen so many beautiful people die. The poet found in his room OD'd with a needle in his arm. He was my best friend. The twenty-year-old drummer who killed himself over a romance gone wrong. Nice kid. The young artist who drank and was found murdered in her Tenderloin hotel room. She was so talented. The buddy who drank and wound up facedown in a river in Pennsylvania, drowned. The ones, so many, who jumped off the bridge or the roof or put a gun barrel to their heads and squeezed the trigger, or in private ate painkillers until found on the floor brain-dead, or perished young of a destroyed liver. That young nurse, a mother of three, who had everything, beautiful children, loving husband, looks to die for, a house with two cars in the garage, who also had this little problem that she couldn't stay sober or stop smoking crack, no matter how many meetings she attended or what advice she tried to follow, and one day returned home to that garage, ran a hose, turned on the ignition, and gassed herself to death.

When you have seen as much of that as I have in my sobriety, in the last twenty years, how can I not regard my own reflection with amazement that I am still here. Why me? How did I get so lucky? Really, I don't know. I want to think that I've done something right, but in truth, I know better. I do believe in a Higher Power and I do work the 12 steps and go to meetings and work with drunks of every kind and description, yet it doesn't seem like enough, it never does. I never feel that I can repay what has been given to me. The love that has been shown. The patience and straight-shooting counsel that has saved my butt time and again. I have met in recovery men and women who are the greatest human beings I have ever known but don't want their names advertised. Anonymous, quiet angels, invaded by death, propelled by light, who move among us with quiet grace and private suffering and seek each day to help those around them without fanfare or reward.

And so I look back on my life and it is divided in parts: my drunk years and my sober ones, and I can hardly believe the beauty, meaning, and victory that have attended my sober years. I have become someone I don't recognize, and yet do. A man I dreamed of as a boy, the kind I admired then. A writer and a soldier, poet and artist, a monk and a public man. He is the father and the brother I never really had, who walks the streets of his city and is known alike in high and low places, greeted by politicians and hugged by the unknown homeless, friend to both the criminal and the cop, the outlaw and the spiritualist, well regarded by persons of every color and creed, occupation and social rank. And if asked by any who I most truly am, I can reply: "My name is Alan. I am an alcoholic. And it is the best thing that has ever happened to me."

Because when death sits on your shoulder each day, whispering, urging you to your end, there is no time to lose, so much light to grasp for, strive for, struggle to embrace. We are struggling with light. And yet we are only human after all, so terribly flawed and foolish, selfish and ridiculous. Sobriety can be so messy. At times, I have seemed to myself the most awful of persons. But even then I am ascending, even then I am going up a ladder of light with eyes wide open and hands outstretched, to clasp the next rung up. And I climb.

★ ★ ★

Then, in 2006, came an email, my very first from Isadora, to say that she was seventeen, about to turn eighteen, would be in New York any day, wanted very much to see me. Could I come?

I was on the next plane out.

Crashed in the East Village in the home of a friend who was away and said I could have it for as long as needed. Didn't even know how long that would be. Isadora hadn't provided many details because she didn't yet have them, or even a phone number where she could be reached. But she had mine and she promised to call. "Dad. It'll be okay," she said. "Trust me."

For almost the whole first day, I didn't hear back. My head got to work. An alcoholic's mind knows just where its opportunities lie, patiently waiting. After a few hours it told me that Isadora was lying on a gurney in a hospital emergency room, comatose, so pale, covered in blood, surrounded by incompetent doctors unable to revive her. In recovery, we like to say that the alcoholic's head is like a bad neighborhood: never go up there alone. I ran to a 12-step meeting in the West Village, where I calmed down and was reminded that once upon a time, not too far from here, I had passed out in doorways, but I was now in town to see my little girl, hoofing about in a French sports jacket with cash in my pocket, and had even brushed my teeth with actual toothpaste that morning. She would call in God's time, not mine.

And she did. She was with Esther at her grandmother's lower Manhattan apartment. Would I meet her in Washington Square Park? Before hanging up she said: "Dad. It'll just be you and me. I want to see you without Mummy. Just us. I'm seventeen now. We can have our own relationship."

"Yes, sweetheart," I said. She sounded so mature. A grown woman! That once tiny little angel puffing breaths in her swaddling blanket had just explained to me exactly how things would be from now on. I had not seen her in three years, but never like this: just us, completely on our own.

Before I'd left San Francisco, Old Ray, who had raised a son, advised: "Look. She's seventeen. So, whatever she says, just don't contradict her. Agree. Okay? You'll be a lot happier. The point is not to be right but to be with her. Huh? Yes?"

I sat in the park at dusk, looking around—at the arch, the trees, the big plaza noisy as always with Village street life, young thugs and singers, lovers and the lost, junkies, mothers with strollers, roller skaters. As a seventeen-year-old, I had sat here hunched just this way, fingering an angry zit, intently looking around, a bit morose, with a brooding hunger, lonely and defiant, the suspicious rebel and poetic innocent, craving companionship, meaning, connection. Just like this. With hands folded so and knowing very little about people, what made them tick. And now to be waiting to meet my seventeen-year-old daughter here, where I had once been a teen, her age. It was time circling memory into strange new loops of continuity, offering glimpses of the eternality of things. Just keep in mind, I told myself, how important everything feels at that age, and honor her need to be met on her own terms, with respect, as an autonomous person.

And there she was. Long thick hair, dyed red. In a black short-sleeved three-quarter-length dress with cowboy boots. Isadora. A dramatic young woman. Her face proud and shy, just as mine was at her age. Grown, matured. Walking toward me self-consciously, filled with the specialness of the moment, which I could feel. And New York, for once, seemed to be filled with the comfort of gray blue fading light, magical, safe, uplifting, through which she moved like a dream.

Mad with love, I stood and waited. She carried a black book in her hand. We embraced.

"Izzy," I said.

"Dad."

I stepped back. "You're so beautiful."

"Thank you," she said with great dignity.

We held hands. Just as naturally as that. For we had both been waiting for years. Began to walk along.

"I can't believe you're here. I'm so happy."

"Me too, Dad."

Even though we can each be hair-trigger reactive, deep down we are long-haul emotional voyagers, Isadora and I, wise in the ways of ourselves, and we know how to wait, even seemingly forever.

We walked and were happy. Found a café. Sat quietly, looking around. We can let love sleep for years, knowing it's there and will someday reawaken. As if time did not separate our encounters. The way she'd leaned against me in Ashdod only minutes into our first reunion, a simple preverbal ease, like now, that had always existed between us since they first laid her in my arms at the hospital, that reappeared every time we met again.

Smiling at each other. Ordered two Cokes. We sipped through straws, looking at each other. My daughter. Fatherhood is a blessing that nature reserves for the lucky, a way to be that is simple and true and doesn't need instructions or explanation, so that our mutual closeness and love lives in the interstices of great solitudes, growing there like flowers from the cracks in a wall.

I asked about her writing. She showed me her black book. Decorated with a photograph of her, it was a sheaf of her poems in Hebrew. I tried to read one but my Hebrew was inadequate.

"How's that for one of life's little jokes? I'm a writer in English whose daughter writes Hebrew poetry that I can't understand."

"Here," she said, taking the book. "Let me try to translate one for you."

And so began a weeklong odyssey around scorching Manhattan summer streets, heads tipped together, working to translate her poems, in apartments, restaurants, streets, tossing out word candidates, pondering, judging, deleting, substituting this phrase for that, struggling to render into English her exact intended meaning, and then reading our joint effort aloud to see how it sounded: a Diasporic Jew and his Israeli daughter, the Exiled and the Redeemed, two writers, one progenitive of the other, doing what made us happiest. It was as if God put a song in my throat that had passed to her.

We also did dumb stuff. Went to see *Pirates of the Caribbean.* She dragged me to see *The Color Purple,* almost the only whites in an audience of mainly black women, some quite large and big-breasted, who for every song performance jumped from their seats to sway and clap. Izzy did too, laughing and loving it and glancing at me disconcerted as I sat there so curmudgeonly, refusing to join in this daytime TV–level middlebrow activity, until I found myself on my feet too, because Izzy was, clapping and cheering because she did, and to my great astonishment feeling like a brassy big-breasted uplifted black woman, full of soulful Oprah love.

She had a camera. It turned out that photography was her other artistic fixation. We went around Manhattan shooting everything and stopping every five seconds on the sidewalk to study the image, marveling at specific effects, Izzy asking for my critiques, considering my views.

One evening, at twilight, we found ourselves at 9th Street and Avenue A in the East Village, Tompkins Square Park.

"Daddy," she said. "Isn't this where you ended up in your drinking?"

I could barely bring myself to look at the park in her presence. "Yes," I said numbly.

"This is where you would go to drink when I was little?"

"Sometimes."

She wanted to see which bench I'd slept on, but the park was closed and the benches welded with metal hoops that prevented using them for a bed. Along the park wall, though, were blacked-out drunks and junkies all in a row, like napping nightmare adult kindergartners, pants down around their naked unwashed bottoms, angelically vulnerable in their incapacity and strangely awesome in their sheer proximity to annihilation. Some looked just days away from a pauper's grave.

"That pretty much was me," I said, nodding their way.

"No. I don't believe it."

"No. Really. That was me."

"I don't believe it. You could have stopped drinking if you wanted to."

"No, Izzy, I couldn't."

"I don't believe it. You could have."

"No, I couldn't have."

"Yes, you could."

"Izzy, I'm telling you, I—"

Suddenly, I heard the voice of Old Ray telling me to remember that she was seventeen, to just agree with anything she said.

"Uh, maybe you're right. Maybe I could have. Sweetheart, I need to get to a meeting. Why don't I drop you at your grandma and then I'll meet you afterward."

"Can I come?"

"You want to come to a meeting with me?"

"Yes."

It was close by. And we found front-row seats. The speaker talked for twenty minutes about how he had been unable under any circumstances to stop drinking, no matter what. Then, one after another, recovering drunks raised their hands and shared that until getting into recovery they were unable to stop drinking.

Halfway through the meeting, a light went on in Isadora's face. She raised her hand. Was called on. I stared, amazed. She said: "My name is Isadora. And this is my father, Alan. He's been sober many years. I'm here for him. I just want to say that until now, until hearing your stories, secretly I never really believed that he couldn't stop drinking. But I now know that he's telling the truth and it's a miracle. He is sober today because of you, and if not for this, I would not be sitting here with my daddy today. I want to thank you people with all my heart."

On our last night, she was to meet her family in Ossining. We rode the train north on the Hudson River line as I pointed out spots along the bank where I had hopped freights in my youth, building bonfires and watching barges drift by. Now I had passed here not only as a touring author but as a father with his grown daughter. Once again, it was time circling memory into strange new loops of continuity, offering glimpses of the eternality of things.

At the station in Ossining we had to say goodbye, and once more it was unbearable. We grew angry with each other. I saw how helpless we were before our need for each other. It made me so sad that we had to pay such a high price for something so natural as family love. But it hurt. All my fears erupted out of me and met all her loss, and we hissed and turned away in disappointment, unable to say goodbye.

By 2007, Isadora had completed her first year in the Israeli Army, during which she had been bombed by terrorist rockets. Since she was now serving in Tel Aviv, I flew out to see her. We arranged to meet off base, in a café in the center of town.

She appeared out of uniform, in a springlike dress cinched at the waist and patterned with flowers, with her hair, restored to natural blondness, combed back and her face fresh, lightly made up, and lovely. As always, my heart in my throat, I hugged her. We sat down and looked each at other, waiting.

Then she said: "Daddy, I have something very important to tell you."

"Yes, sweetheart."

She hesitated, fidgeting with a bracelet. Looked up at me.

"This is very hard for me, Dad. It's so important. I…"

She looked away. Then back at me. "Daddy, I'm gay."

Relieved, my lower lip decompressed. I had thought God knows what. Some fatal illness or something. "Well, how perfect, then, that I live in San Francisco! Your cred there has just shot way up."

She gaped at me, shocked. "Daddy? Did you hear what I just said?

"Yes, you're gay."

"But you— You mean— You don't—?"

"What, honey?"

"You don't care!?"

"Why no. I'm very proud of you, actually. In fact, I'm kind of happy for you. Have you noticed how lonely heteros are? I mean, they have no community. Queers are so, you know, kind of hip. I think you're the cutting edge. I'm actually a little jealous. I'm sick of being hetero myself. It's so fucking boring!"

"DADDY!" She jumped up and threw her arms around my neck and hugged me so hard I almost toppled over backward.

I laughed, blushing. "Honey, what's all the excitement about?"

"DADDY! YOU'RE SO CRAZY!" She shrieked with glee. "I can't believe you! I thought you would be crushed! I should have known. You're not like others!"

"Why would I be crushed?"

DRUNKEN ANGEL

"Well excuse me, Mr. San Francisco Outlaw, but have you noticed that most people want to have straight kids so they can be, you know, have, normal families and things and...."

"Well, but I'm not like them. I don't care about normal. What the hell is that anyway? Half my friends in San Francisco are gay and queer. They're some of the brightest and most talented people I know. Without our gays San Francisco would be like, like, I don't know—like Dallas or something."

"You are *too* much, Daddy!" She just couldn't stop laughing. An explosion of relief. She became wildly expressive, happy, involved, gossipy. Told me all about her girlfriend and then confided that she had once had many. Wanted me to meet them all. Would I? I would? "Oh, Daddy, I'm so excited. I can't wait."

Then the conversation took a serious turn. She told me that she had been molested by the Bosnian, Yaacov. Her mother had known about it but feared losing his love, so she looked away. Isadora told me how she could not bring herself to speak about it to anyone. How when she tried to tell Esther, her mother had told her she was crazy and dragged her to therapists, to be institutionalized. How she had never had a lover her own age. Her first real love had been a grown woman, with whom she carried on an affair when she was fifteen.

"Daddy, I've got a real girlfriend now. She's my age. I want you to meet her! She's so great!"

"I can't wait. You are so brave. You are my hero. I'm so happy that you're gay. Don't ever let anyone make you feel there's something wrong with that. What's wrong is them, not you. You're the most wonderful, beautiful daughter any daddy could ever hope to have, and I love you with all my heart. Come here."

She leaned forward and I held her, her head on my shoulder. My little girl. My Isadora.

She had to return to the base. But this evening she would come by with her girlfriend and they would take me to a club.

That night, she arrived in a tiny military car with her girlfriend, another soldier, both out of uniform, dressed in slinky Tel Aviv club-hopping lesbian chic. While they sat up front, chatting and screeching and singing and laughing and looking over their shoulders at me, I sat hunched in back, grinning like a dope, amazed. How had I gotten here? Squeezed in back of a tiny army car with my queer Israeli soldier daughter and her lover, on our way to an all-night lesbian dance club. I was so happy for her, proud, honored to be the one member of her family she trusted enough to come out to. I closed my eyes to smell the perfumed air of this perfect moment of perfect freedom. Clean and sober, and with the joyful voice of my daughter in my ears, I thanked God from the bottom of my heart.

San Francisco

ABOUT THE AUTHOR

ALAN KAUFMAN is an American novelist, memoirist and poet who was instrumental in the development of the Spoken Word movement in literature and in the rise of alternative Jewish culture. David Mamet has called Kaufman's *Matches* "an extraordinary war novel," and Dave Eggers has written that "there is more passion here than you see in twenty other books combined." Ruth Prawer Jhabvala has praised Kaufman's memoir, *Jew Boy,* as "astonishing...a grand epic of a memoir." Hubert Selby, Jr. has described *Jew Boy* as a work inspiring "wonder and awe." *The San Francisco Chronicle* called *Jew Boy* a "classic coming of age story."

Kaufman is the editor of the bestselling *The Outlaw Bible of American Poetry* and co-editor of *The Outlaw Bible of American Literature,* alongside Barney Rosset and Neil Ortenberg. His other books include *The Outlaw Bible of American Essays* and *The New Generation: Fiction For Our Time From America's Writing Programs.* He has written for *The Los Angeles Times, The San Francisco Chronicle,* and numerous other publications. A lay ordained Zen practitioner and twenty years clean and sober, he is Dean of The Free University of San Francisco, which the *New York Times* recently compared to the Freedom Schools of the Civil Rights Movement of the 1960's.